The Concept of Freedom in Judaism, Christianity and Islam

D1593155

Key Concepts in Interreligious Discourses

Edited by
Georges Tamer

In Cooperation with
Katja Thörner

Volume 3

The Concept of Freedom in Judaism, Christianity and Islam

Edited by Georges Tamer and Ursula Männle

DE GRUYTER

ISBN 978-3-11-056055-8
e-ISBN (PDF) 978-3-11-056167-8
e-ISBN (EPUB) 978-3-11-056063-3
ISSN 2513-1117

Library of Congress Control Number: XXX

Bibliographic information published by the Deutsche Nationalbibliothek
The Deutsche Nationalbibliothek lists this publication in the Deutsche Nationalbibliografie; detailed bibliographic data are available on the Internet at http://dnb.dnb.de.

Printing and binding: CPI books GmbH, Leck

www.degruyter.com

MIX
Papier aus verantwortungsvollen Quellen
FSC www.fsc.org
FSC® C083411

Preface

The present volume contains the results of a conference on the concept of freedom in Judaism, Christianity and Islam held at the Friedrich-Alexander University in Erlangen on May 10 – 11, 2017. The conference was organized by the Research Unit "Key Concepts in Interreligious Discourses" (KCID) in cooperation with the Hanns-Seidel-Foundation.

The Research Unit KCID offers an innovative approach for studying the development of the three interconnected religions: Judaism, Christianity and Islam. With this aim in mind, KCID analyzes the history of ideas in each of these three religions, always taking into account the history of interreligious exchange and appropriation of these very ideas. In doing so, KCID investigates the foundations of religious thought, thereby establishing an "archaeology of religious knowledge" in order to make manifest certain commonalities and differences between the three religions via dialogic study of their conceptual history. Thus, KCID intends to contribute to an intensive academic engagement with interreligious discourses in order to uncover mutually intelligible theoretical foundations and increase understanding between these different religious communities in the here and now. Moreover, KCID aims to highlight how each religion's self-understanding can contribute to mutual understanding and peace between the three religious communities in the world.

In order to explore key concepts in Judaism, Christianity and Islam, KCID organizes conferences individually dedicated to specific concepts. A renowned set of researchers from various disciplines explore these concepts from the viewpoint of all three religions. The results of each conference are published in a volume appearing in the book series "Key Concepts in Interreligious Discourses". Particularly salient selections from each volume are made available online in Arabic, English and German.

In this fashion, KCID fulfills its aspirations not only by reflecting on central religious ideas amongst a small group of academic specialists, but also by disseminating such ideas in a way that will appeal to the broader public. Academic research that puts itself at the service of society is vital in order to counteract powerful contemporary trends toward a form of segregation rooted in ignorance. Mutual respect and acceptance amongst religious communities is thereby strengthened. Such a result is guaranteed due to the methodology deployed by the research unit, namely the dialogic investigation of the history of concepts as documented in the present volume.

We wish to thank all of those who put their efforts into organizing the conference and producing the volume: Dr. Philipp Hildmann from the Hanns-Seidel-

https://doi.org/10.1515/9783110561678-001

Foundation, Dr. Katja Thörner, Ms. Ariadne Papageorgiou, Mr. Fabian Schmidmeier and Mr. Ezra Tzfadya from the Research Unit KCID, along with the student assistants. Our thanks also goes to Dr. Albrecht Döhnert, Dr. Sophie Wagenhofer and their assistants at the publisher house Walter de Gruyter for their competent caretaking of this volume and the entire book series.

Erlangen and Munich in February 2019
The Editors

Table of Contents

Kenneth Seeskin

The Concept of Freedom in Judaism

In Judaism, the first commandment of the Decalogue reads: "I am the LORD your God, who brought you out of the land of Egypt, out of the house of bondage."[1] What is noteworthy about this commandment is the way God introduces himself: not as a metaphysically perfect being, not as creator of heaven and earth, but as a liberator – the one who freed Israel from the grips of Pharaoh. Given the prominence of this commandment, freedom from slavery is not only the central theme of the Passover holiday, known in Judaism as *zman herutaynu* (the season of our freedom), it is a central theme of the Sabbath as well. In fact, if you engage in daily prayer, you cannot live a single day of your life without recalling it.

It could be said therefore that liberation from slavery is the formative event in all of Judaism. In the words of Michael Walzer: "The Exodus is a story, a big story, one that became part of the cultural consciousness of the West ..."[2] It has been invoked by revolutionaries ranging from German peasants to Oliver Cromwell to the American colonists to Martin Luther King.[3] Along these lines, it is also noteworthy that the Liberty Bell, which sits in Philadelphia and symbolizes American independence from Great Britain, is inscribed with the words "Proclaim LIBERTY throughout all the land unto all the inhabitants thereof" a reference to Leviticus 25:10, which announces the Jubilee year when slaves were to be freed, debts forgiven, and land returned to its original owner.[4] Indeed, Deuteronomy 30:19, the rhetorical climax of the Torah, contains a rousing affirmation of free choice: "I call heaven and earth to witness against you this day: I have put before you life and death, blessing and curse. Choose life – if you and your offspring would live."

Against this celebration of freedom, the standard Christian critique of Judaism is that no sooner were the Israelites freed from Egyptian bondage than they were subjected to another form: bondage to a distant, unapproachable God who insists on strict obedience to law.

---

1 Note that Judaism normally parses the Ten Commandments differently than Christianity. For Jewish thinkers, "I am the Lord thy God ..." is usually taken as a commandment to accept the sovereignty of God even though it is not expressed in the form of an imperative. Cf., for example, Maimonides, Moses, *Mishneh Torah 1*, trans. E. Touger, New York/Jerusalem: Moznaim Publishing, 1989, Basic Laws, 1. 1–6.

2 Walzer, Michael, *Exodus and Revolution*, New York: Basic Books, 1985, 7.

3 Ibid., 3–7.

4 It is unclear whether the Jubilee year was an aspiration or a report of an actual practice.

https://doi.org/10.1515/9783110561678-002

Along these lines, it is noteworthy that the Hebrew word for slavery (*avduth*) comes from the same root as the word for service to or worship of God. Strictly speaking if God freed Israel from Egyptian bondage, then by all rights, Israel would be bound to God as a result.

As enlightened a figure as Kant argued that Judaism is not a religious faith in the true sense of the term because it is concerned merely with the outward performance of statutory laws, takes no interest in their moral significance, and leaves the inner life of the person, including his feelings and intentions, unaddressed.[5] If this is true, then it is not until the emergence of Christianity that genuine freedom became possible. In the words of Paul (Gal 3:23–24): "Before faith came, we were imprisoned and guarded under the law ... therefore the law was our disciplinarian [*paidagogos*] before Christ came ..."[6]

Like Islam, Judaism is a religion of law. Although there have been attempts to introduce articles of faith to Judaism, the most notable being that of Moses Maimonides, Moses Mendelssohn was right in saying that articles of faith have always been controversial and have never attained what might be considered official status.[7] Soon after Maimonides introduced his version of them, some people questioned how many he himself was committed to. From a religious point of view, the absence of articles of faith is not necessarily a bad thing. As Kant pointed out, nothing is gained if statutory laws are replaced by statutory beliefs: beliefs one must accept without supporting evidence or rational justification.[8] It is in this spirit that Mendelssohn referred to articles of faith as "shackles of faith."

Even a cursory look at the history of Jewish thought will show that without articles of faith to rein them in, Jewish thinkers have given themselves enormous latitude in choosing systems of thought within which to craft their theories. There have been Jewish Platonists, Aristotelians, voluntarists, Averroists, Spinoz-

---

5 Kant, Immanuel, *Religion within the Boundaries of Mere Reason*, trans. Allen Wood/George Di Giovanni, Cambridge: Cambridge University Press, 1998, 6:125–27.

6 The *paidagogos* was someone assigned to look after young boys for the purpose keeping them out of trouble.

7 Cf. his *Commentary on the Mishnah*, "Sanhedrin, Chapter Ten." For a readily available English translation, cf. Maimonides, Moses, *A Maimonides Reader*, Isadore Twersky (ed.), New York: Behrman House, 1972, 402–23. For discussion of Maimonides' principles as well as their reception by other Jewish thinkers, cf. Kellner, Menachem, *Dogma in Medieval Jewish Thought*, New York: Littman Library, 1986 and idem, *Must a Jew Believe Anything?*, New York: Littman Library, 2006. Even in Maimonides' lifetime, a controversy arose over how deeply he himself was committed to these principles, especially Number 13: belief in resurrection. For Moses Mendelssohn's critique of Maimonides, cf. *Jerusalem*, trans. Alan Arkush, Hanover, N.H.: University Press of New England, 1983, 100–1.

8 Kant, *Religion within the Boundaries of Mere Reason*, 6:166, footnote.

ists, Kantians, Hegelians, Marxists, existentialists, realists, idealists, and almost anything else one could name. In the words of Joseph Albo (1380–1444): "It is clear now that every intelligent person is permitted to investigate the fundamental principles of religion and to interpret the biblical texts in accordance with the truth as it seems to him."[9]

What I propose to do is to look at the concept of freedom in Judaism by examining five central themes: the giving of law, Sabbath observance, repentance, freedom of thought, and messianism. In addition to the biblical text, I will examine a prominent thinker from the middle ages, early modern period, and twentieth century: Maimonides, Spinoza, and Hermann Cohen.

It should come as no surprise that in looking at freedom from so many different perspectives, more than one understanding of it will emerge. It is customary for philosophers to distinguish freedom in a negative sense, i.e. lack of external constraint, from freedom in a positive sense, i.e. self-mastery or self-determination.[10] To take a simple example, I am not free in the first sense if a dictator prevents me from doing what I want. The classic threat to freedom in this sense is, of course, Pharaoh. Suppose, however, that while there are no external constraints to what I can do, there are internal ones. Suppose, in other words, that I am addicted to drugs or alcohol, that I am obsessed with jealousy or revenge, or that my self-knowledge is so distorted that I routinely do things that I come to regret. It could be said that under these circumstances, I am not free because I am at the mercy of harmful or dehumanizing tendencies that spring from within. We do, after all, speak of being a slave to passion. When this happens, even though the problem is internal, it would be fair to say that the person has failed to achieve an adequate degree of self-control and in that sense cannot be said to have acted freely.

---

9 Albo, Joseph, *Sefer ha-Ikkarim*, trans. Isaac Husik, Philadelphia: Jewish Publication Society of America, 1929, Book 1, Ch. 2, 55.

10 The origin of this distinction can be traced at least to Kant's distinction between *Wille* and *Wilkur* and before that to Plato's conception of *boulesis* at *Gorgias* 466b ff. The question raised by Plato is whether I can really be said to do as I wish if my action runs counter to what is in my own best interest. Contemporary philosophers often begin their discussion of this issue by citing Isiah Berlin's famous essay "Two Concepts of Liberty" in: Berlin, Isiah, *Four Essays on Liberty*, London: Oxford University Press, 1969. Berlin is right to point out that the positive conception of liberty runs the risk of becoming another form of tyranny if the question of what is in my own best interest is entirely the hands of other people. It should be clear however that the negative conception of freedom as lack of external constraint runs risks as well, e.g. if a government were to allow people to sell themselves into slavery on the ground that it is up to each individual to decide whether slavery is in his best interest.

As the various conceptions of freedom are developed, we will see that some fit better with the negative conception while others fit better with the positive conception. In the end, I will argue that to understand the role of freedom in Jewish thought, we must do justice to both.

1 The Giving of Law

The normal way to understand the giving of law in a religious context is to invoke the concept of revelation: an omniscient God gives his chosen prophet an authoritative list of do's and don'ts. There are well-defined rewards for obedience and equally well-defined punishments for disobedience. No one doubts that there are passages in the Torah (Pentateuch) that read this way *if viewed in isolation.* As Hegel put it: "All law is given by the Lord, and is thus entirely positive commandment."[11] The fact is however that these passages occur is a larger narrative in which the primary way for God to establish order is not just to hand down law but to offer a covenant (*brit*). There is now general agreement that the model for such covenants was a suzerain treaty between a sovereign and a vassal.[12] But whatever their source, the important point is that a covenant is much more than a simple decree.

In crucial places in the Hebrew Bible, God enters into covenants with Noah, Abraham, the whole Israelite nation, and David. While the latter three deal with the fate of the Jewish people, the Rabbis interpreted the first and oldest, the covenant with Noah, which contains the prohibition against spilling innocent human blood, to apply to all of humanity.[13] In simple terms, this covenant sets forth the basic principles needed to live a civilized life: prohibitions against idolatry, blasphemy, murder, theft, impermissible sexual unions, eating meat from a live animal, and a positive commandment to establish courts of justice.

It goes without saying that not all covenants take the same form. Sometimes they involve a relation between equal parties (Gen 21:32), sometimes between unequal parties (1Sam 11:1), sometimes the relation between a king and his council

11 Hegel, Georg Wilhelm Friedrich, *Lectures on the Philosophy of Religion*, trans. E. B. Spears/J. B. Sanderson, New York: Humanities Press, 1962, vol. II, 211.
12 For the historical background to the biblical notion of covenant, cf. Mendenhall, George, "Ancient Oriental and Biblical Law," *Biblical Archaeologist* 17 (1954), 24–26 as well as idem, "Covenant Forms in Israelite Tradition," *Biblical Archeologist* 17 (1954), 50–76. For further discussion of the philosophic implications of this idea cf. Seeskin, Kenneth, *Autonomy in Jewish Philosophy*, New York: Cambridge University Press, 2001, chapter 2.
13 Talmud, *Sanhedrin* 56a.

(1Chron 11:30), and sometimes a marriage vow (Prov 2:17). Whatever form they take, the important point is that they constitute an invitation. As Exodus 19:5 puts it: "Therefore if you obey my voice and keep my covenant, you will be my treasured possession out of all the peoples of the earth." Note the difference: "*If* you obey my voice," rather than just "Obey my voice." In the former case, the dominant party seeks the recipient's consent; in the latter, consent has no role to play – the recipient is ordered to do something regardless what she thinks about it.

Consent, in turn, is meaningless unless the person who gives it is free to accept the proposal or reject it. To ask for someone's consent is therefore to respect their dignity as a moral agent capable of making up their own mind.[14] Pharaoh ruled as an absolute dictator never asking for anyone's consent. By contrast, God, who is mightier than Pharaoh, asks for consent again and again. In addition to Sinai, the covenant is offered in the plains of Moab, between Mounts Ebal and Gerizim, at Joshua 24, and again at 2 Kings 23. According to Exodus 24: 4, everything God asked of the people was written down so that they could know exactly what they were agreeing to.

At this point, it is necessary to introduce a qualification. When I say that consent implies recognition of human dignity, I do not mean to suggest that the biblical conception of human dignity is a close approximation to ours. We are talking about a culture that accepted slavery, polygamy, arranged marriages, and wars of conquest. It would be thousands of years before someone would argue that every human being is an end in him or herself. A well-known rabbinic passage even has God holding a mountain over the people at Sinai and threatening to drop it on them if they fail to accept what he has offered.[15]

Despite all of this, we should not lose sight of the enormous difference between Pharaoh's way of making law and God's. In addition to issue of consent, there is also that of inclusiveness. When the covenant is accepted at Exodus 24, we are told that all the people answered with one voice and gave their acceptance. At Deuteronomy 29:10, the text goes much further:

> You stand assembled today, all of you, before the LORD your God, the leaders of your tribes, your elders, and your officials, all the men of Israel,

---

14 As I see it, even in those cases where a covenant is given unconditionally as a gift rather than pact or bond (e.g. Genesis 15:18 or Numbers 25:12), the dignity of the recipient is implied.

15 Talmud, *Shabbat* 88a. The rabbis knew that a contract entered into under duress is not valid, hence the suggestion that if this were true, it would destroy the whole Torah. Another suggestion is that the covenant at Sinai was not ratified until the time of Esther, almost a thousand years later. In any case, it is clear from the passage that consent cannot be forced.

> your children, your women, and the strangers who are in your camp, even those who cut your wood and draw your water, to enter into the covenant of the LORD your God, sworn by an oath, which the LORD your God is making with you today.

In a famous essay, Emmanuel Levinas argued that if we were to take all the people who stood at Sinai (the traditional number is 603,550) and multiply it by the number of things the law asks us to do, e. g. to learn, to teach, to observe, and to keep, as well as the number of times it is offered, one would get 48 X 603,550, an enormous number of individual covenants![16]

The exact number is unimportant. What matters is that a God who could destroy heaven and earth just as easily as he created them has asked human beings, from the top of the social register down to the very bottom, to join in a partnership. Why, one may ask, did God go to such lengths to gain the consent of mortal creatures? Why did he not decide that might makes right and rule as Pharaoh did?

From a moral standpoint, the answer is that no matter how much power can be applied, might alone does not make right. While promises of reward and threats of punishment can make it in my *interest* to obey God, they cannot make it my *obligation* to obey. For an obligation to arise, the people must agree to do what God has asked – hence the constant repetition of the act of acceptance. Beginning in the Book of Deuteronomy (31:16–22) and continuing in later prophetic literature, the people's disobedience is compared to sex outside of marriage on the grounds that the people pledged their allegiance to God and now have gone back on their word.[17]

From a theological standpoint, the answer is that God wants more than simple obedience. A famous midrash makes this point by saying: "If you are My witnesses, then I am God ... but if you are not my witnesses, then, as it were, I am not God." It is not that God will cease to exist if the people are not his witnesses but that God's plan for the world will not be complete as long humans and God are estranged.[18] In short, God seeks a partner, and with a partner, the recognition

16 Levinas, Emmanuel, "The Pact," in: Sean Hand (ed.), *The Levinas Reader*, Oxford: Basil Blackwell, 1989, 211–226. The 603,550 figure (Numbers 1:46) is usually taken to refer to men of fighting age. If this number is accurate, the total number of people would have to be close to 2,000,000.

17 Cf., for example, Hosea 1–3, Jer 2, Ezekiel 16.

18 For a modern account of how God can have needs, cf. Novak, David, *The Jewish Social Contract*, Princeton: Princeton University Press, 2005, 179–180. The basic idea is that while there is nothing that God lacks in the sense that getting it would make him a more perfect being, it is

that only a true partner can provide. At Deuteronomy 6:5, he goes further and asks for love. This is what allowed Hosea and other prophets to compare the covenant with a marriage vow. Again the contrast with Pharaoh is telling. An absolute dictator is satisfied with obedience alone; God is not. To rule as a lonely king in heaven without human participation and devotion is contrary to the divine purpose. But such participation and devotion makes no sense unless it is freely given. Absent the element of choice and the result would be a forced marriage rather than a true one.

We can therefore agree with David Hartman, when he says: "The creation of a being capable of saying no to divine commands is the supreme expression of divine love, insofar as God makes room for humans as independent, free creatures."[19] In fact, the ability to say no to God is more than just a remote possibility. Though Abraham is ready to leave his father's house at God's command, and eventually ready to sacrifice his son, it is noteworthy that when God announces his plan to destroy Sodom and Gomorrah, he protests (Genesis 18:25): "Shall not the judge of all earth do what is just?" Despite Abraham's devotion to God, he is willing to say no when God's intention contradicts his own sense of right and wrong.

Then there is Moses. When God first summons him at the burning bush, he is reluctant to take on the role of leader and comes up with so many objections to what God's has asked that he eventually provokes God's anger. Moses' independence of spirit receives further expression in two places where he protests God's plan to destroy the people as a punishment for disobedience. In the first (Exodus 32:13–14), Moses points out that if God carries through on his plan, the Egyptians will form a false impression of the Exodus and God will be breaking the promise he made to Abraham ("You shall be the ancestor of a multitude of nations"). In the second (Numbers 14:13–19), he makes essentially the same points: the nations of the earth will form a false impression and, again, God will be breaking a promise, in this case the one he made to Moses at Exodus 34:5–8 ("The Lord is slow to anger ...").[20]

Abraham and Moses are just two examples of how biblical characters express their independence. One also could cite Job, Jonah, and Jeremiah. It is

---

nonetheless true that God is concerned about the finite beings he has created and wants to see them flourish.

19 Hartman, David, *A Living Covenant*, New York: Free Press, 1985, 24.

20 For further discussion, cf. S. H. Blank, "Men Against God. The Promethean Element in Biblical Prayer," *Journal of Biblical Literature*, 72 (1953), 1–13. For a contemporary version of the same phenomenon, cf. Kolitz, Zvi, *Yossel Rakover Talks to God*, trans. Paul Badde, New York: Pantheon Books, 1999.

not just that God lets these characters talk back to him but that they raise themselves in our estimation by doing so. They are people rather than religious automatons. In many ways, they are fighting our fight, asking the kind of questions that we would ask. Even though their piety is legendary, they do not see piety and the ability to think for themselves as being in conflict with one another. If God wants a real partner, then the terms of the partnership apply equally well whether in heaven or on earth. Mutual recognition has to be given, and promises have to be kept. This is another way of saying that if the partnership is going to amount to anything, then the junior partner cannot be hushed up or forced into submission.

The ability of the junior partner to say no to God or, at the very least, to hold God to account, represents a decisive move in the direction of negative freedom. The dictator has been replaced by a covenant partner. But this should not blind us to the fact that a move has been made in the direction of positive freedom as well. If all that happened is that the dictator was removed, the people would be nothing more than an unruly mob traveling in the desert. At times, e.g. the Golden Calf or the revolt of Korach, this description seems spot on. The truth is, however, that an unruly mob with no external constraints is not the same as a free people. To become the latter, the Israelites must constitute themselves *as* a people, which means that they have to accept the rule of law and commit themselves to a set of goals. What sort of things do they stand for? What sort of things do they reject? The acceptance of a covenant is supposed to answer these questions by having the people commit and recommit to a way of life that insists on the establishment of a civilized order with protections for those at the lower end of the social scale.

It will be objected that if you take the time to examine the covenant that the people accept, you will see a plethora of statutory commandments governing everything from eating to cleaning, from marriage and sexuality to property rights, from holidays to sacrificial rights and priestly vestments. According to tradition, the Torah contains a total of 613 separate commandments.

On the basis of Deuteronomy 4 ("Behold, I have taught you statutes and laws ..."), we can divide the commandments into either of two groups: laws (*mishpatim*) and statues (*chukkim*). The Rabbis argued that the former are ones such that if God had not given them to us, we would have been justified in giving to ourselves.[21] This group would include the prohibitions against murder, lying, or adultery. The latter are completely dependent on God and include such things as the prohibitions against eating pork or wearing a garment with a mixture

21 Talmud, *Yoma* 67b.

of fibers. It is often said that the statutes are what pose a real test of faith because in the absence of a rational reason to obey them, the only reason one can give is that God has commanded them. Since most of the 613 commandments are statutory in nature, it is here that we encounter the criticism that Judaism is a religion of positive commandment issued by a distant and unapproachable God.

Against this way of looking at Jewish law, Maimonides advances two claims. The first is that because God does nothing frivolous or in vain, everything God commands must have a reason behind it.[22] If so, the difference between the laws and statutes must be that in the former case, the reasons for the commandments are plainly visible while in the latter case, the reasons for the commandments have to be investigated. If this is true, then there is no such thing as a commandment that is purely arbitrary. The second is that when God gave the Torah to Israel, he had to take into account the historical experience of the people who received it.[23] Having seen luxurious sanctuaries and a sacrificial cult in Egypt, the people would have expected similar places and practices from Judaism. To give them a religion without animal sacrifice, for example, would be the equivalent of giving modern worshippers a religion without hymns or prayers.

Maimonides buttresses the latter point by engaging in what one might call theological history. Since Abraham came after Noah, we can assume that Abraham was bound by all the commandments contained in the Noachide covenant. As we saw, these laws are binding on the whole human race and are the basic principles needed to live a civilized life. But an atheist could abide by them as long as he did not blaspheme God. Except for the one dealing with law courts, none impels a person to take part in any kind of community practice. A hermit who lived in an isolated location could fulfill them as well. The only commandment that Abraham received that marked him as a Jew is the right of circumcision (Genesis 17:10).

In short, Abraham's religion had nothing in the way of dietary laws, festivals, standardized prayer, special articles of clothing, or Sabbath observance. He sacrificed to God on certain occasions, but for all we know, these sacrifices were spontaneous and did not involve anything in the way of community participation. Maimonides took this to mean that except for circumcision, Abraham's

22 Maimonides, Moses, *Guide of the Perplexed*, trans. Shlomo Pines, Chicago: University of Chicago Press, 1963, 3.28. I should add that according to Maimonides, the search for reasons cannot go into the minute details of worship. While there was a reason why God mandated a sacrificial cult – the people had been accustomed to sacrifice as a mode of worship – it is impossible to say why a ram is needed in one case and a goat in another.

23 Maimonides, *Guide of the Perplexed*, 3.31.

religion was purely intellectual.[24] Thus Maimonides contends that he had good philosophic arguments for the existence of an immaterial God and propagated them as best he could. His arguments were passed on to Isaac and Jacob. As Maimonides sees it, the Israelites abandoned Abraham's religion during the Egyptian captivity not because his arguments were invalid but because people need more than abstract arguments to hold them together as a faith community.

The result is that God had to start the religion all over again at Sinai. Given the failure of Abraham's religion, there was no choice but to introduce festivals, dietary laws, a priestly cast, a Tabernacle where the priests could perform their rights, and Sabbath observance.[25] In addition to reminding people of the promise they made at Sinai, these things would standardize worship and bring them together as a community. Granted that the resulting religion would not be as spontaneous as Abraham's, Maimonides' point is that most people lack Abraham's intelligence and devotion. For the average worshipper, the need for order, tradition, and community involvement cannot be overlooked.

With order, tradition, and community involvement come statutory laws. Just as governments, military regiments, sports teams, and social clubs need ceremonies, standardized clothing, music, and historical markers to hold their members together and reinforce shared commitments, religious communities need them as well. To an outsider, these practices might seem arbitrary, e.g. not boiling a kid in its mother's milk. To an insider like Maimonides, however, these practices direct one's attention to important truths or call to mind collective memories: boiling a kid in its mother's milk was a pagan ritual tied to idolatrous worship.

It follows that if were we to study the history of the ancient Near East, then Maimonides argues, we would find that what at first glance seem like statutory laws forced on the people without rhyme or reason, are in fact meaningful practices designed to teach valuable lessons. So far from the whims of a distant and unapproachable God, they are concessions to human fallibility, in particular the need to band together with like-minded people to pursue common goals.

With Maimonides' theological history in mind, we are in a position to see why it is incorrect to say that in moving from Pharaoh to God, the people traded one form of slavery for another. In addition to the manner in which the law is given – a covenant rather than a marching order – there is also a difference in the content of the law. Pharaoh sought political and economic advantages from the labor of his slaves. By contrast, God seeks only a spiritual partnership.

---

24 Maimonides, *Mishneh Torah*, 1. Laws Concerning Idolatry, 1.2. Needless to say, there is nothing in the biblical text to corroborate this.

25 Maimonides, *Guide of the Perplexed*, 3.32.

It follows that the laws that hold the people together and reinforce the importance of the partnership are mainly for our benefit. Without them religious life would be as futile and chaotic as political life in a state of nature.

The more rational the law becomes, the less it will seem like the arbitrary dictates of a ruler and the more it will seem like the people's effort to achieve a degree of mastery over their own destiny. To see this, it helps to distinguish between simple agreement and genuine consent. To agree to something without proper understanding is not to offer consent. A twelve-year-old girl cannot consent to sexual relations with an adult man no matter how much she may agree to it. By the same token, an adult man in our society cannot consent to slavery even if he is convinced his life would be better if he did. In both cases, the obvious reply would be that the people lack a sufficient understanding of themselves and the values of their society to offer genuine consent. By providing a historical rationale for the statutory dimension of religious law, Maimonides tried to show that in principle the people's consent was informed and therefore represents their considered judgement on how to live a life. To return to Deuteronomy 4:6: "Observe them [the statutes and laws] faithfully, for this is your wisdom and understanding ..."

There is one more issue to take up in regard to the giving of law. It is customary for constitutional democracies to have one branch of government responsible for making the laws and another branch responsible for interpreting them. What do you do when the law is of divine origin? The traditional view is that the revelation that God gave to Moses was perfect in the sense that it lacked nothing. This is based on Deuteronomy 4:2: "You must neither add anything to what I command you nor take anything away from it ..."[26] Thus the rabbis took Leviticus 27:34 ("These are the commandments which the Lord gave to Moses") to mean these are the *only* commandments ..."[27] The problem is that any body of law no matter how extensive is bound to raise questions of interpretation. To take an obvious example, the Torah prohibits work on the Sabbath but provides only a brief description of what counts as work. To fill in the needed gaps, the rabbis went on to write the longest tractate in the entire Talmud. In a moment of self-reflection, they compared the laws of Sabbath observance to a mountain hanging by a thread.[28]

How can one compose a whole tractate if nothing can be added to the original legislation? According to Maimonides, the answer has to do with the justi-

---

26 Cf. Deuteronomy 13:1.

27 Talmud, *Shabbat* 104a, *Yoma* 80a, *Megillah* 2b.

28 Talmud, *Chagigah* 10a.

fication given for the additional material.[29] It is one thing for a person to shed light on the original text by claiming to be the recipient of a divine revelation that provides further instruction and another for a person to shed light on it by advancing a rational argument. Maimonides maintains that the former is committed to saying that the original revelation given to Moses was not complete so that an additional revelation is needed to set things straight. The latter person makes no such claim. In view of this, it is the person who claims to have received a divine revelation who has transgressed the warning "You must neither add anything ... nor take anything away." Maimonides went so far as to say that the former person should be put to death for contravening one of the most sacred principles of the Torah.

The proof text for Maimonides' position is Deuteronomy 30:11–12: "Surely, this commandment that I am commanding you today is not too hard for you, nor is it too far away. It is not in heaven ..."[30] In context, the passage seems to say that the law is not too difficult for human beings to understand and fulfill. But the rabbis and eventually Maimonides took it to say something much stronger: that the Torah is not in heaven. In other words, God gave the entire Torah to Moses at Sinai, from which it follows that after Sinai God has no more Torah to reveal. Thus anything that has to do with the interpretation or application of the Torah cannot be sent from heaven and must derive from human reason alone.[31]

In an important and much-discussed passage in the Talmud, a debate arises in a rabbinic court over how to interpret the law.[32] God enters the debate by working several miracles and eventually proclaiming one side right. At this point, the Rabbi from the other side, the one not favored by God, rises and cites the verse from Deuteronomy 4: "It is not in heaven." Again we have a challenge to divine authority, and again God relents. The result: "God laughed and said: 'You have bested me, my children, you have bested me.'" Here is another case where might does not make right. Having said that the Torah is not in heaven, God must now abide by his own pronouncement. The rabbis took this to mean that rather than deciding legal questions by turning to heaven or listening to a prophet, they would decide them by majority rule of the members of the court.

29 Maimonides, *Mishneh Torah*, Introduction, The Rabbinic Commandments.

30 Maimonides, *Mishneh Torah*, 1. Basic Laws of the Torah, 9.1.

31 In practice, this may have been an anti-Christian polemic because in the eyes of the rabbis, Jesus did claim to bring a second revelation and therefore to supersede the revelation given to Moses at Sinai.

32 Talmud, *Bava Metzia*, 59b.

If one were to look at the Judaism of today and compare it to that of biblical times, one could not help but see a wide range of practices that separate them, including the lighting of candles on Friday night, the wearing of a head covering, the celebration of Hanukkah, Bar and Bat Mitzvahs, and the recitation of standardized prayers. None of these is mentioned in the Torah, which is a way of saying that all are the result of human interpretation. By any estimation, then, the human contribution to Jewish law is considerable. So far from a distant and unapproachable God laying down arbitrary statutes to helpless and unreflective people, what we have is a situation in which the law is shot through with human contributions at practically every level.

To the degree that the human contribution is the result of a majority decision, no single person in heaven or on earth is in a position to dictate what the law requires. This is another way of saying that human choice – the decision of a court – is the deciding factor in determining the direction that interpretation and application must take. Such are the terms of the partnership that God established and that human beings agreed to live by.

2 Sabbath Observance

We owe to Abraham Joshua Heschel the insight that Judaism is a religion that aims at the sanctification of time rather than space.[33] According to the story of creation (Genesis 2:3), God blessed the seventh day and called it holy. As Heschel points out, after creating heaven and earth, we might have expected God to designate a particular region or a particular thing as holy, but that is not how the story goes. To this day, we do not know the exact location of Mt. Sinai or the place where Moses went to die. Though it is true that God commands the construction of a Tabernacle in the Book of Exodus, we should keep in mind that the Tabernacle was intended to be portable.[34] When it was in location A, then A became holy; when it was dismantled and moved on to B, then B became

---

33 Heschel, Abraham J., *Between God and Man*, New York: The Free Press, 1959, 216–8.

34 Although Solomon's Temple was not portable, Solomon himself recognized that neither his building nor the high heavens above it could contain God (1Kings 8:27). Cf. Psalm 139:7–10. On the other hand, there is in Judaism a tradition that regards Jerusalem as the holiest city on earth and the Temple Mount as the holiest place in Jerusalem (Talmud, *Kelim* 1:7–8). The obvious reply is that if holiness reflects the history of what happened somewhere, then this tradition may well be true. In this respect, a battlefield, cemetery, or home of a national hero may be considered holy. But if it is a metaphysical reflection – that somehow God occupies one plot of land in distinction from others, then I submit it cannot possibly be true.

holy. So it was not the ground under the Tabernacle that gave it its special character but the rights performed in it.

The commandment mandating rest on the Sabbath reads as follows (Exodus 20:8–11):

> Remember the Sabbath say, and keep it holy. Six days you shall labor and do all your work. But the seventh say is a Sabbath to the Lord your God. You shall not do any work – you, your son or daughter, your male or female servant, your livestock, or the stranger [alien] who resides in your towns. For in six days the Lord made heaven and earth, the sea, and all that is in them, but rested on the seventh day. Therefore the Lord blessed the seventh and made it holy.

The first thing to notice here is the universality of the wording. The people are to rest because the creator of heaven and earth rested. It is not just the master of the house who gets to rest but everyone within it including servants, landed aliens, even beasts of burden. Again the contrast with space is instructive. Space can be owned, walled off, or fought over. Even if the space we are talking about were as large as North America, it would be all but impossible for a substantial portion of the world's population to occupy it at once. By its very nature, time is different. Everyone on earth can experience sundown on Friday night, no one can have more of it than someone else, and no one can tarnish it or destroy it.

In his critique of Judaism, Hegel argued that a day of idleness was a welcome relief to a band of slaves. For free men and women, "to keep one day in a complete vacuum, in an inactive unity of spirit, to make the time dedicated to God an empty time," is a sign of melancholy and estrangement from God rather than closeness.[35] Against this, it should be noted that Judaism does not denigrate work. Even in Paradise, Adam was given work to do (Genesis 2:15). The Mishnaic tractate *Ethics of the Fathers* (2:2) says that study of the Torah ought to be combined with a worldly occupation lest it lead to sin. While a period of rest is often viewed with relief, the question is *why* one rests. When God rested on the seventh day, it was not because he was exhausted from all his labors and needed to take some time off; rather the fact that he rested is a sign that his labor was not forced but freely chosen. A slave cannot decide when to work and when not to; free men and women can. In other words, the fact that God could decide to cease working when he wanted means that his decision to start working was also freely chosen.

35 Hegel, Georg Wilhelm Friedrich, *Early Theological Writings*, trans. T. M. Knox, Chicago: University of Chicago Press, 1948, 193–4.

As with God, so with human beings. When Moses first encounters Pharaoh at Exodus 5, he asks whether the Israelites can go out to the wilderness to celebrate a festival in honor of God. But Pharaoh, the ultimate taskmaster, objects that this will mean that the people get time off from work. Seen in this light, rest is more than just a way of dealing with exhaustion and more than a way of getting back to work refreshed and ready to go. At its core, rest is a sign that one has achieved mastery of her situation, that even if she enjoys her work, she is not defined by it.

In addition to the issue of choice, there is also the issue of status. For most people, work is hierarchical: there are bosses to please and clients to serve. Cessation of work means that for a short period of time, these hierarchies and the inequalities they introduce are dissolved. In principle, bosses and laborers, free men and servants, and native born and aliens all confront each other as equals. In the words of Deuteronomy 5:14: " ... that your male and female servant may rest as well as you." Because it is forbidden to use money, the same can be said for rich and poor.

Granted that hierarchical relations are reinstated the minute the Sabbath ends. The important point is that if we can look beyond them for even a short time, we put ourselves in a position to see that social hierarchies are not ultimate. While they may be necessary for society to function, they do not reflect the true nature of our humanity – the fact that every human being from the mightiest king to the lowliest worker is a moral agent made in the image of God. If choosing when to work and when to rest is an essential part of freedom, so too is the recognition that our dignity as human beings is not determined by our wealth or social status.

According to Leviticus 25:4, not only must people and animals rest every seven days, the land must rest every seven years. While the land was not created in the image of God, letting it rest is the Torah's way of saying that it too has a certain dignity and cannot take it for granted. It is as if the land has a right to be seen as something more than a resource to be exploited but as something to be cherished and appreciated in its own right.

As noted earlier, we can justify cessation from work on the grounds that time away from the job enables one to return to it refreshed and ready to go. The problem with this view is that it assumes that work and production are the final ends of human life: that we cease working in order to work even harder when we return. Hermann Cohen was therefore right to say that the final end of human life cannot be realized as long as we remain cogs in civilization's machinery.[36] The problem is that civilization's machinery often treats us as means to a greater end – wealth production – rather than ends in ourselves.

We saw that negative freedom concerns the absence of external constraints. What Cohen is getting at here is that such constraints are not limited to the whims of a dictator or taskmaster. Sometimes social structures can become so entrenched that people feel trapped in their jobs or family roles. How free is an unemployed worker who must take on dangerous or demeaning work to support his family? Strictly speaking, no one is interfering with his decision. But if we consider how things look to him, it is hard to avoid the conclusion that he must swallow his pride and do something he would rather not do. Though Sabbath observance alone cannot remedy this situation, it allows us to see that economic production is not the only perspective from which to view human life. For Cohen, as for any thinker in the Kantian tradition, it is only when we take the time to view ourselves as ends *in* ourselves that genuine freedom is possible.

That brings us to the issue of idleness, which suggests sluggishness, lethargy, and lack of commitment. By the same token, rest is often associated with amusement or self-indulgence. The truth is that when the Bible talks about the Sabbath, it generally mentions three things: to remember (Exodus 20:8), to observe (Deuteronomy 5:12), and to delight (Isaiah 58:13). To remember and to observe are active verbs. Normally they find expression in prayer and study. To delight is also active and finds its expression in a ritual meal, wine, song, and merriment.

To follow up on Cohen, these activities are intended to get us to the point where we can look beyond the barriers that divide people and detract from their dignity as moral agents. In words made famous by Martin Buber, it is on the Sabbath that we are most able to leave the network of I-IT relations, where everything has a market value, and enter the world of I-THOU. In fact, the rabbis tell us that the Sabbath is a foretaste of the world to come – a kind of heaven on earth.[37] I mention all of this because gaining such a perspective on human life is not easy; in fact, it may be one of the hardest things we are ever asked to do.

Social hierarchies exist for a reason. Without them factories could not make products, hospitals could not care for the sick, armies could not defend nations, and universities could not teach students. They require our attention for six out of every seven days. The issue is whether we can accustom ourselves to look be-

36 Cohen, Hermann, "Affinities Between the Philosophy of Kant and Judaism," in: Eva Jospe (ed.), *Reason and Hope*, New York: W. W. Norton, 1971, 87.
37 Talmud, *Berakoth 57b.*

yond them – at least temporarily. Can someone at the top of the social scale and someone at the bottom deal with each other as people rather than winners and losers in a competitive system? Or, for that matter, can we look at ourselves as people rather than employers or employees?

For many the answer is not without difficulty. To return to Heschel, who we are depends on what the Sabbath is for us.[38] To the degree that Sabbath observance asks us to look at the world differently from how we normally do, it is connected with the issue of messianism. I will take up messianism in a later portion of this essay; for the present, it is enough to say that both messianism and Sabbath observance ask us to recognize that the way the world is, is not the way it has to be or the way it ought to be.

3 Repentance

On the importance of repentance in Judaism there can be no doubt. A classical rabbinic text asks us to repent one day before our death.[39] Since most of us do not know when we will die, the upshot is that we should repent every day of our lives. The same source tells us that one hour of repentance and good deeds on this earth is better than a whole life in the world to come.[40]

Yet another tells us that where the truly penitent stand, not even the perfectly righteous can stand.[41] Of all the themes taken up in this essay, the connection between repentance and freedom is the easiest to see because to repent in a sincere manner, one must accept responsibility for past mistakes and make a concerted effort not to repeat them. Simply put, to repent means to undergo a change of heart. Unless we were free to make this change, repentance would be a meaningless ritual.

In fact, Maimonides goes so far as to say that for repentance to be genuine, a person must revisit the circumstances that led him to sin and chose the right path instead. In his treatise on the Laws of Repentance, he leaves no doubt about the importance of human freedom:[42]

---

38 Heschel, Abraham J., *The Sabbath*, New York: Farrar, Straus, and Giroux, 1951, 89.

39 *Ethics of the Fathers*, 2.14.

40 Ibid., 4.22.

41 Talmud, *Berakhot* 39b.

42 Maimonides, *Mishneh Torah*, Laws Concerning Repentance, 5. 1–2. Cf. Maimonides' letter on Astrology in *A Maimonides Reader*, 466: "Know, my masters, that every one of those things concerning judicial astrology that (its adherents) maintain—namely, that something will happen one way and not another, and that the constellation under which one is born will draw him

> Free will is granted to all men. If one desires to turn himself to the path of good and be righteous, the choice is his. Should he desire to turn to the path of evil and be wicked, the choice is his. Each person is fit to be righteous like Moses, our teacher, or like Jeroboam. [Similarly] he may be wise or foolish, merciful or cruel, miserly or generous, or [acquire] any other character traits.

In saying that free will is granted to everyone, Maimonides rejects any suggestion that God has identified who will be saved and who will be damned prior to the time they are put on this earth.[43] Unless this were true, he argues, then it would be senseless for God to give commandments of the form "Do this" or "Do not do that." Not only does "ought" imply "can," as Edwin Curley reminds is, it also implies "cannot."[44]

Confronted with Exodus 14:4, where God says that he will harden Pharaoh's heart, Maimonides argues that Pharaoh had chosen of his own accord to commit grievous sins against the Israelites. In fact, these sins were so grievous that God had to exact a severe punishment. That punishment consisted in God's taking away the chance for Pharaoh to repent. If Maimonides is right, then the hardening of Pharaoh's heart came *after* he chose the path of wickedness and did nothing to interfere with it.

Maimonides' commitment to freedom can also be found later on in the *Guide of the Perplexed*, where he says: "It is a fundamental principle of the Law of *Moses our Master*, peace be on him, and of all those who follow it that man has an absolute ability to act; I mean to say that in virtue of his nature, his choice, and his will, he may do everything that it is within the capacity of man to do."[45] Unfortunately the issue of free choice in Maimonides is complicated by two factors. The first is a passage where he claims that every event has a proximate cause, which itself has a cause, which terminates in the will of God. Although the line of intermediate causes that links an event to God is sometimes omitted in the Bible, Maimonides insists that it is God who sets the causal chain in motion. This passage has led to a debate among scholars as to whether, de-

---

on so that he will be of such and such a kind and so that something will happen to him one way and not another—all those assertions are far from being scientific; they are stupidity."

43 Maimonides, *Mishneh Torah*, Laws Concerning Repentance, 5.3.

44 Curley, Edmund, "Kissinger, Spinoza, and Ghenghis Khan," in: Don Garrett (ed.), *The Cambridge Companion to Spinoza*, New York: Cambridge University Press, 1996. 321. For a medieval Jewish statement of the same principle, cf. Gaon, Saadia, *Book of Beliefs and Opinions*, 4:3, 186: "I am of the opinion that the ability to act must precede the act itself to the point where an equal opportunity would be granted to man either to act or desist from acting."

45 Maimonides, *Guide of the Perplexed*, 3.17, 469.

spite his defense of freedom in earlier writings, and in occasional places in the *Guide*, Maimonides was a determinist at heart.[46]

The second factor is the issue of divine foreknowledge. Critics of free will protest that if God's knowledge is perfect, he must already know what a person is going to do, in which case, the person is not free to do anything else. The classic Jewish pronouncement on this issue is that of Rabbi Akiva, who said that everything is foreseen yet free will is given. Unfortunately he did not say how the two are compatible.[47] Maimonides' typical response to the problem is to emphasize that God's knowledge is not like ours so that God's knowing that a contingent even will happen does not rob the event of its contingency.[48] But this leaves several questions unanswered. If, as Maimonides and most of the medieval philosophers believed, God is not subject to change, then God cannot gain any new knowledge by observing the world. Granted that God's knowledge is unlike ours, if it is knowledge at all, its object must be true, in which case anything that God knows must eventually come to pass. How, then, can an agent make a free choice between two options?

The problem of divine foreknowledge is complicated by the fact, that following Aristotle, many medieval philosophers had a more restrictive understanding of knowledge than we have today. For them, knowledge was limited to truths that are universal and eternal. To say that God's knowledge is perfect would mean that in his infinite wisdom, God knows everything that is know*able* but not

46 For the determinist reading, cf. Pines, Shlomo, "Notes on Maimonides' Views concerning Free Will," in *Studies in Philosophy,_Scripta Hierosolymitana*, 6 (1960), 195–98 and Altmann, Alexander, "Free Will and Predestination in Saadia, Bahya, and Maimonides," in: Alexander Altmann (ed.), *Essays in Jewish Intellectual History*, Hanover, N.H.: University Press of New England, 1981, 35–63. Against the determinist reading, cf. Gellman, Jerome, "Freedom and Determinism in Maimonides' Philosophy", in: Eric L. Ormsby (ed.), *Moses Maimonides and His Time*, Washington, D.C.: Catholic University Press of America, 1989, 139–150. The crux of Gellman's position is that God determines only *that* we choose (by endowing us with free will) not *what* we choose. For further defense of free will in Maimonides, cf. Hyman, Arthur, "Aspects of the Medieval Jewish and Islamic Discussion of 'Free Choice'", in: Charles H. Manekin/Menachem M. Kellner (eds), *Freedom and Moral Responsibility. General and Jewish Perspectives*, Bethesda: University Press of Maryland, 1997 and Stern, Josef, "Maimonides' Conceptions of Freedom and the Sense of Shame," in: Charles H. Manekin/Menachem M. Kellner (eds), *Freedom and Moral Responsibility. General and Jewish Perspectives*, Bethesda: University Press of Maryland, 1997. Note in particular Stern's argument that for Maimonides, as for much of the Aristotelian tradition, the fact that an action is caused in the sense that it follows from the agent's choice and deliberation does not necessarily mean that it is necessitated in the sense that the agent could not have done otherwise.

47 *Ethics of the Fathers*, 3:19.

48 Maimonides, *Mishneh Torah*, Laws Concerning Repentance, 5.5; *Guide of the Perplexed*, 3.20.

things that are unknowable and happen by chance. If, as Aristotle argued, there is no science of the individual in its individuality, then God would know individuals to the degree that they exemplify universal forms or patterns but not to the degree that they take action peculiar to themselves. In other words, God would know that as a human being, I must eat to survive but not what I am going to have for dinner tonight.

At *Guide of the Perplexed* 3.17, Maimonides says that he accepts a modified form of the Aristotelian view: people participate in divine providence to the degree that they perfect their intellect; to the degree that they do not, they are subject to chance. This implies that to the degree that my actions are guided by temporal concerns rather than eternal truths, God is not aware of them. Hence the problem of divine foreknowledge does not arise. In this and other chapters, however, Maimonides insists that nothing is hidden from God. Again we must ask: nothing knowable or nothing at all?

Whichever way Maimonides came down on this issue, it is worth noting that one of his best -known successors Levi ben Gershon (1288–1344) came down squarely on the side of saying that God's foreknowledge does not include contingent events.[49] More precisely, God knows *that* there are contingent events but not how they will turn out. Since their outcome is unknowable in principle, this does not compromise divine omniscience. The problem with this view is not hard to see. If God is unaware of most of the decisions people make, how can he reward or punish them for what they do?

The great outlier in medieval Jewish philosophy was Hasdai Crescas (1340–1410), a strict physical determinist. Considered by itself, the will can assent or dissent; considered from a wider context – as an event in the natural order – it is determined by its causes.[50] When we say that an act is voluntary, what we mean is that it is in harmony with the agent's feelings and appetite. By contrast, an involuntary act is one in which the agent is compelled. But all acts are foreseen by God and come about as consequences of a causal chain with God as the ultimate source.

The problem with this view is also easy to see. As Albo, a student of Crescas, remarks: it accomplishes nothing to say that an action is possible when viewed in itself if it is determined by a chain of causes that go all the way back to God.[51] For Albo, the only legitimate understanding of freedom is one in which the agent

49 Gersonides, Levi ben, *Wars of the Lord*, vol. 2, trans. Seymour Feldman, Philadelphia: Jewish Publication Society, 1987, Book Three, 116–134.

50 *Or Adonai*, 2.5.3. For an English translation, cf. Harvey, Warren Zev, *Physics and Metaphysics in Ḥasdai Crescas*, Amsterdam: J. C. Gieben, 1988.

51 *Sefer ha-Ikkarim*, 4.1, 7.

is free to choose one course of action or a different one without causal interference. Though God knows what I will choose, the important point is that God is not the cause of what I choose.[52] It is this insight that allows Albo to say that divine foreknowledge is compatible with free will.

As Jewish philosophy moved from the medieval period into the early modern, the influence of Aristotle waned and was eventually replaced by that of Kant. The Kantian influence on Jewish philosophy is most readily seen in the thought of Cohen. Like Kant, Cohen was skeptical of metaphysics and approached religious questions from a practical rather than a theoretical standpoint.

By his own admission, Cohen's analysis of repentance takes its cue from the prophet Ezekiel. It was Ezekiel (18:2–4) who stressed that children would not be punished for the sins of their parents so that "It is only the person who sins that shall die." According to Cohen, this insight set in motion the whole idea of the individual's responsibility for her own actions.[53] Again from Ezekiel (18:20): "The righteousness of the righteous shall be his own, and the wickedness of the wicked shall be his own." Along with the idea of individual responsibility came an emphasis on the individual's ability to renounce sin and set out on a new path, a process that Cohen describes as self-transformation.[54] As Ezekiel (18:31) implores us: "Cast away from you all the transgressions that you have committed against me, and get yourselves a new heart and a new spirit." By taking responsibility for his own sin and experiencing the power to create for himself a new heart, writes Cohen, the moral individual comes to full fruition.[55]

In this way, no family history or decree of fate stands in the way of the individual's ability to make himself into a new person. In Cohen's words:[56]

> Only now does man become the master of himself; no longer is he subject to fate. It was fate that would not allow man to abandon the way of sin. Man becomes free from this fate through the teaching that sin does not become a permanent offense for man, a permanent reason for stumbling. Through this, man first becomes

---

52 For a similar defense of free will in light of divine foreknowledge, cf. Gaon, *The Book of Beliefs and Opinions*, 191. For more on Albo and the free will debate in medieval Jewish philosophy, cf. Feldman, Seymour, "A Debate concerning Determinism in Late Medieval Jewish Philosophy," *Proceedings of the American Academy for Jewish Research*, 51 (1984), 15–54 and Weiss, Shira, *Joseph Albo on Free Choice*, New York: Oxford University Press, 2017, esp. Chapter 2.
53 Cf. Cohen, Herrmann, *Religion of Reason out of the Sources of Judaism*, trans. Simon Kaplan, New York: Ungar, 1972, 191ff.
54 Ibid., 193.
55 Ibid., 194.
56 Ibid.

> an individual who is not absolutely dependent on the relations of the social plurality in which he is enmeshed. He is an autonomous spiritual unity ...

One more thing is needed for a person to become master of himself. It is not just that the individual is punished for his sin, for punishment is often inflicted from an external source, but that the individual must confess his own guilt, and by so doing, come to punish himself.[57] This too must be freely chosen to have genuine moral significance.

It should be understood that by "autonomous," Cohen does not mean the ability to do whatever one pleases but rather, as Kant understood it, self-imposition of the moral law, which is to say the self-imposition of a law of which one can regard oneself as author.[58] To say that one must be able to *regard* oneself as author is not to say that one must *be* the author in fact. I am not the author of the commandment that prohibits murder; quite possibly no human being is. But I have no trouble viewing this commandment as my own in the sense that it expresses my deepest conviction on how a human life should be lived. To return to Deuteronomy 30, the passage that begins by saying that the law is not in heaven ends by saying that it is written on the heart, meaning that it is part of the moral conscience of every person.

It is here that we come to the crux of positive freedom. To be free is not to have an arbitrary or unpredictable will but to have a will that adheres to a law with which the agent can identify even if she is not the source of the law in a historical sense. Put otherwise, I am free to the extent that the law I impose on myself can be viewed as *part* of myself. Along these lines, Cohen argues that the origin of the moral law is not in question.[59] Rather it is the validity of the law that matters whatever its origin. In a genuine act of repentance, then, the individual first must accept her guilt, then confess her guilt, and finally set herself the task of living according to a law that expresses her own considered judgment about what to do to set things right.

Although repentance, or more generally the task of sanctification, always takes place *before* God, Cohen insists that it is not something that can be brought about *by* God. As he puts it: "... the brining about of redemption is man's independent action."[60] This means that not even an omnipotent God can bring about

57 Ibid., 195.

58 Kant, Immanuel, *Groundwork of the Metaphysics of Morals*, trans. Mary Gregor, Cambridge: Cambridge University Press, 1998, 4:431.

59 Cohen, *Religion of Reason*, 202.

60 Ibid., 202–3.

repentance in a person unless the person himself makes the effort to change his ways.[61] That is why "Cast away ..." is directed to the sinner, not to the God before whom the sinner asks to be forgiven. In keeping with Leviticus 11:44 ("Sanctify yourselves therefore, and be holy"), Cohen understands the process of sanctification as *self-sanctification.*[62] The command is directed to human recipients and can only be accomplished by human actors. In this way, the decision to renounce the past and set out on a new and better path is tantamount to achieving mastery of oneself, which for Cohen and Kant constitutes the very essence of freedom.

Where then does God enter the picture? Cohen continues: "Man himself must cast off his sin, but whether his own deed succeeds, whether it leads to the goal, this he cannot know. His concern is only the task of casting off sin; he is deprived of the knowledge of the result and the success of his action."[63]

Although one cannot demand a guarantee of success, one can hardly say that the person who undertakes the process of self-sanctification can be unconcerned with it. The success of the action is of course the forgiveness of sin by God – in a word, redemption. Unless this were true, unless God had a role to play, self-sanctification would cease to be a religious ideal. For Judaism redemption has always involved two agents. Thus Zechariah 1:3: "Turn back to me – says the Lord of Hosts – and I will turn back to you."[64]

In Cohen's eyes, the forgiveness of sin becomes the ultimate expression of God's goodness. In fact, he goes so far as to say that the entire monotheistic worship is based on the forgiveness of sin.[65] Recall that it was the forgiveness of sin that caused Moses to confront God at crucial places in Exodus and Numbers. Though forgiveness of sin becomes God's special function, it would be a mistake to think that Cohen was following in the footsteps of Heinrich Heine, who said on his deathbed: "*Dieu me pardonnera c'est son metier.* [God will pardon me; that's his job]." It is not that God's act of forgiveness is compelled by some sort of inner necessity but rather that God and God alone is in a position to decide whether our act of repentance is sincere. If it is, then God's act of forgiveness will be forthcoming but as an act of mercy rather than an effect necessitated by a prior cause.

---

61 Cf. Kant, *Religion within the Boundaries of Mere Reason*, 6:44: "The human being must make or have made *himself* into whatever he is or should become in a moral sense, good or evil."
62 Cohen, *Religion of Reason*, 204–5.
63 Ibid., 206.
64 Here it is worth noting that the Hebrew word normally translated "repentance" (*teshuvah*) actually mean to turn or return.
65 Cohen, *Religion of Reason*, 209.

All this means that in repentance, God and the penitent person confront each other as free agents – a relation that Cohen describes as *correlation.* Absent such freedom on either side and repentance would lose any moral significance it has. If Cohen is right in saying that God's willingness to forgive sin is the ultimate expression of God's goodness, then the entire system of religion that Cohen has constructed is built on the assumption that whether in heaven or on earth, freedom of action is essential. In the case of God, whose moral perfection is already in hand, freedom is an essential feature. In the case of humans, whose moral perfection is a task yet to be completed, freedom is an aspiration in the sense that we have to work to become masters of ourselves. The important point is that without freedom, the relation between God and humans would be causal – God as creator – rather than moral – God as the source of mercy. For Cohen this would entail a naturalistic conception of God and thus the death of ethical monotheism.

Not every Jewish thinker would be willing to march under the banner of ethical monotheism. By his own admission, Cohen's view of Judaism is a rational reconstruction: the religion of reason derived from Jewish sources. In effect, he tried to do for Judaism what Kant had done for Christianity, which is to identify and justify its moral core. What emerges is therefore an idealized version of Judaism rather than an account of the religion as actually practiced. But whether one identifies with ethical monotheism or not, there is no getting around the fact that Cohen has put his finger on something important. Like Maimonides before him, Cohen sees divine and human freedom as essential components of the Jewish worldview. Not only do they allow us to make sense of repentance, we have seen that they also crucial for understanding the notion of covenant.

4 Freedom of Thought

In addition to the question of free will, there is also the question of political freedom, by which I mean the ability of a person to think and say what he wants without interference from the government. Unlike Christians and Muslims, Jews have had to deal with minority status for most of their history. There is no need to review the record of oppression, forced conversion, expulsion, and violent opposition except to say that all of the major thinkers mentioned in this essay were in some sense outsiders in the communities in which they lived. Maimonides had to flee his native Cordova at an early age and may have been forced to practice Islam when he lived in Fez.[66] Spinoza was the son of Portuguese parents who had to flee their native land when it was discovered that they had been practicing Judaism in secret. Mendelssohn did not have the rights of a German citizen. Cohen was the first Jew to be appointed Professor at a German university. Levinas spent several years of his life in a Nazi prison camp.

In view of this history, it is easy to understand why most Jews have understood political freedom to involve two things: (1) a return to their homeland, and (2) the ability to practice their religion as they see fit. As late as the Eighteenth Century, Mendelssohn was asked why, if he could convert to Christianity and become a German citizen, he wanted to remain a Jew. The question "Why do you want to remain a Jew?" was hardly novel. Napoleon asked the Jews of France the same question after the *ancien régime* was overthrown and became frustrated with them when they said that they considered themselves both Jewish and French.

From a philosophic standpoint, one of the early champions of free thought and religious toleration was Baruch Spinoza. In the Preface to the *Theological-Political Treatise*, he points out that one of his purposes in writing it is to show that not only can freedom of thought be granted without endangering piety and the peace of the commonwealth, but, on the contrary, piety and the peace of the commonwealth depend on it.[67]

In defense of this claim, Spinoza makes a distinction between civil and religious authority. The former deals with outward behavior such as laws that protect the life and property of the citizens. In this sphere, there need to be courts and judges for the simple reason that if every person were free to interpret the

---

66 For a brief account of Maimonides' life, cf. Kraemer, Joel, "Maimonides. An Intellectual Portrait," in: Kenneth Seeskin (ed.), *The Cambridge Companion to Maimonides*, New York: Cambridge University Press: 2005, 10–57. For a fuller account, cf. idem, *Maimonides. The Life and World of One of Civilization's Greatest Minds*, New York: Doubleday, 2008. Maimonides debt to Islamic thought, especiall al-Fārābī, is well-established. For a recent study, cf. Stroumsa, Sarah, *Maimonides in His World*, Princeton: Princeton University Press, 2009.

67 Spinoza, Baruch, *Theological-Political Treatise*, trans. Samuel Shirley, Indianapolis: Hackett, ^{2}1998, 3. It is well known that the metaphysics advanced by Spinoza in Book One of the *Ethics* is strongly deterministic. It should be pointed out however that while he denied the existence of free will if by that we mean the ability to decide to do or not do something, it is still true that he conceived of himself as a philosopher of liberation. I say this because the overall purpose of the *Ethics* is to free us from superstition and with it the false hopes and fears that it engenders. For Spinoza, the ultimate in human freedom is achieved when one abandons the hope or fear that things might go differently from what they are and accept the necessity of things as a direct consequence of the infinite power of God. This in turn leads to the intellectual love of God as described in *Ethics* Book Five.

civil law as he chose, there would be no such thing as public right and the result would be anarchy.

Religion is a different matter because it is concerned with internal matters or what Spinoza calls matters of the heart as such. According to Spinoza, it is impossible for matters of the heart to be imposed by the state. This is not to deny that states have tried to do exactly that. His point is that if they do, they are taking on an impossible task. How can you tell what someone else is thinking, and even if you could, how can you force them to think something else? In the last analysis, all one can do is rely on persuasion, a good upbringing, and (perhaps) sound judgment. Summing this up, Spinoza concludes with a spirited defense of freedom of thought:[68]

> Therefore, as the sovereign right to free opinion belongs to every man even in matters of religion, and it is inconceivable that any man can surrender this right, there also belongs to every man the sovereign right and supreme authority to judge freely with respect to religion, and consequently to explain it and interpret it for himself.

Why is it inconceivable that the right to free opinion cannot be surrendered? To answer this question, we need to look more closely at Spinoza's understanding of right. The basis of Spinoza's view of the state is that the right of anything is coextensive with its power.[69] Since it is a law of nature that every individual does its best to preserve itself in being, it follows that every individual has the sovereign right to do whatever it takes to achieve this end.

In a state of nature, there is no law, which means that everyone has the right to press his advantage by whatever means are necessary. Since no one's life is free from anxiety in this situation, and everyone's life is wretched as a result, it is in everyone's interest to band together to form a state. Here too the right of the state to do something is a function of its power, the power it derives from the people who came together to form it.

It follows that to the degree that a state can no longer exercise its power, it relinquishes its right to do so. By contrast, the state retains a sovereign right over everything within its power. Because the citizens have surrendered their power to the state, they are bound to obey it in all things. But even if we grant this, it is in the state's interest to issue reasonable commands, lest the citizens rise

---

68 Spinoza, *Theological-Political Treatise*, 103. This line of thought would later be adopted by Mendelssohn, who argued that while the state can persuade or coerce, all the church can do is persuade. Cf. Mendelssohn, *Jerusalem*, 45: "The state [which is content with outward compliance] gives orders and coerces, religion [which seeks inner conviction] teaches and persuades."
69 Spinoza, *Theological-Political Treatise*, 173–4.

up against it and usurp its power. In a democracy, where the rulers are elected by the people, the chances of the people rising up against the state are minimal. Accordingly: "... in a democratic state nobody transfers his natural right to another so completely that thereafter he is not to be consulted; he transfers it to the majority of the entire community of which he is a part."[70]

Spinoza qualifies this position to some extent by saying that no person can transfer all of his rights and therefore all of his power to another. This means that even after the state is formed, each person reserves part of his natural right to himself.[71] Recall Spinoza's claim that it is impossible for the state to exercise control over a person's thoughts. "It will certainly never come to pass," he insists, " that men will think only what they are bidden to think." If the state has no power to control people's thoughts, then by Spinoza's argument, it has no right to do so. Put otherwise, no person can surrender his right to think as he pleases, and any state that fails to recognize this is set on doing the impossible. The result of trying to do the impossible is tyranny and the social chaos and hardship that typically come with it. In a spirit of optimism, Spinoza quotes Seneca to the effect that tyrannical governments never last long.[72]

Against Spinoza, one might object that his view of religion amounts to an oversimplification. Most religions do require some form of outward behavior, especially in regard to the ritual or ceremonial part of their doctrine. Does Judaism not ask one to rest on the Sabbath and refrain from eating pork? Does Christianity not ask for baptism and communion? To the degree that religions do require outward behavior, then, contrary to Spinoza's suggestion, their observance can be mandated by the state. Granted that Spinoza had little sympathy with this aspect of religion. For him true religion is universal and comes down to love of neighbor and justice and mercy for everyone. But religions as practiced are much more particularistic.

One way to defend him on this matter is to turn to Mendelssohn, who pointed out that even when religions ask for outward behavior, they still want such behavior to be motivated by internal states like honesty and sincerity. In his words: "Religious actions without religious thoughts are mere puppetry, not service to God."[73] If this is right, then Spinoza's query is still valid: How can you tell what someone else is thinking, and even if you could, how can you force her to think something else?

70 Ibid., 179.
71 Ibid., 185.
72 Ibid., 178.
73 Mendelssohn, *Jerusalem*, 44.

At bottom, the purpose of the state is to allow people to practice their natural right to think and speak as they please without fear of violence or retaliation – either from civil or religious authorities. Or, to put it another way, the purpose of the state in Spinoza's words is freedom – albeit negative freedom as introduced earlier.[74] A ruler who does not recognize this proceeds at his own peril.

Although some have viewed Spinoza as a proponent of separation of church and state, I agree with Steven Nadler that this interpretation is wide of the mark.[75] Spinoza is adamant that the sovereign is the sole interpreter of religion. Thus: "... no one can properly obey God unless his practice of piety – which is the duty of every man – conforms with the public good, and consequently, unless he obeys all the decrees of the sovereign.[76] We must be careful however lest we conclude that Spinoza wanted to establish a state religion in the usual sense of the term. As we saw, Spinoza's idea of true religion comes down to love of neighbor and justice and mercy for all people. It is the job of the sovereign to do whatever is necessary to ensure that this kind of religion, in effect a secular religion, is adhered to.

To promote the public good, the sovereign can promulgate beliefs, interpret books, and pass laws. To that extent, Spinoza brings in a certain degree of positive freedom as well. Still, it is negative freedom that carries the day: the sovereign cannot force people to pledge alliance to a particular church or prosecute them for heresy if their views of religion depart from established norms.

Spinoza's defense of the authority of the sovereign can be better understood if we view it as an outgrowth of his distrust of the authority of the priesthood. In his opinion, it is the priests who sow divisions among the people, insist on strict adherence to statutory laws, impede the development of science, and prosecute heretics. In his overview of the ancient Israelite state, he argues that political life was relatively secure when the authority of the priests was subordinate to and therefore held in check by Moses. Recall that it was Aaron the priest who allowed worship of the golden calf to proceed and Moses, God's appointed ruler, who put a stop to it. In Spinoza's view, it was in later ages, when the priests usurped the power of the sovereign and eventually took it upon themselves to govern the state, that civil war ensued and security was lost. Worse, the religion that the priests espoused degenerated into superstition and corrupted the plain and simple meaning of the prophets.

---

74 Ibid.

75 Nadler, Steven, *A Book Forged in Hell*, Princeton: Princeton University Press, 2011, chapter 9.

76 Spinoza, *Theological-Political Treatise*, 216.

Spinoza therefore maintains that the priests can function only at the pleasure of the sovereign. While this gives the sovereign more authority over religious matters than we might like, when viewed in its context, it takes authority away from those whom Spinoza thinks have made religion the primary source of intolerance. It is well known that he himself was excommunicated by the rabbinical court of Amsterdam in his early 20's. Moreover by putting all authority in the hands of the sovereign, Spinoza thinks he has eliminated any possibility that church and state could come into conflict and divide the loyalty of the citizens.

Finally in Spinoza's opinion, it is the state, not the church, that is most in tune with natural law. Without the state, life as we know it would be impossible. The same cannot be said for the various faiths that have arisen since ancient times. To the degree that they try to control what people can think and say, these faiths sin against natural law. Because nature's laws are nothing but God's decrees, Spinoza argues that those who insist on the supremacy of one faith at the expense of others have contravened the will of God.[77]

It is not hard to see that the crux of Spinoza's philosophy is his naturalism, in particular the claim that right is coextensive with power. Because the power of nature is infinite, nothing nature does can be considered unjust or immoral. Whatever we may think of them, nature "does not frown on strife, or hatred, or anger, or deceit, or on anything at all urged by appetite."[78] Does this not legitimate tyranny? Spinoza's only reply would be to fall back on the claim that history shows that tyrannical governments are inherently unstable. Thus it behooves a ruler to look to the common good and rule according to the guidance of reason.

The question is whether Spinoza's optimism is warranted. Here one is inclined to object, with Curley, that Stalin ruled the Soviet Union for nearly 30 years while Hitler ruled Germany for 12 years.[79] Aside from the length of their rule, there is the untold suffering and devastation that occurred during it. Do we want to say that their right to do what they did was coextensive with their power to do it? I take it that the answer is a resounding no.

The answer is all the more emphatic for a minority people powerless in the face of a modern totalitarian state, who were almost annihilated by its desire to seek a Final Solution to the "problem" of their existence. While Spinoza's defense of free speech and religious toleration promised a better life for Europe's Jews, even before the twentieth century, his naturalism raised serious questions. Hav-

77 Ibid., 39.
78 Ibid., 174.
79 Curley, "Kissinger, Spinoza, and Genghis Khan," 334.

ing suffered at the hands of tyrants of nearly every description, Jews were much more likely to accept a theory that said not only that power *can* be misused but that it often is. It is to such a theory that we now turn, a theory that makes a principled distinction between what is and what ought to be.

Although some may think that the battle for religious toleration has been fought and won, the issue is still with us. It is not that long ago that Protestants and Catholics were at each other's throats in Northern Ireland. Sunni's and Shiites are actively at war in the Middle East. Conflicts between secular and orthodox Jews are commonplace in Israel as are conflicts between secular and religious Muslims in Turkey and parts of Europe. Abortion, prayer in the public school system, and the right to discriminate against homosexuals are pressing issues in the United States, where large groups of people still insist on having "Creation Science" taught as a viable alternative to the theory of evolution. Last, of course, is the ever-present specter of religious terrorism in virtually every corner of the world.

Although Spinoza saw priests as the source of the problem and secular rulers as the source of the solution, in our day, it is hard to generalize. There are tolerant priests who are comfortable with science and secular rulers who appeal to bigotry. What then? The first thing to notice is that whether we are talking about the Seventeenth Century or the Twenty First, Spinoza's universal religion – love of neighbor and justice and mercy for all – is not a religion at all as most people understand the term. There is no transcendent God to issue commandments and no rituals to induce a mood of piety. What he calls a religion would for most people be the foundation of a theory of universal rights.

The second thing to notice is that Spinoza needs to go into more detail about what "the sovereign" consists of. If we ask in what kind of society people's rights have the best chance of surviving, the answer is not one in which one person or even one institution is in charge. To take account of this, Spinoza would have to extend his understanding of democracy to include more than popular sovereignty. As we know all too well, popular opinion can get things tragically wrong – even to the point of handing the government over to a tyrant. In short, a true democracy would have to include a variety of institutions that increase the participation of the citizens and act as a check on any one institution acquiring too much power, e.g. a constitution, a free press, an independent judiciary, and civilian control of the military. Not only would this prevent one person or institution from gaining too much power, it would prevent him (or them) from putting forward a single view of what "true religion" requires. The priests could still practice traditional religion, provided that they obeyed the same laws that apply to every other citizen.

5 Messianism

Although it is often said that monotheism is Judaism's great contribution to world culture, I have argued at length that an equally important contribution is the idea that the future will be better than the past.[80] In simple terms, messianism amounts to repentance writ large for it claims that one day the evil and suffering we see around us will be eliminated making way for an age of justice and peace. We have seen that for Jews "justice" normally involves an end to exile and return to national sovereignty. Maimonides expressed the hope for a better future as follows:[81]

> King Messiah will arise and restore the kingdom of David to its former state and original sovereignty ... He who does not believe in a restoration or does not wait the coming of the Messiah denies not only the teachings of the prophets but also those of the Law of Moses our Teacher.

Strictly speaking there is no mention of the coming of a Messiah in the Torah, and it is questionable whether most modern Jews would be happy with the reinstitution of a monarchy. For my purposes, what is important here are the assumptions that underlie Maimonides' position.

The first such assumption is that human history is not destined to repeat its past mistakes: no divine decree or tragic fate prevents humanity from righting the wrongs that it has inflicted on itself. This is another way of saying that we are free to set out on a new and better course if we choose to do so. The second assumption is that either with God's help or by coming to its senses, humanity will one day make this choice. This, in turn, is another way of saying that not only are we free to set out on a better course but that it is reasonable to hope that we will. Putting the two together, we get the claim that the way things are is not the way they should be or in time the way they will be. Thus Isaiah 43:18–19: "Do not remember the former things, or consider the things of old. I am about to do something new."

The theme of newness is evident in the Hebrew Bible right from the start. With the words "In the beginning ..." the Bible raises the possibility that there might also be a middle and an end. Much of the narrative of the first five books involves the theme of travel. Abraham is asked to leave the house of his

80 Seeskin, Kenneth, *Jewish Messianic Thoughts in an Age of Despair*, New York: Cambridge University Press, 2012, chapter 1.
81 Maimonides, *Mishneh Torah*, 14, Kings and Wars, 11.1.

father and go to a new land. Jacob is constantly fleeing his adversaries. Moses escapes the Egyptian authorities and takes up residence with the Midianites. Finally there is the Israelites' 40-year journey through the wilderness to the Promised Land. Note, as Walzer does, that unlike the *Odyssey*, where the title character returns home, these stories have people traveling to places they have never seen before.[82] Not only do the biblical characters go from A to B, but in so doing they often experience new and unprecedented events. In short, these narratives encourage the reader to think that the future is not predetermined but open to new possibilities.

Even when the Israelites finally enter the Promised Land, obstacles remain. There are wars to fight, including civil wars, corrupt rulers to deal with, and prophetic utterances to the effect that the people have neglected the poor and strayed from God. Shortly before Moses dies (Deuteronomy 31:16–18), God tells him that the people will lust after strange gods and that his anger will be kindled against them. The result is that however momentous their entry into the Promised Land, it cannot serve as the end of the story. Something else must happen if the promise of the early books is to be fulfilled. It is hardly surprising, then, that the prophets introduce the idea that history will culminate in a cosmic upheaval in which evil will be swept away and the proper order installed.

According to Amos (8–9), the Day of the Lord will be a bitter, awful time when no light will shine and famine will destroy the land. The punishment for sin will be so severe that no one from those in Sheol to those at the top of Mt. Carmel will escape. This will be followed by a glorious period in which the House of David will be rebuilt and Israel's fortunes restored. Jeremiah (4) proclaims that the earth will be waste and void, the heavens will have no light, the mountains will quake, cities will lie in ruins, and one disaster will follow upon another. Isaiah (6) asks God to stop up the people's ears and close their eyes so that cities will be ruined and the land will be desolate. He then (Isaiah 11) proclaims that a king will come forth from the house of David and rule over a reconstituted Israel (Isa 11). That king will be the Messiah.

The word *messiah* simply means the anointed one of God. Originally it referred to kings or priests who were anointed in special ceremonies.[83] Eventually it came to mean not just a king but a redeemer who would preside over a new world order. Thus Isaiah 11:9: "The earth shall be full of the knowledge of the Lord, as the waters cover the sea" and Ezekiel 37:5: "I will cause breath to enter you and you shall live again." It is impossible to overestimate the impor-

82 Walzer, *Exodus and Revolution*, 11.

83 Cf., for example, Exodos 29:41, where Moses is told to anoint Aaron's sons.

tance of these sentiments for our understanding of history. As Kant tells us: "The hope for better times, without which an earnest desire to do something that benefits the general good would never have warmed the human heart, has always influenced the work of the well-intentioned."[84] Similarly Reinhold Niebuhr writes that: "Without the ultrarational hopes and passions of religion no society will ever have the courage to conquer despair and attempt the impossible."[85]

If causal determinism is the enemy of freedom from a metaphysical standpoint, then despair is its enemy from a moral one because it encourages us to think that we have no choice but to continue doing what we have always done even if the results are unsatisfactory. The prophetic utterances just mentioned say otherwise. A cosmic upheaval may have a devastating impact on those affected by it, but if it were to occur, it would allow humanity to forget the past and start over again, much as God does after the flood. Even if there is nothing so dramatic in store, a society that has the courage to attempt what might seem impossible to some still could accomplish a great deal. Again it is important to consider the political realities that helped shape this literature. A small nation sandwiched between much larger ones does not want to be told that all it has to look forward to is one power play after another. Reduced to simplest terms, the prophets looked forward to an age when justice would triumph over power.

This view is unrealistic, to say the least. No historical evidence supports it, and common sense argues against it. What the prophets are asking us is to put historical evidence and common sense aside and look at the world in moral rather than natural terms. In the words of Emmanuel Levinas: "This most ancient of claims is its [Judaism's] claim to a separate existence in the political history of the world. It is the claim to judge history – that is to say, to remain free with regard to events, whatever the internal logic binding them. It is the claim to be an eternal people."[86] If the debate over freedom and determinism in medieval philosophy is focused on the metaphysical space for freedom, Levinas' remarks about history are focused on the moral space. In his opinion, Judaism is distinguished by its belief that we can pledge ourselves to ideals that go well beyond anything that history can validate. From the fact that something has not happened yet, it does not follow that it can never happen.

---

84 Kant, Immanuel, "Theory and Practice," in: *Perpetual Peace and other Essays*, trans. T. Humphrey, Indianapolis: Hackett, 1983, 86.

85 Niebuhr, Reinhold, *Moral Man and Immoral Society*, Louisville: Westminster John Knox Press, 1932, reprint 2001, 81.

86 Levinas, Emmanuel, *Difficult Freedom*, trans. Sean Hand, Baltimore: Johns Hopkins University Press, 1990, 199.

If such thinking has preserved Judaism over the centuries, it has also cost it dearly. As the historian Heinrich Graetz put it, messianism is both Pandora's box and the elixir of life.[87] It is an elixir to the degree that it allows a people to overcome despair. But it can be Pandora's box to the degree that it opens people to false hopes, especially in times of crisis. Even a casual observer cannot help but notice that the history of Judaism is littered with false hopes, false messiahs, and wild speculation about the circumstances in which the true one will appear. Though hope is needed when things get difficult, it is precisely when things get difficult that people are most susceptible to folly.

We can see this by looking at the Roman occupation of Judea, during which two attempts at revolution failed. In regard to the first, Josephus writes:[88]

> Their chief inducement to go to war was an equivocal oracle
> also found in their sacred writings, announcing that at that time
> a man from their own country would become Monarch of the world.
> This they took to mean the triumph of their own race, and many
> of their own scholars were wildly out in their interpretations.

This led to the destruction of Jerusalem, civil war between competing Jewish factions, numerous massacres and crucifixions, and a large number of people being taken away as slaves. In the second attempt, the Jews were led by Bar Kochba, a man proclaimed the Messiah by no less an authority than Rabbi Akiba. But the revolution was defeated by a scorched earth policy meant to teach the Jews a lesson for all time.

The failure of the second attempt at revolution raised a number of questions. The first and most obvious one asks what the Messiah is supposed to be: a warrior who will put an end to foreign domination or a Torah scholar who will lead the people back to the religion as it supposed to be practiced? The second question returns us to the fundamental problem: What is the proper response to misfortune – despair or hope? Faced with these issues, rabbinic authorities in late antiquity were deeply ambivalent about the status of messianic longings. Given the horrors of exile and oppression, they were hardly in a position to squelch a belief that gave the people something to hope for. At the same time, they could not be completely comfortable with a doctrine that had led to two dis-

---

87 Graetz, Heinrich, "The Stages in the Evolution of the Messianic Belief," in: Ismar Schorsch (trans. and ed.), *The Structure of Jewish History and Other Essays*, New York: Jewish Theological Seminary, 1975, 151–52.

88 Josephus, Flavius, *The Jewish War*, trans. G. A. Williamson, Middlesex: Penguin, 1959, 6.312–3.

astrous wars, spawned a rival religion, and on some interpretations puts more emphasis on military prowess than on observance of the commandments.

One will look in vain through rabbinic literature for a coherent view of what the Messiah will do or when he will come.[89] Rather one will find a variety of suggestions, each with a different idea of what the Messiah will be and when he will come. The Messiah will come when Israel repents and observes a single Sabbath in accordance with established rules.[90] The Messiah will come when human behavior becomes utterly intolerable and desperate measures are needed to correct it.[91] The Messiah has already come so that all we can do is commit ourselves to improved behavior.[92] The Messiah will usher in an apocalypse.[93] The Messiah is already here in the person of a leper bandaging his wounds outside the gates of Rome.[94]

It was amidst such chaos that Maimonides tried to introduce order into the discussion. Following yet another rabbinic precedent, he argues that the only difference between life now and life then is that Israel will regain political sovereignty, be at peace with the rest of the nations, and rather than constantly preparing for war, be able to devote itself entirely to study and worship.[95] In his opinion, then, there will be no cosmic upheaval or apocalypse. All references to such upheavals in the works of the prophets should therefore be read as predicting the downfall of political regimes rather than natural disasters. By the same token, Isaiah's vision at 11:6 ("The wolf shall dwell with the lamb ...") is only a way of saying that Israel will live in peace with its neighbors. In fact, human behavior will be largely the same as it is now, except of course for the absence of war. There will still be rich and poor, strong and weak. In time, the Messiah will die a natural death.

As Maimonides sees it, the significance of the messianic age is that it will free people from the economic and political realities that make the current order burdensome and allow them to devote themselves to the things that really matter. In his words: "The sages and prophets did not long for the days of the Messiah that Israel might exercise dominion over the world, rule the heathens, or be exalted by the nations, or that it might eat, drink, and rejoice. Their aspi-

---

89 For further discussion, cf. Neusner, Jacob, "Messianic Themes in Formative Judaism," *Journal of the American Academy of Religion*, 52 (1984), 357–74.

90 Talmud, *Sanhedrin* 97b, *Taanit* 64a.

91 *Sanhedrin* 97a.

92 *Sanhedrin* 97b.

93 *Megilla* 11a, *Sanhedrin* 97b.

94 *Sanhedrin* 98a.

95 Maimonides, *Mishneh Torah* 14, Kings and Wars, 11.3, 12.1. For rabbinic precedents, cf. Talmud, *Berakhot* 34b, *Shabbat* 63a, 151b, *Sanhedrin* 91b, 99a.

ration was that Israel be free to devote itself to the Law and its wisdom."[96] Again we have the joining of a negative conception of freedom with a positive one. Because peace will reign, other nations will be able to follow Israel's lead and devote themselves to the acquisition of wisdom. There is even a passage, often deleted from editions of the *Mishneh Torah*, in which Maimonides suggests that Christianity and Islam will be educate people on the virtues of monotheism.[97]

It should be understood that for Maimonides, the acquisition of knowledge involves more than the gaining of information as we understand it but rather a gradual shift in orientation from material matters to spiritual and from temporal truths to eternal. In the *Guide of the Perplexed* (3.11), he goes so far as to say that the major evils that people inflict on each other all stem from ignorance. If ignorance could be replaced by knowledge, then "they would refrain from doing any harm to themselves and to others. For through cognition of the truth, enmity and hatred are removed and the inflicting of harm by people on one another is abolished." It should also be understood that as Maimonides understands it, the messianic age will not be a utopian paradise in which people acquire immense wealth, eat lavish meals, and enjoy generous amounts of leisure time. Since these things have nothing to do with perfecting our nature as human beings, they have no place in the picture.

The thinker for whom messianism plays the most important role is Hermann Cohen. But before we can examine his views, we have to return to Kant. Kant makes clear at the outset of the *Critique of Pure Reason* (Bxx) that by its very nature reason seeks the unconditioned, or as we might say, the absolute. Given a series of causal interactions such that A causes B, which causes C, etc., reason posits the idea of a first cause which is responsible for the entire series. Given the judgment that one institution is more just than another, reason is led to the idea of perfect justice. There is nothing wrong with this so long as we do not make the mistake of thinking that because reason has arrived at a certain idea, it has grounds for asserting the existence of something outside the mind to which that idea corresponds. In Kant's terms, the ideas of reason are regulative rather than descriptive. Thus:[98]

> Plato made use of the expression *idea* in such a way that we can readily see that he understood by it something that not only could never be borrowed from the senses, but that even goes far beyond

96 Maimonides, *Mishneh Torah* 14, Kings and Wars, 12.4.

97 Ibid., 11.

98 Kant, Immanuel, *Critique of Pure Reason*, trans. Paul Guyer/Allen Wood, New York: Cambridge University Press, 2009, A313/B370.

> concepts of the understanding (with which Aristotle occupied himself), since nothing encountered in experience could ever be congruent to it.

Seen in this way, reason offers us awareness of things to which no experience can ever be adequate. No experience can present us with a first cause or a society that is perfectly just. But that does not mean that these ideas are worthless. On the contrary, they are indispensable for practical purposes. The fact that no society on earth has ever been perfectly just has no tendency to show that we should ignore the idea of perfect justice when it comes to evaluating the societies we currently inhabit. Without the idea of perfect justice, we would succumb to a tendency to become content with *imp*erfect justice, which would amount to a capitulation to evil. This is part and parcel of Kant's distinction between *is* and *ought*. It is the job of reason to keep the latter squarely before our minds and to supply a target at which we should aim. If we were to derive our idea of virtue from experience alone, in Kant's view, we would make of it "an ambiguous non-entity."[99]

If no experience can ever be adequate to the kind of idea Kant is talking about, how can we use such ideas as targets? Kant answers that we follow such ideas "only as asymptotically, as it were, i.e. merely by approximation, without ever reaching them ..."[100] Or again: "It is man's duty to *strive* for ... perfection, but not to *reach* it (in this life), and his compliance with this duty can, accordingly, consist only in continual progress."[101] What is true of individual agents is also true of humanity as a whole. Although it must strive for the Kingdom of God, it cannot realize it by undertaking a finite series of steps.

Applying this conception of progress broadly, we arrive at the view that it is instructive to regard human history messianically – not as achieving perfection but as trying to approximate it. Accordingly we can say that religion has advanced from superstition and primitive forms of worship to more advanced forms that stress the inner life of the individual and her freedom to transform it. Political history has marched, however slowly, toward the institution of a democratic republic founded on equal rights for all citizens. Most important, from Kant's perspective, humanity has begun to throw off the bonds of its self-incurred tutelage and embrace the idea of enlightenment.

99 Ibid., A315/B371.

100 Ibid., A663/B691.

101 Kant, Immanuel, *The Metaphysics of Morals*, trans. Mary Gregor, Cambridge: Cambridge University Press, 1991, 446:241.

Here we must be careful. Kant is not arguing that empirical evidence gathered from history supports the claim that humanity has made moral progress. Although it may seem as if progress has been made if we look at certain periods of time, the opening remarks of *Religion within the Boundaries of Mere Reason* dispel any notion that Kant was an optimist about human behavior taken as a whole. Rather, Kant's position is that for practical reasons it is beneficial to regard human history *as if* it makes progress lest we come to believe, as many do, that moral progress is impossible. The problem with the latter belief is that it would amount to another way of capitulating evil.

That brings us to Cohen. In keeping with the idea that experience can never furnish us with the unconditioned, Cohen characterizes the coming of the Messiah by saying: "his coming is not an actual end, but means merely the infinity of his coming, which in turn means the infinity of development."[102] In this way, the messianic age is always ahead of us. Along these lines, Steven Schwarzschild, a disciple of Cohen maintained that: "the Messiah not only has not come but also will never have come … [rather] he will always be coming."[103] No matter how much progress humanity makes in creating the conditions necessary for the arrival of the Messiah, there will always be more progress to be made. In support of this, Cohen argues that man "always feels himself to be innately infirm and defective" and cites Ecclesiastes 7:20 ("For there is not a righteous man on earth, who does good and sins not.").[104]

If the messianic age is a moral ideal, then for Cohen it must be stripped of any taint of mythology. The first thing he does is to point out that it is not a return to a Golden Age or a recovery of lost innocence. At no point do the prophets

102 Cohen, *Religion of Reason*, 314–5.

103 Schwarzschild, Stephen, *The Pursuit of the Ideal*, Menachem Kellner (ed.), Albany: SUNY Press, 1990, 211. Cf. Patterson, David, "Though the Messiah May Tarry: A Reflection on Redemption," *May Smith Lecture on Post-Holocaust Christian Jewish Dialogue*, Florida Atlantic University, January 26, 2009, 16: "the Messiah is by definition *the one who tarries*, signifying a redemption that is *always yet to be*, always future, because what we do now is never *enough*." This idea can also be found in post-modernists like Blanchot and Derrida, who stress that the future must always contain an element of openness or indecidability so that the Messiah can never actually be present. Cf. Blanchot, Maurice, *The Step Not Beyond*, trans. Lycette Nelson, Albany: SUNY Press, 1992, 108, 137 and Derrida, Jacques, *Specters of Marx*, trans. Peggy Kamuf, New York/London: Routledge, 1993, 81–82. The difference is that for Schwarzschild, the messianic has the content of a Kantian regulative idea while for Derrida, who upholds the notion of the "messianic without messianism," it has no content. For Derrida, then, there is no set doctrine or structure that will be realized at a future point, only an eternal oppeness to the possibility of what could be. For further comment on Derrida, cf. Kavka, Martin, *Jewish Messianism and the History of Philosophy*, New York: Cambridge University Press, 2004, 195–98.

104 Cohen, *Religion of Reason*, 211.

suggest that the culmination of history will be a return to the Garden of Eden before Adam and Eve ate the forbidden fruit. In fact, the text of Genesis (3:24) makes it clear that such a return is impossible. Rather than going back to an imagined age before the emergence of culture and civilization, what the prophets envision, and what later Jewish thinkers like Maimonides insisted on, is a future age in which the impediments to culture are removed and knowledge becomes widespread. Thus: "All peoples transfer the Golden Age into the past, into the primeval time; only the Jewish people hopes to see in the future the development of mankind. Messianism alone maintains the development of the human race, while the Golden Age represents the idea of a decline."[105]

Along these lines, Cohen credits Maimonides with removing any hedonistic overtones from the idea of the messianic age.[106] As we saw, Maimonides claims that the prophets did not long for the days of the Messiah in order to achieve political power or to eat, drink, and be merry. They did so in order that people could devote themselves to study and worship without having to worry about war or social inequality. For Maimonides, study would have included natural science, astronomy, and mathematics in addition to the Torah and Talmud. We also saw that Maimonides rejected the idea that the messianic age will involve miracles and insisted that human nature would remain as it now is. Cohen therefore credits him with the realization that messianism is not utopianism.[107]

Cohen's next step is to purify the idea of a messianic age by arguing for its universality. True messianism involves more than just the redemption of the Jewish people but the redemption of mankind as a whole.[108] In that sense, it is similar to Kant's idea of the Kingdom of Ends. For all of his ethical sophistication, Plato did not have the idea of mankind because in Cohen's view, he lacked the central insight of all monotheistic religion: that whatever their differences, all people have a common origin in God. For Cohen, the idea of humanity is central to morality, whose primary rule is that any maxim must have universal applica-

105 Ibid., 289.
106 Ibid., 310–11.
107 Ibid.
108 Cohen (*Religion of Reason*, 262) argues that the prophets did adhere to a national consciousness but argues that this does not exhaust the full moral significance of their thought, which he takes as universalistic. Along these lines, it is important to recall that Cohen was not a Zionist. Cf. "An Argument Against Zionism: A Reply to Dr. Martin Buber's Open Letter to Hermann Cohen," in: Cohen, *Reason and Hope*, 170: "We invoke all those Biblical utterances which proclaim, without resorting to imagery, the One God as 'the Lord of the whole earth' (Micah 4:13)."

bility to be valid.[109] So while the prophets talk about Israel, Cohen argues that they really have a broader focus: "Thus Israel, as a nation, is nothing other than the mere symbol for the desired unity of mankind."[110]

In this case, unity means mutual recognition of the dignity of all people as ends in themselves, or as the Bible puts it, as creatures made in the image of God. Accordingly: "Messianism is the straightforward consequence of monotheism."[111] Thus the two tasks of the Messiah are the ideal of morality and the unity of mankind. To repeat: the ideal of morality does not refer to a sinless state reminiscent of the Garden of Eden but rather to a state of reconciliation between mankind and God, where mankind is honest about confessing its sins and its sins are forgiven as a result.

Finally Cohen goes to great lengths to insist that messianism refers to an age rather than the appearance of a particular person. There is, then, no cult of personality in Cohen's view of the Messiah. This means that empirical questions like how we will separate the real Messiah from pretenders, when and where the Messiah will arrive, and exactly what the Messiah will do are eliminated. As an idea of reason, the content of the messianic age is known a priori.

The connection between messianism and freedom should now be clear. Humanity is not compelled to repeat past mistakes but has the ability to renounce the pursuit of power and pleasure and set itself on a new path. According to the prophets, not only *can* this happen, but in time it *will*. In Cohen's words: "The Messianic idea offers man the consolation, confidence, and guarantee that not merely the chosen people but all nations will, at some future time, exist in harmony, as nature does today."[112]

Beyond the confidence that humanity will start on a new path, there is the conviction that as it comes closer to the ideal of a unified humanity in correlation with a forgiving God, people will be coming closer to the ideal of rational self-determination or positive freedom. Kant insists that to be moral, an action must be done not just in accordance with duty but for the sake of duty. The only way we can act for the sake of duty, which is to say the only way we can

109 For those unfamiliar with Kant's terminology, a maxim is simply the rule or principle on the basis of which a person performs an action. For example, if I give money to charity, my maxim is "One should give to charity whenever possible," or "Giving to charity is good." It should be noted that maxims can be either moral or immoral. An example of the former is "One should give to charity whenever possible." An example of the latter is: "One should lie if it is in one's interest to do so."

110 Cohen, *Religion of Reason*, 253.

111 Ibid., 255.

112 Cohen, "The Messianic Idea," in: *Reason and Hope*, 126.

guarantee the universal applicability of the maxim according to which we act, is to follow the dictates of reason. According to the positive conception of freedom, then, it is reason that makes us free by setting us on the path to morality.

As humanity overcomes its obsession with power and pleasure and begins to devote itself to the goal of achieving universal human dignity, in Cohen's eyes, it is moving from self-imposed bondage to desire and inclination to freedom in the true sense of the word. In its own way, this transition would as momentous as the Exodus from Egypt – perhaps more so. The difference is that while the Exodus from Egypt was completed in the space of a generation, according to Cohen, the days of the Messiah would require the effort of multiple generations and always be a step ahead of us.[113]

6 Conclusion

It is not my purpose to argue that there is a consistent line of development that stretches from the story of the Exodus to the thought of Cohen and Levinas. It should be clear by now that Jewish thought contains several conceptions of freedom and that not all of its spokesmen would agree with other. But it should also be clear that under some description or another, freedom plays a critical role in Judaism's self-understanding. One could almost say that without the concept of freedom, the standard Christian critique of Judaism would have merit: it would be a collection of statutory laws that leave the inner life and the aspirations of its followers unaddressed. Under these conditions, service to God would resemble service to a tyrant.

Fortunately that is not the case. The dignity of the moral subject, her right to think for herself, speak for herself, redirect the course of her life, and work to correct the injustices of the past are everywhere present. Even "present" may be too weak, as we have seen, it could be replaced by "celebrated." We have also seen that as various understandings of freedom are examined, it is natural to distinguish between a negative and a positive conception. Important as it is, release from Egyptian bondage is only part of the story. There also has to be an end of the story, which is to say an age when human beings come to realize their full potential as moral agents.

If there is a philosophic lesson to be learned, it is that the obstacles to freedom come in a variety of shapes and sizes. The most obvious is the tyrant. But we could make no greater mistake than to think that once the tyrant has been

113 Cohen, *Religion of Reason*, 314–15.

removed, freedom is guaranteed. In addition to the tyrant, there is divine predestination, social inequality, lack of self-awareness, stubbornness, laziness, close-mindedness, and, of course, despair. If the first three are external threats, the others are internal.

For those of us fortunate enough to live in a constitutional democracy, it may be that the most formidable threat to freedom are the internal ones, in particular the view that because history has always turned out a certain way, there are no alternatives worthy of consideration – that we are destined to repeat past mistakes no matter how hard we try to avoid them. More than anything else, it is this attitude that limits our choices and prevents us from realizing our full potential. Freedom, as Emmanuel Levinas reminds us, is difficult. But then Judaism is difficult too and for exactly the same reasons.

Bibliography

Albo, Joseph, *Sefer ha-Ikkarim*, trans. Isaac Husik, Philadelphia: Jewish Publication Society of America, 1929.

Altmann, Alexander, "Free Will and Predestination in Saadia, Bahya, and Maimonides," in: Alexander Altmann (ed.), *Essays in Jewish Intellectual History*, Hanover, N.H.: University Press of New England, 1981.

Black, S. H., "Men Against God. The Promethean Element in Biblical Prayer," *Journal of Biblical Literature*, 72 (1953), 1–13.

Blanchot, Maurice, *The Step Not Beyond*, trans. Lycette Nelson, Albany: SUNY Press, 1992.

Berlin, Isaiah, *Four Essays on Liberty*, London: Oxford University Press, 1969.

Cohen, Hermann, "Affinities Between the Philosophy of Kant and Judaism," in: Eva Jospe (ed.), *Reason and_Hope*, New York: W. W. Norton, 1971.

Cohen, Hermann, *Religion of Reason out of the Sources of Judaism*, trans. Simon Kaplan, New York: Ungar, 1972.

Curley, Edmund, "Kissinger, Spinoza, and Ghenghis Khan," in: Don Garrett (ed.), *The Cambridge Companion to Spinoza*, New York: Cambridge University Press, 1996.

Derrida, Jacques, *Specters of Marx*, trans. Peggy Kamuf, New York/London: Routledge, 1993.

Feldman, Seymour, "A Debate concerning Determinism in Late Medieval Jewish Philosophy," *Proceedings of the American Academy for Jewish Research* 51 (1984), 15–54.

Gaon, Saadia, *The Book of Beliefs and Opinions*, trans. Samuel Rosenblatt, New Haven: Yale University Press, 1948.

Gellman, Jerome, "Freedom and Determinism in Maimonides' Philosophy," in: Eric L. Ormsby (ed.), Moses Maimonides and His Time, Washington, D.C.: Catholic University Press of America, 1989.

Gersonides, Levi ben, *Wars of the Lord*, vol. 2, trans. Seymour Feldman, Philadelphia: Jewish Publication Society, 1987.

Graetz, Heinrich, "The Stages in the Evolution of the Messianic Belief," in: *The Structure of Jewish History and Other Essays*, trans. Ismar Schorsch, New York: Jewish Theological Seminary, 1975.

Hartman, David, *A Living Covenant*, New York: Free Press, 1985.
Harvey, Warren Zev, *Studies in the Physics and Metaphysics of Ḥasdai Crescas*, Amsterdam: J. C. Gieben, 1988.
Hegel, Georg Wilhelm Friedrich, *Early Theological Writings*, trans. T. M. Knox, Chicago: University of Chicago Press, 1948.
Hegel, Georg Wilhelm Friedrich, *Lectures on the Philosophy of Religion*, trans. E. B. Spears/ J. B. Sanderson, New York: Humanities Press, 1962.
Heschel, Abraham J., *The Sabbath*, New York: Farrar, Straus, and Giroux, 1951.
Heschel, Abraham J., *Between God and Man*, New York: The Free Press, 1959.
Hyman, Arthur, "Aspects of the Medieval Jewish and Islamic Discussion of 'Free Choice'" and in: *Freedom and Moral Responsibility: General and Jewish Perspectives*, Charles H. Manekin/Menachem M. Kellner (eds), Bethesda: University Press of Maryland, 1997.
Josephus, Flavius, *The Jewish War*, trans. G. A. Williamson, Middlesex: Penguin, 1959.
Kant, Immanuel, *Perpetual Peace and Other Essays*, trans. T. Humphrey, Indianapolis: Hackett, 1983.
Kant, Immanuel, *The Metaphysics of Morals*, trans. Mary Gregor, Cambridge: Cambridge University Press, 1991.
Kant, Immanuel, *Religion within the Boundaries of Mere Reason*, trans. Allen Wood/George Di Giovanni, Cambridge: Cambridge University Press, 1998.
Kant, Immanuel, *Groundwork of the Metaphysics of Morals*, trans. Mary Gregor, Cambridge: Cambridge University Press, 1998.
Kant, Immanuel, *Critique of Pure Reason*, trans. Paul Guyer/Allen Wood, New York: Cambridge University Press, 2009.
Kavka, Martin, *Jewish Messianism and the History of Philosophy*, New York: Cambridge University Press, 2004.
Kellner, Menachem, *Dogma in Medieval Jewish Thought*, New York: Littman Library, 1986.
Kellner, Menachem, *Must a Jew Believe Anything?* New York: Littman Library, 2006.
Kolitz, Zvi, *Yossel Rakover Talks to God*, trans. Paul Badde, New York: Pantheon Books, 1999.
Kraemer, Joel, "Maimonides. An Intellectual Portrait," in: Kenneth Seeskin (ed.), *The Cambridge Companion to Maimonides*, New York: Cambridge University Press, 2005.
Kraemer, Joel, *Maimonides. The Life and World of One of Civilization's Greatest Minds*, New York: Doubleday, 2008.
Levinas, Emmanuel, "The Pact," in: Sean Hand (ed.), *The Levinas Reader*, Oxford: Basil Blackwell, 1989.
Levinas, Emmanuel, Levinas, *Difficult Freedom*, trans. Sean Hand, Baltimore: Johns Hopkins University Press, 1990.
Maimonides, Moses, *Guide of the Perplexed*, trans. Shlomo Pines, Chicago: University of Chicago Press, 1963.
Maimonides, Moses, *A Maimonides Reader*, Isadore Twersky (ed.), New York: Behrman House, 1972.
Maimonides, Moses, *Mishneh Torah*, trans. E. Touger, New York/Jerusalem: Moznaim Publishing, 1989.
Mendelssohn, Moses, *Jerusalem*, trans. Alan Arkush, Hanover, N.H.: University Press of New England, 1983.
Mendenhall, George, "Ancient Oriental and Biblical Law," *Biblical Archaeologist*, 17 (1954), 24–26.

Mendenhall, George, "Covenant Forms in Israelite Tradition," *Biblical Archeologist* 17 (1954), 50–76.
Nadler, Steven, *A Book Forged in Hell*, Princeton: Princeton University Press, 2011.
Niebuhr, Reinhold, *Moral Man and Immoral Society*, Louisville: Westminster John Knox Press, 1932, reprint 2001.
Neusner, Jacob, "Messianic Themes in Formative Judaism," *Journal of the American Academy of Religion* 52 (1984), 357–74.
Novak, David, *The Jewish Social Contract*, Princeton: Princeton University Press, 2005.
Patterson, David, "Though the Messiah May Tarry. A Reflection on Redemption," *May Smith Lecture on Post-Holocaust Christian Jewish Dialogue*, Florida Atlantic University, January 26, 2009.
Pines, Shlomo, "Notes on Maimonides' Views concerning Free Will," *Studies in Philosophy, Scripta Hierosolymitana* 6 (1960), 195–98.
Schwarzschild, Stephen, S., *The Pursuit of the Ideal*, Menachem Kellner (ed.), Albany: SUNY Press, 1990.
Seeskin, Kenneth, *Autonomy in Jewish Philosophy*, New York: Cambridge University Press, 2001.
Seeskin, Kenneth, *Jewish Messianic Thoughts in an Age of Despair*, New York: Cambridge University Press, 2012.
Spinoza, Baruch, *Theological-Political Treatise*, trans. Samuel Shirley, Indianapolis: Hackett, [2]1998.
Stern, Josef, "Maimonides' Conceptions of Freedom and the Sense of Shame," in: Charles H. Manekin/Menachem M. Kellner (eds), *Freedom and Moral Responsibility. General and Jewish Perspectives*, Bethesda: University Press of Maryland, 1997.
Stroumsa, Sarah, *Maimonides in His World*, Princeton: Princeton University Press, 2009.
Walzer, Michael, *Exodus and Revolution*, New York: Basic Books, 1985.
Weiss, Shira, *Joseph Albo on Free Choice*, New York: Oxford University Press, 2017.

Suggestions for Further Reading

Cohen, Hermann, *Religion of Reason out of the Sources of Judaism*, trans. Simon Kaplan. New York: Ungar, 1972.
Hartman, David, *A Living Covenant*, New York: Free Press, 1985.
Heschel, Abraham J., *The Sabbath*, New York: Farrar, Straus, and Giroux, 1951.
Mendelssohn, Moses, *Jerusalem*, trans. Alan Arkush, Hanover, N.H.: University Press of New England, 1983.
Seeskin, Kenneh, *Jewish Messianic Thoughts in an Age of Despair*, New York: Cambridge University Press, 2012.
Walzer, Michael, *Exodus and Revolution*, New York: Basic Books, 1985.
Weiss, Shira, *Joseph Albo on Free Choice*, New York: Oxford University Press, 2017.

Nico Vorster

The Concept of Freedom in Christianity

Introduction

The central statement of the Christian faith is that God revealed himself in Jesus Christ, who liberated humanity from the bondage of sin. This confession that God saves, liberates, and redeems his children through Christ and that this act of God brings about true human freedom is essential to Christianity and informs the core content of this religion. Christianity can therefore be described as a salvific religion.

In a sense, it is not possible to speak about the origins of the Christian concept of freedom as if it is just one metaphor among many other Christian metaphors that developed in parallel during the course of Christian history. Instead, freedom encapsulates what Christianity is all about. Scholars such as Larry Hurtato, Martin Hengel, James Dunn and others have shown through the study of Christian hymns and other early Christian documentation that the confession of Jesus as Lord was part and parcel of early Christian worship.[1] From very early on, Christians understood themselves as the saved children of God, liberated and freed by the grace of God in Christ to serve God through the power of the Spirit.

Having said this, the Christian concept of freedom is not static, but has evolved over the centuries. Theologians were consistently forced to refine their understanding of human freedom in response to doctrinal controversies and in reaction to philosophical, political and social developments.

I commence by providing a short overview of the basic terminology and images used in the Bible for the concept of freedom. Since the meaning attached to biblical concepts is usually related to specific social, theological and philosophical contexts, due consideration is given to the semantic domains and theological frameworks within which these terms are employed. The most outstanding and consistent feature of biblical terminologies on freedom is that they are shap-

1 Cf. Hurtado, Larry W., *Lord Jesus Christ. Devotion to Jesus in Earliest Christianity*, Grand Rapids: Eerdmans, 2003; Hengel, Martin, *The Son of God. The Origin of Christology and the History of Jewish Hellenistic Religion*, trans. John Bowden, Philadelphia: Fortress Press, 1976; Dunn, James, *Christology in the Making. A New Testament Inquiry into the Origins of the Doctrine of the Incarnation*, London: SCM Press, [3]1992.

https://doi.org/10.1515/9783110561678-003

ed decisively by the confession that freedom finds its basis in God, who revealed himself in and redeemed humanity through Jesus Christ.

The second section focuses on the essential features of the Christian concept of freedom. The question that the section probes is: What are the main theological and philosophical principles that govern the Christian understanding of freedom? Admittedly, Christianity is a diverse religion within which different strands have formulated a wide variety of concepts of freedom. At times, these concepts diverge quite considerably. Conversely, we must not overstate the differences to trivialize the Christian concept of freedom. Ferguson[2] rightly warns that variety can be emphasized to "the neglect of the extent of the central core of the Christian faith." The Christian notion of freedom indeed exhibits some essential features that mainstream Christianity has accepted as normative through the ages.

Evidently, we cannot understand the true complexity of the Christian concept of freedom without tracing its historical development. The third section subsequently analyzes the historical evolution of the Christian concept of freedom. As noted above, various controversies through the ages have forced Christian theologians to revisit traditional Christian dogmas. These reformulations often impacted either directly or indirectly on Christian understandings of freedom. Revisions were, however, not only inspired by theological interests, but also by the rise of philosophical and intellectual movements such as the Enlightenment, Renaissance and Postmodernism; and changing political and social contexts such as the establishment of the Holy Empire, the European religious wars, the demise of monarchy, the devastating two World Wars of the twentieth century and the decolonialization period of the 1960's and beyond.

The fourth section compares some features of the contemporary Protestant, Roman Catholic and Orthodox understandings of Christian freedom. Though these mainline traditions share some fundamental Christian premises on freedom, there are also divergences, specifically when it comes to their understanding of the relation between human autonomy and the sovereignty of God's will; God's grace and the freedom of the creature to respond to it; the organization of the church and the church's relation to public authority.

The monotheistic religions Judaism, Christianity and Islam share the common premise that all human beings are created by God and that share a common descent. Yet there are also fundamental differences. Modern Christianity, for instance, is profoundly influenced by the Western notion of personhood, whereas the Islamic worldview is more communal and hierarchical in outlook. The three

2 Cf. Ferguson, Everett, *Backgrounds of Early Christianity*, Grand Rapids: Eerdmans, ^{3}2003, 612.

religions seem to exhibit common features with regard to their doctrines on creation and notions of divine freedom and sovereignty, but they diverge sharply as far as their soteriologies are concerned. The fifth section identifies the areas where the Christian concept of freedom overlaps with Judaist and Islamic notions of freedom. Possible dialogical elements are identified, while the profound differences are kept in mind.

The sixth section reflects on the contemporary influence of the concept of freedom on Christianity and Christian theological research. Specific attention is given to the rise of liberation theologies, Pentecostalism and postmodern theology within Christianity, as well as their effects on the contemporary Christian notion of freedom.

The last section concludes by discussing the present and potential future impact of Christian concepts of freedom on broader culture. The influence of the contemporary Christian tradition on human rights discourse is probed and the possible positive effects that it can have on modern culture are identified. The argument put forward is that the Christian concept of freedom can be fruitfully utilized to correct the individualistic, hedonistic and anarchistic distortions of freedom in modern culture and, conversely, to counter the coercive and dehumanizing extremes of totalitarianism and collectivism.

1 Basic Biblical Terminology

We should be cautious when assessing the terminology that the Bible uses for freedom, because biblical authors sometimes use the same expression to express different ideas. The semantic, textual, socio-historical and theological contexts within which expressions are used have a significant influence on the meaning of a concept and the intent behind its use. The term freedom, for instance, can be used in a socio-ethical, moral, legal, theological or purely practical sense, depending on the issue at hand. Biblical writers, furthermore, often appropriated Hellenistic and Stoic terminology and molded it into their own theological understanding of freedom. Though the terminology used remained the same, the ideological content changed.

The Old Testament mainly employs the term freedom in a socio-theological sense. Jones[3] notes that the Hebrew term for 'free' and 'freedom' (*חופש*) and its

3 Jones, F. Stanley, "Freedom," in: David Noel Freedman (ed.), *The Anchor Bible Dictionary*, vol. 2, New York: Doubleday, 1992, 855.

derivatives usually appear in discussions on slavery and manumission. In the vast majority of cases, it refers to slaves being set free by or from their owners.[4] We probably find the most sophisticated theological notion of freedom in the Deuteronomic biblical tradition, which locates it in the redemptive acts of God who liberated his people from the slavery and oppression of Egypt. Being freed from the rule of the Egyptians, the Israelites now stand under the rule and dominion of YWHW. Notably, freedom is not grounded in the social significance or the "psychological appeal" of the Exodus event itself, but in the redemptive acts of God who brought Israel out of Egypt to become his servants.[5] YHWH establishes a new covenantal society based on justice, which is opposite to the degrading slave system from which Israel escaped. The Israelites are exhorted to respect the freedom of others in the knowledge that they once were slaves themselves.[6] The Sabbath is depicted in the Deuteronomic Decalogue as a day of commemoration during which the Israelites have to remember the oppression they suffered and reflect anew on the redemption God provided during the Exodus event:

> Remember that you were slaves in Egypt and the Lord your God brought you out with a strong hand and an outstretched arm, and for that reason, the Lord your God commanded you to keep the Sabbath day.[7]

By exhorting the Israelites to remember their suffering, the Deuteronomists encouraged Israel to resemble God in their actions by granting freedom to those who are weak and economically dependent.[8]

The word used in the New Testament for freedom is *ἐλευθερια*. It depicts the state of being free and is used to indicate a negation of control, domination or constraint.[9] The derivative word *ἐλευθερόω* means 'to set free' and is used in passages such as John 8:35 to signify that Christ is the source of the Christian's freedom. The most extensive use of the term is found in Pauline literature. In passages such as Galatians 3:28, Colossians 3:11 and Ephesians 6:8, freedom is depicted as an internal freedom that is not dependent on one's external social status. Ac-

4 Cf. Exodus 21:2,5; Deuteronomy 15:12–13, Jeremiah 34:9–11, Exodus 21:26–27. Also cf. Harris, R. Laird/Gleason L. Archer/Bruce K. Waltke (eds), *Theological Wordbook of the Old Testament*, Chicago: Moody Press, 1980, 312.

5 Cf. Braulik, Georg, "Deuteronomy and Human Rights," *Skrif en Kerk* 19/2 (1998), 215.

6 Cf. ibid., 212. Deuteronomy 6:21–5.

7 Deuteronomy 5:15.

8 Braulik, "Deuteronomy and Human Rights," 214.

9 Louw, Johannes P./Nida, Eugene A., *Greek-English Lexicon of the New Testament Based on Semantic Domains*, vol. 1, Cape Town: Bible Society of South Africa, 1989, 488.

cording to Jones[10], this approach is strongly reminiscent of Hellenistic statements on freedom. Pauline literature also uses *ἐλευθερόω* to claim that the Christian is free from legalistic constraints such as abstaining from certain kinds of food or practicing meaningless rites.[11] Freedom, however, does not justify license or anarchy, but demands an obedience to the law according to God's real intent. The Christian obeys God's law out of a gratitude for being set free from the bondage of sin, not to earn her own salvation through good works.[12] In Johannine literature, *ἐλευθερόω* is used within the context of not sinning. Since Christ sets the believer free, she is no longer a slave of sin.[13]

The term *σώτηρια* refers to divine salvation and specifically denotes the state of being saved,[14] or depending on the context, the process of being saved.[15] The New Testament uses a wide variety of images to articulate the believer's salvation in Christ.[16] Victory images[17] depict Christ's death on the cross as a triumph over the evil forces of this world. Christ is portrayed as the Cosmic Redeemer who conquers the principalities and demonic forces of this world and reconciles the whole of the cosmos to God. Cultic images account for most of the biblical imagery used and portray Jesus' death as a sacrifice for the sins of the world that appeases God's anger and reconciles believers to God. The cross delivers believers from guilt and purifies them from sin. God no longer holds them accountable for their sins because of the substitutionary sacrifice of Christ.[18] Legal metaphors are often employed, intertwined with cultic imagery. They present Christ as the one who redeemed us from the curse of the law by being cursed in our place. Through his perfect obedience, Christ fulfils the entire law and makes possible a renewal of the covenant between God and his children.[19] In his letters to Romans and Galatians, Paul speaks of a change in the legal status of the believer before God. Guilty sinners are acquitted of their guilt before God in light of Jesus'

---

10 Jones, "Freedom," 857.

11 Galatians 5:1; Romans 7:2–3; Galatians 2:4–5, 1Corinthians 10:29.

12 Galathians 5:13; Romans 8:2–4.

13 John 8:36.

14 Cf. 2Corinthians 7:10, 1Peter 1:9.

15 Acts 13:26.

16 Cf. Vorster, Nico, "The Nature of Christ's Atonement," in: Eddy van der Borght/Paul van Geest (eds), *Strangers and Pilgrims on Earth. Essays in Honour of Abraham van de Beek*, Leiden: Brill, 2013, 140. Also cf. Blochner, Henri, "Biblical Metaphors and the Doctrine of Atonement," *Journal of the Evangelical Theological Society*, 47/4 (2004), 629–645.

17 Cf. Collosians 2:1; 1Corinthians 6:20; 15:24; Philippians 2; 10; Revelation 5:10, 12:11; 15:2–3.

18 Cf. John 1:29; 19:14; Revelation 5:5–6, Hebrews 10:28.

19 Cf. Hebrews 5:8, 9 and Galatians 3:13.

sacrifice on the cross.[20] Financial and exemplarist imagery are mainly utilized, together with other metaphors. The financial images[21] portray Christ's death as a payment for sins that secures the release of the sinner, who is depicted as either a slave, prisoner or debtor. Pauline literature specifically refers to Christians being adopted as children of God, thus sharing in the inheritance rights and glory of Jesus Christ.[22] Exemplarist concepts depict Christ's death as an illustration of God's love for the world. Believers are called to conform to the image of Christ and to participate in the legacy of Christ by imitating his example.[23]

2 Essential Theological and Philosophical Features

Michael Welker[24] rightly asserts that Christianity is typified by and set apart from other religions by the confession that Christ is Lord. God identifies with humanity, he gives shape and orientation to human life and he brings humanity into eternal communion with himself through the historical events of the crucifixion, death and resurrection of Jesus Christ and the continuing revelation of Christ through the Spirit, Word and revelation. This essential premise of the Christian concept of freedom is accompanied by four related foundational confessions, namely:

a) that humans are creatures in bondage, who are slaves of sin, evil and death;
b) that humans find their redemption in Christ, who alone is able to overcome the principalities and powers of this world;
c) that the Spirit of Christ draws human beings into communion with Christ and empowers them to enact a praxis of freedom in their lives;
d) that freedom is a gift of God's grace that invokes in the believer a sense of responsibility and discipleship.

2.1 Humanity in Bondage

Over and against utilitarian and expressivist notions of freedom that define the human as an essentially free and autonomous being, Christianity posits the

20 Cf. Romans 5:2; Gal 4:24.
21 Cf. 1Peter 1:18–19; Mark 10:45, Romans 3:9; Revelation 5:9.
22 Romans 8:14–16; Gal 4:5.
23 Cf. John 12:25; Luke 9:6; Ephesians 5:1; 1Thessalonians 1:6.
24 Cf. Welker, Michael, *God the Revealed. Christology*, Grand Rapids, Eerdmans, 2013, 48.

qualified nature of human freedom. Even though God created humans free, creaturely life is constantly threatened by individual and collective violence, cruelty, suffering, illness, distress, anxiety and mortality. The Christian tradition ascribes this human bondage to the existence of sin and evil. There is considerable disagreement between various Christian traditions on the origin of sin, the manner in which it is transmitted through generations and the degree to which sin perverts the human will and distorts the human's image of God. Yet, mainstream Christianity concurs that sin and evil exist; that this has radical implications for the divine-human relationship; that sin is a pervasive and comprehensive force that distorts human and creaturely life; and that it prevents humans from realizing their divinely created purpose and destiny. At the same time, mainline Christian traditions are united in maintaining that God created his creation good and that God is in no way responsible for sin and evil.

Our sinful nature weakens the human mind to such a degree that we are unable to know God adequately and to comprehend the nature of our depravity from within ourselves. Alienated from God and the transcendent, we become trapped in ourselves, inclined to create all sorts of idols in the place of God. To escape our bondage, we need the revelation of God to enlighten us and to guide us to God. Mainstream Christianity holds that God, in a free act of love, attaches himself to human beings by revealing himself to them through his creative acts, the incarnation of Christ and Scripture that contains God's law and the Gospel of redemption. God's law reveals to us the nature and extent of our sins, the guilt that we all share, and the curse that sin brings. It reveals that sin and evil stand under God's judgment and that all human beings are culpable before God. The Gospel contains the good message of God's redemption and victory over sin and death. Though the various Christian traditions disagree on the precise relationship between the Law and the Gospel, mainstream Christianity holds that the human being cannot be saved through obedience to the Law or his own good works. The Law is incapable of liberating the human being from the bondage of sin because human works can never carry out the full demands of God's law. Yet the law is not unimportant or obsolete, because it allows us to discern sin, to comprehend the full range and impact of sin, and it reminds us that humans cannot save themselves. It engenders in us a yearning for a Redeemer that can break the power of sin and the bondage that human nature experiences. The Gospel attests to who that Redeemer is.

2.2 Redemption in Christ

McGrath[25] rightly notes that Christianity regards human salvation as "manifested in and through and constituted on the basis of the life, death and resurrection of Jesus Christ." It follows that Christ's incarnation, crucifixion and resurrection represent the three pivotal moments in salvation history that shape and determine human redemption.

Christianity regards the incarnation of Christ as a redemptive event. The Son of God had to be incarnated because humanity fell from grace and humans are unable to redeem themselves. Western Christianity largely understood the need for Christ's incarnation in legal terms: human nature cannot redeem itself because it is enslaved to sin. Human nature requires a Divine Redeemer to be redeemed. Yet, only a human person can be held culpable for the sins of human nature. As a result, the divine had to become human to simultaneously bear God's curse on sin and redeem humanity. Eastern Christianity, in contrast, largely approached the incarnation in terms of deification: divine nature had to become human, so that human nature can be taken up in divine nature.

Despite the abovementioned differences, Christianity in general agrees that the incarnation reveals that God in Christ has entered creaturely reality; a reality characterized by sin, distress, suffering and culpability. As is the case with creation, the incarnation is a free act of God; a kenotic event where God empties himself by creatively suspending his majesty and sovereignty for the sake of the other and taking on the form of a servant.[26] God's kenotic action sets the tone for the Christian concept of freedom. Christ's incarnation teaches us that freedom is not a freedom *of* others, but a freedom *for* others and it entails creatively withdrawing ourselves to allow space for the free self-realization of others. The kenotic action of Christ displayed through his incarnation and life on earth is the same kind of free action that God demonstrates when he creates and sustains all things. The Trinitarian God's free actions are characterized by a 'Christ-like' shape, that is, actions that create space for the world and the other.

Christians do not regard the event at the cross as an isolated event relevant only to a specific time and place, but as an occurrence with a definitive impact on the past, present and future of human existence. Christian cross-theology maintains that God is active in human history through the Crucified by acting "in him" and "through him."[27]

25 McGrath, Alister, *Christian Theology. An Introduction*, Oxford: Wiley-Blackwell, [5]2011, 275.
26 Cf. Phillipians 2:5–11.
27 Cf. Welker, *God the Revealed*, 173.

For Christians, the cross at once depicts God's judgement over humanity and the saving power of God.[28] According to Michael Welker, Christian cross-theology upholds the Old Testament law tradition's paradoxical understanding of the relation between justice and mercy. The cross as judgement reveals the profound sinfulness of humanity and how human beings distance themselves from God's loving presence.[29] Human beings not only turned against Jesus and rejected his reign, but they closed themselves off from the creative love of God. As such, the cross is an event of divine–human confrontation where the worldly powers turn against God by handing over his Son for execution and God judges humanity by abandoning it. God completely abandons, not only the crucified Jesus, but also the whole of the world. By handing over the world to its own power, God confronts humanity with the resulting sense of God-forsakenness, weakness, frailty and self-endangerment.

Yet, the cross paradoxically reveals the life-affirming power of God's mercy that is also prevalent in the Old Testament scriptures. Whereas human beings close themselves off from God, God opens himself up to human beings by entering the realm of suffering and death and bearing the curse of sin. As noted earlier, the New Testament uses, amongst others, the metaphor of a sacrifice to describe the atoning significance of Christ's death on the cross.[30] Through Jesus Christ's substitutionary and vicarious self-sacrifice, God's judgement on sin is revealed and his mercy is bestowed on human beings. God's mercy makes possible reconciliation between the divine and human realms.

The events of the cross cannot be separated from the resurrection of Christ. Without the resurrection, the cross will be devoid of all soteriological and salvific meaning. Welker[31] states it well:

> That Jesus Christ 'not only was but is', indeed that he not only is but is also present in the power of his creative spirit – all this hinges on the resurrection. What first turns faith in Jesus Christ into 'good news,' into a genuine message of salvation, is the confession that the Jesus Christ who is present not only touches human beings through his life and message, but also takes up their lives into his own.

---

28 Cf. Barth, Karl, *The Humanity of God*, trans. Thomas Wieser, Louisville: Westminster John Knox Press, 1960, 46–47.

29 Cf. Welker, *God the Revealed*, 187. In his Christology, Welker emphasizes that the powers of religion, law, politics and public opinion all conspired to kill Jesus. In this the violent nature of worldly powers are revealed.

30 Ephesians 2:14; Hebrews 9:14; John 1:29; John 6:54; Revelation 1:5.

31 Welker, *God the Revealed*, 104.

The New Testament depicts Christ's resurrection as a historical event. However, there is disagreement among mainstream theologians on whether the resurrection amounted to a physical revivification, Christophanies that actually happened in time and place, or a transphysical combination of both. Even though the Gospels posit a continuity between the pre-Easter and post-Easter Christ, they also suggest a discontinuity in the sense that the post-Easter Christ exhibits features that the pre-Easter Jesus did not possess. The Gospels depict the resurrection of Christ as much more than a mere continuation of his physical existence, but as a new type of existence "in a decidedly new form" that inaugurates a new aeon.[32] Though the resurrection of Christ remains a rather mysterious and elusive concept in Christian theology, it undoubtedly belongs to the essence of the Christian faith.

Mainstream Christianity understands the salvific meaning of the resurrection as a sign of God's victory over the powers of sin, evil and death. The powers of sin and evil bring Christ to the cross and eventually murder Jesus, but God overcomes these dark powers by resurrecting Jesus Christ. The resurrection of Christ constitutes a new reality that is already present in the here and now. This new reality is a liberating reality that mediates the salvific powers of the resurrected to the present. With the resurrection, God makes human participation in the divine life possible, thus anticipating the eternal life with God. Michael Welker[33] states it as follows:

> Blessed, eternal life is already anticipated here on earth in the experiences and acts of love and forgiveness, in the dignified celebration of worship and sacrament that seeks knowledge of God, in God-fearing prayer and in self-forgetting joy, but also in the persistent pursuit of liberating truth and justice.

2.3 Freedom and the Spirit

Jesus Christ's outpouring of the Spirit on his disciples, his missionary directive to his followers, his ascension and the Pentecost are important moments in the post-Easter narratives and indicate the restorative power of God. They are indications of Christ's victory over sin and the restitution of God's reign in this world. The Christian Scriptures identify the Spirit as the Spirit of Christ that links the

32 Ibid., 117; 124.
33 Ibid., 15.

believers to the Resurrected. The result is that believers are able to share and participate in the life of Christ, sharing in his strength and power.[34]

The Christian praxis of freedom is strongly informed by the Christian faith's understanding of the believer's participation in Christ. The Spirit of God unites the faithful to Christ and into living communities by working faith in them, infusing them with love, inculcating obedience in them and bestowing on them a wide variety of spiritual gifts. These features of the Christian life are exhibited in the sacraments of baptism and the Holy Communion.[35] The outpouring of the Spirit creates complex and diverse plural societies that are characterized by the interplay between various members. Paul calls this new community of believers the spiritual body of Jesus Christ, not only since they are constituted by the Spirit of Christ, but also because the Spirit acts through them in the world.[36] Human beings who participate in the life of the resurrected, gain in the words of Welker "a share in a power that has already shaped and is continuing to shape the world itself, a power revealed in the bodily resurrection of Christ."[37] The church is therefore called into being by God's salvation, but it is also a vehicle of his salvation by proclaiming and promoting his redemptive reign in the world.[38]

The community of believers that the Spirit creates is free and equal in nature. Paul hence states in Galatians 2:28:

> There is no longer Jew or Greek, there is no longer slave or free, there is no longer male and female for all of you are one in Christ.[39]

The implication is that the Spirit of God suspends and relativizes the hierarchical, biological and social differences between people and unites them into a body of believers who have an equal status before God. This does not entail a rigid uniformity; instead, the variety of *charismata* that the Spirit bestows on the church makes the church a unity in diversity, where the unity is served through individuals that freely exercise their individual gifts to the benefit of all.[40]

---

34 Ibid., 141; 217.

35 Cf. Calvin, John, *Institutes of the Christian Religion*, trans. Henry Beveridge, Peabody: Hendrickson, 2008, 4.15.16.

36 1Corinthians 12:11.

37 Welker, *God the Revealed*, 140.

38 Cf. Matthew 5:13–16; 28:19.

39 Also cf. 1Corinthians 12:13.

40 Welker, *God the Revealed*, 289.

2.4 Freedom as Gift and Responsibility

The Christian faith regards freedom as a divine gift that demands a response of gratitude that is exhibited in a sense of responsibility to God and others. Karl Barth encapsulates the Christian notion of freedom as follows:

> Human freedom is the gift of God in the free outpouring of his grace. To call a man free is to recognize that God has given him freedom. Human freedom is enacted within history, that history which leads to the ultimate salvation of man. Human freedom never ceases to be the event wherein the free God gives and man receives his gift.[41]

God's gift of mercy transforms the lives of believers through the power of the Spirit and inspires them to a concrete Christian praxis that bears testimony to God's liberating presence in the world despite the sufferings that human beings and creation experience. Through the transformed lives of believers and the power of the Spirit, the exalted Christ's reign enters the creaturely realm and brings hope and liberation to the oppressed and weak. True freedom can therefore never be exercised without love. In fact, love is "the proper exercise of freedom."[42]

The doctrine of *munex triplex* (the three offices of Christ) is probably the best premise from which to approach the Christian understanding of freedom as both gift and responsibility. This doctrine developed relatively late in the Christian tradition, but soon acquired an ecumenical status. According to Michael Welker,[43] John Calvin first developed the notion; where after Johann Gerhard introduced it to Lutheran theology. It was developed further by influential theologians such as Schleiermacher, Barth and Wainwright and eventually found its way to Catholic and Eastern Orthodox dogmatic handbooks. The doctrine is based on the Old Testament's arrangement of the public offices of Israel and is congruent with the Old Testament legal and prophetic traditions. It is also related to the pre-Easter and post-Easter work of Christ to which the New Testament, specifically the book of Hebrews, often alludes.

The *munex triplex* expresses the threefold nature of Christ's reign as King, Priest and Prophet, both in a pre-Easter and post-Easter sense. Christ's pre-Easter activity as King was characterized by his victory over the powers of sin, evil and death on the cross, while his post-Easter Kingship denotes his reign over the

---

41 Barth, *The Humanity of God*, 75.

42 Cf. Slater, Jennifer, "Freedom: The Liberative Value and Ethical Credential for Christian Living in South Africa," *Journal of Theology for Southern Africa* 148 (2014), 50.

43 Welker, *God the Revealed*, 213.

church, as well as his eternal spiritual reign over all things through the power of the Spirit. His pre-Easter Priesthood denotes his work as Mediator and consisted in him atoning for the sins of humankind, while his priestly work in the post-Easter dispensation is characterized by his continuous intercessory work for all believers. As prophet, the pre-Easter Jesus proclaimed the good news of salvation and the coming of God's kingdom, while the post-Easter Christ's prophetic work consists in him revealing God's will through the power of the Spirit and the Word.

The threefold nature of Christ's reign defines the gift of freedom that believers receive. The faithful are recipients of the benefits of Christ's spiritual reign over all things. They are inheritors of his Kingdom, beneficiaries of Christ's atoning and intercessory work as Priest, and they receive constant strength, vitality and guidance through the testimony of Christ's Spirit and the revelational power of Christ's Word.

John Calvin and his followers also applied the three offices of Christ to individual believers and their calling as disciples of Christ. According to Calvin, God pours out his Spirit to enable believers to participate in Christ's three offices.[44] Christians are kings, priests and prophets in their own right who have to respond to God's gift of salvation by acting responsibly. Believers are enabled to be a community of truth, justice and mercy through the spiritual gifts that Christ bestows on them. The royal dimension of the church is exhibited in its search for truth and justice and a self-withdrawal for the sake of others. Its priestly nature is displayed in its diaconal activities that entail a self-sacrifice for the sake of others, while the prophetic dimension consists of preaching the Gospel, education and teaching. All three of these dimensions are highly important for the Christian notion of freedom. The prophetical and law traditions in the Christian canon, as well as the classical Christian cross theology consistently posit justice (royal dimension), truth (prophetic dimension) and mercy (diaconal dimension) as prerequisites for the realization of true freedom.[45] Freedom without justice leads to license; freedom without truth and obedience leads to anarchy, disorder and lawlessness; and freedom that shows no mercy and love to the weak leads to oppressive forms of inequality. By fulfilling their callings as kings, priests and prophets in response to God's liberating acts, Christians become agents of freedom in all spheres of life.

---

44 Cf. Calvin, *Institutes*, 2.15–16.

45 Cf. Welker, *God the Revealed*, 209–217.

3 The Historical Development of the Christian Concepts of Freedom

Christian concepts of freedom evolved gradually within a wide variety of political, social and cultural contexts. Constantly forced to respond to political, cultural, philosophical and scientific developments, Christians had to refine their understanding of freedom and develop counterarguments to polemic challenges. Often Christian theologians would appropriate views from non-Christian traditions to consolidate their arguments and to add more intelligibility to their understanding of freedom. The logic of Judaism, Hellenism, Neo-Platonism, Aristotelianism, Rationalism, Skepticism, Idealism, Romanticism, Marxism and Postmodernism, to name a few, influenced Christian discourses profoundly. These appropriations were mostly inspired by a conscious desire to synthesize Christian views with secular idioms to make the Christian faith more intelligible to the spirit of the times. Yet, every so often Christian theologians uncritically appropriated secular vocabulary without realizing that these ideas actually did not correspond with Scripture. Christianity's adoption of dualist Platonic categories and Hellenistic notions of divine impassibility is a case in point.

A brief examination of the history of Christian dogma reveals that the same themes tend to resurface in Christian doctrinal controversies on freedom, but often from a new angle. Sometimes Christian theologians would reach relative consensus on a controversial issue that would last for centuries, only for anomalies to appear that force theologians to revisit old answers. We now turn to these recurring themes in Christian discourses on freedom.

3.1 Divine Sovereignty and Human Agency

From the times of the early Christian writers, the human being was seen as a person with an individual and social identity capable of free agency. McGrath[46] explains the Christian understanding of personhood as follows:

> For early Christians the word "person" is an expression of the individuality of a human being, as seen in his or her words and actions. Above all, there is an emphasis upon the idea of social relationships. A person is someone who plays a role in a social drama, who relates to others. A person has a part to play within a network of social relationships.

46 McGrath, *Christian Theology*, 206.

Personhood necessarily entails that the human possesses a certain individuality and creaturely freedom to act. The question that arose in Christian theology was: How should creaturely freedom be understood in relation to God's sovereignty? Is it possible to speak about God's omnipotence, omnipresence, goodness, sovereignty and providence while affirming creaturely freedom at the same time? Invariably, the issue involves questions about the nature of evil and sin, its relation to God and its effects on human agency. Christian theologians have proposed various answers. The discussion that follows is limited to a very brief outline of the most influential approaches.

3.1.1 Irenaeus of Lyon (130–200 AD)

Irenaeus of Lyon described human nature as created with the potential to grow from immaturity to a maturity which eventually finds its destiny in God. Though Irenaeus believed that God created all things good, he did not equate goodness with perfection. Instead, he understood the first creation narrative's description of humans as created in the image of God as prophetic utterances. When God created humans, he intended that they would grow in wisdom and obedience to the point of deification, that is, in God's likeness and image. However, the immaturity of the original human beings led them astray and made them fall into sin. Yet evil, sin, pain and suffering serve as necessary tools to effect spiritual growth. Without the challenges that these forces represent, humanity will never grow to its destiny. To enable humanity to attain maturity, God first introduced the Law and thereafter the person of Jesus Christ, through whom humans can grow in understanding.

The Irenaeun line of thought found its most influential modern exponent in John Hick (1922–2012). John Hick posited that humans were created incomplete. To fulfil their created destiny, they have to participate in life, which is a process of "soulmaking." Soulmaking entails that human beings need to be confronted by choices between good and evil in order to grow; otherwise they would not be free agents. Human experiences of evil, suffering and pain serve as a necessary tool in the process of soulmaking.[47] Though Hick's understanding of divine sovereignty and human agency is reconcilable with modern evolutionary worldviews, it does award evil a positive and constructive role in human existence, which is difficult to reconcile with the logic of the Christian biblical canon.

47 Cf. Hick, John, *Evil and the God of Love*, London: MacMillan Press, ^{2}1977.

3.1.2 Augustine (354–430 AD)

Augustine and Christian theologians of his time were confronted with the dualist views of Gnosticism and Manichaeism. These philosophies made a sharp distinction between the invisible spiritual realm, which is inherently good, and the visible material world, which is corruptible and contains evil. Some forms of Gnosticism also distinguished between a Supreme God who is the origin of the spiritual realm and a lesser deity, the Demiurge, who created the visible realm. The implications of both the Gnostic and Manichaeist views are that creation is not inherently good; that parts of reality exist outside of God's creative will and that evil itself is an independent reality embedded in matter.

Augustine responded by positing that God is the only Creator of the world; that creaturely life is good because it was created by a good God; and that evil is not an independent reality with its own substance, but rather the absence of good (*privatio boni*). The question that naturally arose was: How did sin and evil enter God's creation if it was not part of God original creation? Augustine's answer was that God created human beings with a free will. Drawing on the creation narratives, he posited that humans were initially created with the freedom to choose between right and wrong. Unfortunately, human beings abused their freedom and under the temptation of Satan, chose evil. The result was that the created order became contaminated with evil. Once free, humans now became slaves of sin who transmit sin through the generations.

Augustine's unitary perspective on reality and his notion of the human as originally created with a free will, had a major impact on Western Christian thought and provided a theologically intelligible perspective from which to approach the conundrum on the relation between divine sovereignty and creaturely freedom. His doctrine on the original free will of the human being, however, exhibits the weakness that it portrays evil as a choice available to the first human beings. The question that naturally arises is: Is this premise compatible with Augustine's notion that evil does not constitute a reality of its own?

3.1.3 The Scholastic Tradition

Thomas Aquinas approached the relationship between divine sovereignty and creaturely freedom from the perspective of secondary causes. This doctrine, which was strongly influenced by Aristotle's philosophy of causation, held that God is the Prime Mover who, unmoved himself, governs his creation through a chain of causes. Aquinas distinguished between the *causa prima* (first cause), the *causa secunda* (second cause) and the *causa finalis* (final cause). The *causa prima* refers to God, who through his eternal decree initiates a chain of events. The other causes that emanate from God's decree are relative to the first cause and are continuously taken up in a wide network of other causes.[48] The first cause is always in an indirect manner involved in secondary causes, while secondary causes execute the order determined by first cause.[49] Yet, secondary causes are contingent. While the chain of causes can be related back to the Prime Mover and are indeed guided by God towards their final goal (*causa finalis*), they do possess an agency and integrity of their own. Evil, suffering and pain are therefore not due to the direct action of God, but to the vulnerable agency of secondary causes within the natural order. They possess no *causa finalis*, but are *privatio boni* (the absence of goodness), because they emanate accidentally from the chain of secondary causes. Though these powers affect the chain of events, they have no meaning of their own, nor can they change the *causa finalis* determined by God.[50]

William of Ockham (1285–1347) introduced the notion of divine self-limitation to theology. He distinguished between God's two powers, namely the *potentia absoluta* and the *potentia ordinata*. The *potentia absoluta* (God's absolute power) refers to the options available to God before creation. In his omnipotence, God could have embarked on any course or action of his choosing. The *potentia ordinata* (ordained power of God) refers to the way things are after God created the physical reality. By creating the world, God committed himself to a certain course of action that necessarily excluded other courses of action. For example, after God created the world, the option of not creating the world is no longer available. In other words, God freely limited himself by choosing a certain course of action and staying committed to that course while setting aside other options available to him.

Ockham's concept of divine self-limitation received new attention in the nineteenth and twentieth centuries from theologians who entertained the notion of kenoticism. The kenotic approach is specifically associated with Gottfried Thomasius, who argued that the incarnation involved Christ relinquishing his divine attributes. The argument is based on Philippians 2:6, which speaks of Christ emptying himself (*kenosis*) to take on the form of a human. Kenotic views eventually found their way from Christology to discussions on the relationship between divine sovereignty and creaturely freedom. According to this line of thought, which is particularly evident in process theology, God does not over-

48 Cf. Van de Beek, Abraham, *Een Lichtkring Om Het Kruis. Scheppingsleer in Christologisch Perspectief*, Zoetermeer Boekenzentrum: Meinema, 2014, 359.
49 Ibid., 359; 369.
50 Ibid., 369–370.

power the human being through his omnipotence, sovereignty and omnipresence; but his creative acts involve an element of divine self-withdrawal to allow space for the other. God could have created the human being as a perfect being without the ability to sin, yet this would negate human individuality and agency. God therefore created human beings with free wills and the resulting potential to choose against God.

3.1.4 The Reformers

Whereas the Scholastic tradition held that God's involvement with creation is indirect and intermediary in nature, Reformed theologians posited that God enters directly into our world through his providential reign that sustains the world. John Calvin, for instance, understood divine sovereignty as ruling out the existence of chance. Nothing that happens falls outside of God's decree. However, he maintained that divine determination does not obliterate human agency but is, in fact, the basis for free choice and human agency.[51] Without God's providence, there can be no free and contingent human will. The Fall causes humans to sin necessarily, yet voluntarily. While sin corrupts the human will to such a degree that the human's moral judgement can no longer be trusted, sin does not excuse human beings from acting morally, because humans possess an innate sense of the good through God's natural law. Yet, true freedom in the salvational sense of the word is only possible if God regenerates us. Through his regenerative grace, God changes the inclination of the will from doing evil to embracing the good. He does this not by destroying our original will or changing the ontological nature of the human being, but by changing the disposition of our will.[52] God's freedom to act and to bestow grace therefore becomes the basis for our freedom and choice as human agents.[53]

3.1.5 Deism

Deism rose to prominence in the late seventeenth and eighteenth centuries among Enlightenment theologians and philosophers such as John Locke and Matthew Tindal. It was shaped by the Newtonian emphasis on nature's mechan-

51 Cf. Marko, Jonathan S., "'Free Choice' in Calvin's Concepts of Regeneration and Moral Agency. How Free Are We?," *Ashland Theological Journal* 42 (2010), 42.
52 Calvin, *Institutes*, 2.5.15.
53 Cf. Marko, "How Free Are We?", 49.

ical regularity and orderliness and the resulting skepticism in supernatural concepts such as miracles. Deism suggests that the world is governed by divinely created natural laws that mechanically sustain the universe. By discovering and analyzing these laws, human beings can acquire knowledge of God. Since God's creation is self-sustaining, God does not get involved in the universe, nor does he ever intervene in ways that suspend the natural laws. Instead, God sets creation in motion and then withdraws himself. This approach naturally leads to the question: Do we need the concept of God at all if the world is self-sufficient and God's involvement is not needed at all?

3.1.6 Process Theology

Process theology emerged in the twentieth century and can be traced back to the philosopher Alfred North Whitehead (1861–1947), who conceived of reality as a process that is always in a state of becoming. This theology draws to some degree on the Scholastic two-causes argument that understands the becoming of reality as a chain of events. Yet, it deviates from Scholastic thought in the sense that God is not seen as transcendent, but as part of the process itself. Existing entities are on the one hand influenced by God, who is the only immortal and eternal entity, and conversely by previous finite entities. The various entities influence each other mutually through physical and/or mental interaction. God himself determines the rules of the process, but not in a deterministic sense. To safeguard creaturely freedom, God does not influence creatures through coercion, but by persuasion. Entities enjoy creaturely freedom and are therefore able to remain unresponsive to God's persuasion or to reject it. This suggests that God cannot be held accountable for the existence of moral and natural evil. Though God intends the good for creation and acts in creation's best interests himself, his self-imposed option to persuade rather than coerce in order to safeguard creaturely freedom inevitably prevents him from deterministically imposing himself on human decision making.

3.1.7 The Orthodox Tradition

When it comes to divine freedom, Orthodox theology emphasizes God's ontological sovereignty and absolute freedom to act in love. God is not limited in his actions by any primordial substance, as was argued by some ancient Greek philosophers, but acts freely according to His will. As famously articulated by John

Zizioulas (1931–), God's absolute freedom is manifested in the Person of the Father who begets the Son eternally and brings forth the Spirit.[54]

Orthodox theology generally understands God's creation as an act of love *ex nihilo* that allowed human beings the right to choose whether or not to enter into a loving and reciprocal relationship with God.[55] The Fall is considered as an event where human beings exercised their freedom, but in a wrong manner. Though sin is pervasive and threatens authentic human existence, it does not destroy human freedom or the human's createdness in the image of God.[56] In fact, freedom is seen as a precondition for the ability of humans to be transformed and to re-enter a right relationship with God.[57]

John Zizioulas considers freedom as closely connected to personhood. Personhood indicates that God created us with an ability to seek communion with Him. Our biological hypostasis, finiteness, fallen condition and enslavement to sin threaten our freedom and being.[58] However, through the Incarnation of Christ, God takes the *ecclesia* up in his Trinitarian existence and orients our personhood through the Spirit to the *imago Dei*. The end result is a new mode of existence no longer bound to the "laws of biology" but founded in our eternal relationship with God.[59] *Humanum* is, in the words of Vigen Guroian "grounded in the being and act of God."[60] The incarnation not only signifies that God became human, but that "God is human."[61] The end result of our deification is the eternal life in Christ who breaks down the power of "death and dissolution."[62]

54 Cf. Groppe, Elizabeth, "Creation ex Nihilo and Ex Amore. Ontological freedom in the Theologies of John Zizioulas and Catherine Mowry Lacugna," *Modern Theology* 21/3 (2005), 463–495.
55 Cf. Prodromou, Elizabeth H., "Orthodox Christian Contributions to Freedom. Historical Foundations, Contemporary Problematics," in: Timothy Samuel Shah/Allan D. Hertzke (eds), *Christianity and Freedom, vol. 1: Historical Perspectives*, Cambridge: Cambridge University Press, 2016, 306.
56 Uertz, Rudolf/Schmidt, Lars Peter (eds), *Die Grundlagen der Lehre der Russischen Orthodoxen Kirche über die Würde, die Freiheit und die Menschenrechte*, Moscow, Auslandsbüro der Konrad-Adenauer-Stiftung, 2008.
57 Cf. Prodromou, "Orthodox Christian Contributions to Freedom," 306.
58 Groppe, "Creation ex Nihilo and Ex Amore," 474.
59 Groppe, "Creation ex Nihilo and Ex Amore," 475–476.
60 Guroian, Vigen, "Human Rights and Modern Western Faith. An Orthodox Christian Assessment," in: Elizabeth M. Bucar/Barbra Barnett (eds), *Does Human Rights need God*, Grand Rapids: Eerdmans, 2005, 47.
61 Ibid.
62 Groppe, "Creation ex Nihilo and Ex Amore," 476.

Unsurprisingly, the Orthodox tradition tends to be skeptical of Western notions of human autonomy.[63] Though opposed to monism, Orthodox theology rejects individualist rationalities that bifurcate reality dualistically into object-subject, I-Thou categories. Individualism signifies separation, isolation and estrangement. God, in contrast, calls us to a sacramental life of "communion, relation and catholicity."[64]

3.2 Salvation and human freedom

As noted earlier, the New Testament canon uses a wide variety of metaphors to explain the redemptive significance of Christ's death on the cross. These metaphors are often used interchangeably to complement each other.[65] During the course of Christian history, various theologies of salvation were developed that relied on images used in the New Testament. Though these theologies emphasize different aspects of Christ's salvational work, they do not necessarily exclude each other or invalidate other approaches.

3.2.1 Salvation as Atonement

The sacrificial and legal imagery used by the New Testament to describe the meaning of Christ's death inspired some of the early church fathers to understand Christ's death in terms of atonement. Athanasius (296 AD–373 AD) argued that Christ's sacrifice was a perfect sacrifice that accomplished what the Old Testament sacrifices were unable to do. Whereas the Old Testament offerings could never be perfect because humans sin every day, Christ's perfect obedience to God's law enabled him to bring a sacrifice with eternal significance. Augustine described Christ as both priest and victim. Christ, who is God himself, took on the form of a servant and sacrificed himself, because no other sufficient sacrifice to appease God's anger exists.

Anselm (1033–1109) provided a sophisticated theory of salvation that drew upon both biblical sacrificial and legal imagery. His theory stressed God's righteousness, the offensive nature of human sin and the need for satisfaction. According to Anselm, God originally created human nature righteous so that hu-

---

63 Pollis, Adamantia, "Eastern Orthodoxy and Human Rights," *Human Rights Quarterly* 15 (1993), 341.
64 Groppe, "Creation ex Nihilo and Ex Amore," 475
65 Cf. Vorster, "The Nature of Christ's Atonement," 140.

manity could attain eternal blessedness. Humanity, however, fell in sin, which not only negated the original purpose of their creation, but also offended the honor of God. The offended honor of God demands satisfaction. However, no human being can provide such satisfaction because human nature sins compulsively. Hence, the incarnation of a God-man is required. He must be divine, because only a divine person can bring the perfect sacrifice required. He must be a human, because human nature has sinned against God and therefore has to be held accountable.

Reformed theology of the sixteenth and seventeenth century developed substitutionary and covenantal perspectives on human salvation. According to the substitutionary view, Christ dies on the cross on account of our sins. He takes our guilt on him so that the righteousness that he achieves through this sacrifice might become ours. The righteousness bestowed on believers is a gift from God based on Christ's vicarious sacrifice. The covenantal approach portrays Christ as the Representative of a new covenant of grace that came to replace the old covenant with Israel. Through faith, believers partake in the new covenant between God and his children and receive the promises and blessings of the new covenant. Baptism is a sign and seal of entry into the new covenantal community.

3.2.2 Salvation and the Example of Christ

The Abelardian understanding of salvation is an extension of the theology of the early Antiochene School, who attached special importance to the humanity of Christ and his moral example. Though Petrus Abelard acknowledged the sacrificial nature of Christ's death, he emphasized the existential significance of Christ as providing us with an example of the godly life. Christ inspires us to follow his example by revealing the nature of a life that resonates with God's will.

Abelard's distinctive subjective approach to salvation received new impetus with the rise of Liberal Protestantism. Friedrich Schleiermacher (1768–1834) presented a religious-exemplarist understanding of the cross. According to Schleiermacher, Jesus did not attempt to establish a new moral system, but to create a God-consciousness in humanity. Jesus possessed such a perfect and powerful God-consciousness that he was able to captivate and transform the lives of people and evoke love for God. Hence, Jesus was an exemplary person in two senses. First, he was the embodiment of the ideal human God-consciousness (Urbildlichkeit), and secondly he was able to evoke in people a God-consciousness (Vorbildlichkeit).[66]

The eighteenth and nineteenth centuries were characterized by a growing skepticism in Christian notions of original sin, a supernatural redeemer that appeases God's judgement through a satisfactory death, and the event of a resurrection. These doctrines were deemed as implausible and irreconcilable with the rationalist and scientific worldview of the time. In an attempt to challenge purely rationalist and moral-exemplarist approaches to the cross, liberal Protestant theologians such as Albrecht Ritschl (1822–1889), Wilhelm Hermann (1846–1922) and Hastings Rashdall (1858–1924) argued that the Abelardian moral theory of salvation is more plausible to modern culture than substitutionary theories of atonement. The fact and nature of Jesus' pre-Easter historical life, his religious personality and existential significance is important, not the post-Easter narrative of Christ that is based on an implausible and outdated worldview. They reinterpreted Jesus' death on the cross as an illustrative event, not a constitutive one, an example of self-giving love that inspires similar acts of self-giving and unconditional love. Jesus was not a supernatural redeemer, but a moral teacher who provided a compelling ethical example that ought to be assimilated by believers.

3.2.3 Salvation as Deification

The notion of salvation as deification occupied both Western and Eastern Christian thought from the earliest times. According to this view, human salvation consists of being taken up and sharing in the life of the triune God. The Alexandrian school, which was strongly influenced by Hellenistic philosophy, suggested that God had to become human so that humans can partake in the divine. Athanasius held that the divine *logos* is imparted to human nature through the incarnation so that humans are able to participate in the being of God. The Alexandrian school understood deification as a union with the substance of God (*theosis*). In contrast, the Antiochene school regarded deification as becoming like God (*homoiosis theoi*) through a holy moral life.[67]

The Thomistic tradition was mainly an extension of the Alexandrian school. Aquinas held that all things participate analogically in God because they derive their origin from God, who is the supreme *esse*. Since finite creatures possess no

---

66 Cf. McGrath, *Christian Theology*, 346.
67 Cf. ibid., 351.

being of their own, but derive their being from God through a hierarchic process of causation, the finite cannot sustain itself. Instead, the infinite upholds the finite. Thomas hence understood *theosis* in terms of humans participating ontologically in the being of God.

The Orthodox tradition does not conceive of redemption in juridical or legal terms, but as consisting of the participation of human life in divine life. Inner moral renewal and change is seen as imperative for a change of the creature's relation to God.[68] The Hesychastic controversy that broke out in the Eastern Church of the thirteenth century concerned the manner in which human beings participate in the being of God. The earliest proponent of Hesychasm was Simeon the New Theologian (949–1022), who claimed that he had direct encounters with God through visions of light. His views were developed further by Gregory Palamas (1296–1359), who taught that humans could receive direct visions of God through inner introspection and prayerful contemplation. This raised questions regarding the nature of the human's union with God and whether God's essence is accessible to human beings. If so, does such a position not obliterate the difference between Creator and creature? In response, Palamas developed a doctrine that distinguished between divine essence and divine energies. He stated that God unites himself to humans through uncreated divine energies such as visions of light, but that humans cannot enter God's essence. Introspection and contemplation enable believers to encounter these divine energies, but it does not effect an ontological unity with God's essence. The end result of the controversy was that three Councils of Constantinople (1341, 1347 and 1351) accepted Hesychasm as a fundamental tenet of Eastern Christian spirituality.

The Reformers understood the mystical union between God and believers in relational terms. Our union with God is a union in faith. Luther described the human-divine union as an exchange of properties. What belongs to Christ becomes the property of the soul, and what belongs to the human soul becomes the property of Christ. Our sins and vices that reside in the intellect and will of our souls become Christ's property during the event of the cross, while his righteousness and freedom become our property. In the process, our souls are freed from the slavery of sin.[69] John Calvin's doctrine of participation was characterized by a descent-ascent schema that denotes a cycle of exchange between the infinite God and finite beings: We can ascend to heaven because of Christ's

68 Cf. Guroian, "Human Rights and Modern Western Faith," 45.

69 Luther, Martin, *Luthers Werke*, Arnold E Berger (ed.), Leipzig: Bibliographisches Institut, 1917, LW 31:351. Also cf. Moltmann, Jürgen, "Sun of Righteousness Arise! The Freedom of a Christian – then and now – for the Victims and Perpetrators of Sin," *Theology Today* 69/1 (2012), 10.

descent to earth; through Christ's assumption of mortality, we inherit immortality; and because Christ submits himself to weakness, we receive heavenly strength.[70] This whole cycle of descent and ascent is enacted in Christ through the Spirit, who unites us to the Father. The union that the Spirit establishes between God and the believers consisted for Calvin in *koinonia*, that is, a relation of mutual indwelling. The believers dwell in Christ through faith and Christ dwells in the believer through his Spirit.[71]

In the last two decades, the Radical Orthodoxy movement has attempted to re-affirm and revitalize the Thomistic understanding of *theosis*. According to John Milbank, Protestantism's relational understanding of the divine-human encounter and its radical separation of God and creation has led to a "model of distance" that thinks of God as an infinite being beyond finitude who can only be known through the imposition of the divine will, which reveals itself through the Word and requires faith.[72] In doing so, Milbank argues, Protestantism separated faith and reason and contributed to the construction of a space for secular knowledge considered to belong to the natural realm.[73]

3.2.4 Salvation, Grace and Justification

One of most controversial issues that plagued Christian theology with regard to human salvation centered on the question: How is God's grace facilitated to human beings?

The infamous Pelagian controversy broke out in the fifth century AD. Pelagius (354 AD – 420 AD) reacted against what he perceived as the moral decline of the Western Church by stressing the need for human responsibility. Pelagius held that sin does not deprive human beings from their self-sufficiency, nor does it control human nature. He stated it as follows:

---

70 Calvin, *Institutes*, 4.17.2.

71 Cf. Hunsinger, George, "A Tale of Two Simultaneities. Justification and Sanctification in Calvin and Barth," in: John C. McDowell/Mike Higton (eds), *Conversing with Barth*, Hampshire: Ashgate, 2004, 71.

72 Milbank, John, "Participated Transcendence Reconceived," *Stanton Lecture* 5 (2011), 1–32, http://theologyphilosophycentre.co.uk/2011/03/12/john-milbanks-stanton-lectures-2011/comment-page-1/ (Accessed Nov 2, 2011).

73 Milbank, John, *Theology and Social Theory. Beyond Secular Reason*, Oxford: Blackwell, 2006, 16.

> God wished to bestow on the rational creature the gift of doing good of his own free will and the capacity to exercise free choice, by implanting in man the possibility of choosing either alternative.[74]

According to Pelagius, humans are created with a total freedom of the will and are therefore capable of both taking the first initiative in their salvation and earning their salvation through good works. God rewards human beings for their moral purity. Because humans are perfectly able to do right, they only need guidance in what a moral life entails. Christ subsequently became human to serve as the prime human example of the good moral life, thus inspiring human beings to imitate Him by living a holy life. Pelagius defined grace as a form of divine guidance "that informs us what our moral duties are; it does not, however assist us to perform them."[75]

Augustine (354 AD – 430 AD) reacted strongly to the teachings of Pelagius. Whereas Pelagius' argument was premised on the principle of human autonomy and agency, Augustine approached the issue from the perspective of God's grace as the only means to overcome the power of sin. Augustine understood the Fall as contaminating the whole human race with sin. Sin is inherently part of human nature and corrupted and tainted the human will to such a degree that the human person is inclined to do evil and to turn away from God. Though sin did not destroy the human will or prevent humans from taking free decisions, the freedom of the human will became distorted and biased towards evil. While the free will still exists, it is no longer autonomous and self-sufficient as Pelagius suggests, but weak, fallen and corrupted. This state of affairs prevents human beings from taking the initiative in their salvation and makes it impossible to earn salvation through good works. Salvation is only possible if God intervenes in the human state of affairs through his grace and restores the free will of the human being. Augustine understood God's grace as the liberating and transforming power of God that changes us from within and enables us to live a new life in Christ. God's grace is a totally undeserved, unmerited gift located outside the agency of humans. Whereas Pelagius regarded humanity as justified through works, Augustine believed in salvation through the gift of grace alone.

Augustine's understanding of sin and grace eventually gained the upper hand. The Council of Carthage condemned Pelagianism in 418 AD and endorsed the views of Augustine. This temporarily resolved the controversy.

---

74 Pelagius, *Pelagius's Commentary on St Paul's Epistle to the Romans*, trans. Theodore De Bruyn, Oxford Early Christian Studies, Oxford: Oxford University Press, 1993, 116.
75 McGrath, *Christian Theology*, 366.

With the advent of the Reformation, the question on the nature of the believer's salvation again came to prominence largely as a result of Luther's reflections on the question: How can the sinner be saved? His answer was that the sinner can only be justified through faith. This central theme of the Lutheran Reformation was inspired by earlier developments in late scholastic theology. Thomas Aquinas held that God does not stand in a direct relationship with human nature, but only relates with human beings through intermediate stages. Accordingly, God justifies humanity by means of created habits. Aquinas described 'habits' as supernatural entities of substance infused by God in human souls in order to prepare the soul for God's habitation. The habits enable human souls to ascend to God in an ontological sense. God's grace then does not suspend human nature, but works within the conditions of human nature. Personal decision is included in the reception of grace because the free will of the human being is a human condition that enables God's grace to work in the person.[76]

William of Ockham rejected Aquinas's notion of intermediate created habits as an unnecessary hypothesis not essential for justification. He argued that justification simply implies the acceptance of the sinner by God based on God's gracious favor. Justification is therefore dependent on God's attitude rather than divine substances in the human soul.[77] Ockham as a result prepared the way for the Reformation's personalist approach to justification.[78]

Luther signifies a radical break with Scholasticism. He held that we do not encounter God in Scripture as a Mover behind everything created.[79] Luther was convinced that some traditions within Catholicism, most notably the scholasticism of Aquinas, fell into Pelagianism by positing that the human has to give an appropriate moral response to God's grace in order to be rewarded. Luther specifically objected to Aquinas's notion that God has the obligation to recognize the value of some human actions and to reward them accordingly. According to him, this leads to a doctrine of salvation based on merit that emphasizes human works rather than God's grace.

Luther and the Protestant Reformation brought about a fundamental change in vocabulary. McGrath[80] notes that whereas the Augustinian and medieval tradition used the term "salvation by grace," the Reformers coined the term "justification by faith" to emphasize that salvation is based on an external forensic act

76 Cf. Iwand, Hans Joachim, "The Freedom of the Christian and the Bondage of the Human Will," trans. Jacob Corzine, *Logia* XVII/2 (2008), 9.
77 Cf. McGrath, *Christian Theology*, 370
78 Cf. ibid., 37.
79 Cf. Iwand, "The Freedom of the Christian," 10.
80 McGrath, *Christian Theology*, 372.

of God. Luther and other Reformers argued that God justifies the sinner through his grace without taking into account any form of human merit. God's grace is a free, unmerited and undeserved gift that Christians ought to accept in faith. For the Reformers the term "justification by faith" did not mean that the sinner is justified because he believes, this would make faith a human work, but instead the sinner believes because he receives God's grace. Sinners are justified based on God's grace and they receive God's grace through a faith that is worked in them by the Spirit.

Luther consequently developed the doctrine of *iustitia aliena*. This entails that the believer's righteousness is not located in herself; but is an alien righteousness imputed to the believer by virtue of Christ's sacrifice. Because righteousness is an externally imputed gift, sin cannot negate the righteous status of the believer before God. According to Luther, the believer is at once righteous and a sinner (*simul iustus et peccator*). In reality, the believer is a sinner, but before God, he is righteous. In developing the doctrine of alien righteousness, Luther departed from the Roman Catholic tradition that regarded justification not so much as a forensic act, but as something imparted to the believer; that is; the believer is made righteous by God through his grace that transforms the inner life of the believer.

For the Reformers, justification and sanctification had to be distinguished in order to avoid the notion of salvation through good works. Justification is a forensic act, while sanctification denotes the process of regeneration by the Spirit. John Calvin[81] subsequently developed the doctrine of double grace. Grace consists of the believer being united with Christ through faith. This union leads to justification and regeneration, which are two aspects of God's grace that are logically, but not temporally distinguishable. Justification entails that the believer is declared just before God based on Christ's sacrifice, while regeneration comprises the sanctifying work of the Spirit that cultivates a pure life.

The Council of Trent (1545) was summoned to produce a response to Luther's doctrine on justification. They stated that justification is not an extrinsic forensic act, but that it denotes a change to both the outer status and inner nature of the human being. Trent argued that the Reformed doctrine on justification through faith alone undermines the importance that the New Testament attaches to good human works. For Trent, justification is not only the remission of sin, but it entails that an unrighteous person becomes righteous by accepting the gift of being infused with God's grace. Justification is therefore based on an internal righteousness, not an alien righteousness. It is not an imputation on the

81 Calvin, *Institutes*, 3.11.2.

basis of someone else's sacrifice that makes one righteous before God, but God's infusion of faith and grace in the believer on the basis of Christ's sacrifice, which transforms the inner life of the believer. The Reformers, for their part, did not deny that a holy life follows justification, but they argued that sanctification emanates from justification, rather than it being the cause of justification.

3.2.5 Salvation and Divine Election

Both the Catholic and Reformed understanding of justification had theological implications for the scope of God's salvation and human autonomy. If grace is a free and irresistible gift from God, it follows that God withholds his grace from some, since not all people believe in God. Moreover, if grace is an irresistible gift, it naturally implies that salvation is not related to human choosing. In response, Augustine developed the doctrine of election that entails that God elected some from the mass of sinners to save them from perdition. Their election rests on the sovereign will of God and is not related to any human merit or choice. Reformed Orthodoxy developed the notion of double predestination, which entails that God elected some and actively rejected others for damnation. Christ died for all people in the sense that his sacrifice is sufficient for all, but it is not efficient for all. Only the elected are saved.

Arminius (1560 – 1609) and his followers rejected the doctrine of predestination because it was perceived as compromising the universal significance of Christ's work and suspending human autonomy. Arminius held that Christ died for all people, not only the elect. When Scripture refers to predestination, it refers to God foreseeing before creation who will respond in faith to Christ's sacrifice.[82] Arminianism therefore retained the notion of predestination, but gave it new content. Grace is not an irresistible gift, but it is offered to all and requires a free response from all. The human will is depraved by sin, but not totally corrupt. Human beings are despite the effects of sin, capable to choose for or against God. In the end, salvation depends on a combination of God making salvation possible through Christ and offering us grace based on Christ's sacrifice, and humans being able to respond to God's grace. Whereas the magisterial Reformation regarded the human will as totally depraved in the sense that humans are incapable of contributing to their own salvation through choice, Armi-

82 Cf. Arminius, James, "Analysis of the Ninth Chapter of St Paul's Epistle to the Romans," in: *The Works of James Arminius*, vol. 3, trans. William Nichols, Grand Rapids: Baker Book House, 1986, 506; 516.

nianism upheld a semi-Pelagian notion of salvation that understood salvation as a synergistic and cooperative event between God and human beings. Arminianism eventually exercised a major influence on eighteenth century evangelicalism and was forcefully supported within Methodism by Charles Wesley (1707–1788).[83]

Karl Barth is probably the most influential exponent of a universalist understanding of election. For Barth, divine predestination consists of the election of Jesus Christ through whom God has chosen to enter human reality and to become a partner of humanity. God demonstrates his commitment to humanity not only by redeeming humanity, but also by bearing the cost and pain of redemption. This entails that God rejects Jesus Christ so that sinful humanity can escape God's judgement. Barth therefore deviated from the Reformed Orthodox notion of human beings being elected for condemnation. Instead, the whole of humanity is rejected in time because of sin and elected in Christ in eternity.[84] The implication of Barth's position is that humanity cannot be condemned because God has already made a choice for humanity in Jesus Christ.

3.3 Freedom and Responsibility

The close relationship between freedom and responsibility is emphasized throughout the biblical traditions. The law and prophetic traditions in the Old Testament depict God's righteousness as consisting in Him bringing about justice for the poor and oppressed. Because the sojourners, poor, widows and orphans of Israel are vulnerable to judicial arbitrariness and social exploitation, the rights of the weak ought to be protected. The exhortations are often combined with references to the just character of God, who acts in the interests of the weak.[85] The Israelites ought to remember that they were slaves in Israel and that God liberated them from their bondage. As a freed people, the Israelites have a responsibility to care for those who experience similar conditions of bondage.[86] The Gospels follow the same line of thought. Jesus is depicted as the Messiah who liberates us from the bondage of sin. He directs the liberating message of the Gospel to the poor, sick and outcasts of society.[87] The believers who experience God's salvation in Christ have specific responsibilities to the

83 McGrath, *Christian Theology*, 384.
84 Cf. Barth, Karl, *The Epistle to the Romans*, trans. E. Hoskyns, London: Oxford, 1968.
85 Cf. Deuteronomy 1:15, Amos 1:6–7, Deuteronomy 23:7, Deuteronomy 15:9.
86 Cf. Deuteronomy 15:15.
87 Cf. Matthew 9:36, Luke 4:18–19.

poor, because those who care for the poor and for the outcasts, care for Christ himself.[88]

The New Testament understanding of responsibility is strongly informed by the notion of fellowship (*koinonia*). Since God created my neighbor in his image, fellowship is a God-given demand that obliges me to care, serve and devote myself to my neighbor. Authentic fellowship does not allow for any notion or practice of freedom that fosters indifference towards others. Instead, fellowship obliges the Christian to enact his personal freedom in ways that serve the wellbeing of others.

The Christian-Aristotelian tradition, specifically Scholasticism, emphasized the importance of cultivating virtue. Aquinas held that human responsibility requires that the human being, who has been infused with God's grace, must strive to reach his divinely intended purpose by living a virtuous life. Aquinas distinguished between theological virtues such as charity that are supernatural in origin and cardinal virtues that are natural in origin. The theological virtues, of which charity is the most important, inform and direct the natural virtues to their end.[89]

The Reformation moved away from teleological ethics to a more formal ethics of duty and obligation. Luther's famous dictum in his book *The Freedom of the Christian* (1520) was that the Christian is a free lord over all things and subject to no-one, yet the Christian is also a servant of all things and subject to everyone.[90] The Christian is subject to none because she shares in the resurrection of Christ and the victory over sin and evil. This freedom cannot be taken away from the believer, no matter the circumstances. Yet, the Christian is also subject to all in the sense that he is freed to serve others.[91] The inner freedom we gain in Christ leads to an outer servitude to the neighbor and the world.[92] With servitude Luther does not mean a dehumanizing bondage, but in the words of Kristin Largen, a "humanizing activity of being bound to one another in relationships of care and responsibility."[93] Understood this way, freedom and servitude do not diminish or constrain each other, but freedom realizes itself through a compassionate servitude to others.

88 Matthew 25:39.

89 Cf. Thomas Aquinas, *Disputed Questions on the Virtues*, E.M Atkins/Thomas Williams (eds), trans. E.M Atkins, Cambridge: Cambridge University Press, 2005, 246.

90 Luther, *Luthers Werke*, 31:344, 358.

91 Cf. Moltmann, "Sun of Righteousness Arise," 11.

92 Cf. Largen, Kristin, "Freedom From and Freedom For. Luther's Concept of Freedom for the Twenty-First Century," *Dialog: A Journal of Theology* 52/3 (2013), 236.

93 Largen, "Freedom From and Freedom For," 235.

Calvin distinguished between three forms of Christian freedom, namely freedom from the law, freedom of conscience and freedom to obey God's will.[94] Freedom from the law entails that Christ abrogated the law by removing the curse of the law. Obedience to the law is not required for justification, but it does provide us with guidelines to live according to the will of God out of an inner gratitude for the gift of God's grace.[95] Freedom of conscience entails that Christ liberated us from the bondage of a conscience that fears the curse of death and God's eternal judgement. By embracing God's mercy, our consciences can be at peace and the believer can move beyond seeking righteousness through obedience to the law.[96] Freedom to obey God's will entails that, freed from the yoke of the law, the Christian is free to serve God spontaneously.[97] True freedom is to love God wholeheartedly, to serve and obey God keenly and to submit willingly to God's spirit.[98]

Calvin's positive understanding of freedom led him to develop a doctrine on vocation. Every person receives a particular vocation in life, that is, a divine calling to a distinct duty and mode of life within a specific context.[99] Calvin regarded society as a neighborhood where individuals serve each other through their respective gifts within their assigned vocational context.[100] Christian responsibility and ethical appropriateness of our actions are therefore determined by the type of vocation we receive from God.

Dietrich Bonhoeffer considered freedom not in the first place as an "individual right but a responsibility."[101] He was alarmed that people who believe in salvation by faith alone so often separate faith from responsible moral actions. Bonhoeffer described such responses to God's grace as "cheap grace."[102] He specifically objected against abstract theistic conceptions of God that underemphasize the importance of human agency by locating God in the transcendent realm from where he deterministically governs all things, irrespective of human agency. For Bonhoeffer, Christian ethics is not shaped by abstract meta-

94 Cf. Hesselink, John, "John Calvin on the Law and Christian Freedom," *Ex Auditu* 11 (1995), 77–89.

95 Calvin, *Institutes* 2.7.14, Comm Rom 6:15.

96 Calvin, *Institutes* 3.19.2, Comm Rom 8:15.

97 Calvin, *Institutes* 3.19.4.

98 Cf. Hesselink, "John Calvin on the Law," 84.

99 Cf. Calvin, *Institutes* 3.10.6.

100 Calvin, Comm 1 Cor 7:20.

101 Cf. Nickson, Ann L., *Bonhoeffer on Freedom. Courageously Grasping Reality*, Oxford: Ashgate, 2002, 124.

102 Cf. Duff, Nancy J., "'Stages on the Road to Freedom': A Brief Introduction to Dietrich Bonhoeffer," *Theology Today* 71/1 (2014), 9.

physical theories that provide deceptively safe norms and principles, but the person of Christ and the reality of God's reconciliation with humanity.[103] Conversely, Bonhoeffer attacked existentialist and pietistic forms of Christianity that locate God's working in the innermost self-interiority of the human being. Bonhoeffer regarded such notions as complicit in creating an empty bourgeoisie Christianity with no sense of social calling and responsibility. Instead, God is both beyond and in the midst of our lives, an integral part of our multidimensional and polyphonic reality.[104] Responsibility starts not with an adherence to universal principles and an autonomous self, but in knowing the world, acknowledging it and responding to it.[105] Our actions ought to be informed by the living God who revealed himself in the Christ who was incarnated, crucified and resurrected.[106] Living according to the reconciliation that Christ brought about means that freedom is costly; it requires that the vicarious action of Christ becomes the life principle of the believer.[107] Freedom is not to be free from the other, but to be free for the other. Only by being bound in relationship to the other and sacrificing myself for the other, am I free.[108]

Karl Barth approached the theme of Christian responsibility from the perspective of the *eschaton*. This approach was necessitated by the collapse of the nineteenth century philosophy of progress. Barth initiated a move away from the Liberal Protestant understanding of history as an advance to a more mature and enlightened future, to an understanding of Christian action as relevant and powerful only because of its eschatological character.[109] The way in which we act towards our neighbors is determined by our understanding of our heavenly citizenship. The Christian's eschatological citizenship entails that the Christian can be free in Christ while inhibited by the world and that the Christian can find

103 Bonhoeffer, Dietrich, *Ethik*, vol. 6, *Dietrich Bonhoeffer Werke (DBW)*, Ilse Tödt et al. (eds), München: Chr Kaiser Verlag, 1992, 31.

104 Bonhoeffer, Dietrich, *Letters and Papers from Prison*, vol. 8, *Dietrich Bonhoeffer Works*, John De Gruchy (ed.), Minneapolis: Fortress Press, 2010, 429, 366–67. Also cf. Welker, *God the Revealed*, 27.

105 Cf. Rowe, Terra S., "Freedom Is Not Free? Posthumanist, Ecological Reflections on Christian Freedom and Responsibility," *Dialog: A Journal of Theology* 54/1 (2015), 67.

106 Cf. Duff, "Stages On The Road to Freedom," 9.

107 Cf. Bonhoeffer, Dietrich, *Sanctorum Communio*, vol. 1, *Dietrich Bonhoeffer Werke (DBW)*, Joachim von Soosten (ed.), München: Chr. Kaiser Verlag, 1986, 99.

108 Bonhoeffer, Dietrich, *Creation and Fall*, vol. 3, *Dietrich Bonhoeffer Works*, John De Gruchy (ed.), Minneapolis: Fortress, 2007, 37.

109 Quash, Ben, "Exile, Freedom and Thanksgiving. Barth and Hans Urs van Balthasar," in: John C. McDowell/Mike Higton (eds), *Conversing with Barth*, 90–120, Hampshire: Ashgate, 2004, 96.

homage in Christ while being an exile in the world.[110] The duty of the Christian is to show solidarity with the world and the exiles within it.[111] For Barth, freedom is not a precondition for ethical action, but it emanates from a response to God's calling; it is "an effect of being occupied in the service of God."[112] Obedience as a loyal response to God's command therefore precedes freedom.

3.4 Freedom and Politics

The Jesus movement not only originated in times characterized by political and social conflict, but the Gospel accounts of Jesus' life are pervaded in the words of Gerd Theißen by symbol-political conflicts.[113] We can identify a host of symbol-political conflicts in the Gospel narratives. The Gospel of Matthew places the birth of Jesus within the context of the worldly empire of Augustus. Whereas the worldly king Augustus was lauded as ruler of peace, Matthew depicts Christ as the true Inaugurator of the kingdom of peace. Other symbol-political conflicts include Herod Antipas's fear of an upheaval after hearing of the promised Messiah's birth, Jesus's criticisms of the temple; his calling of the twelve disciples to represent the new Israel; Jesus' outreach to the socially ostracized such as women and tax collectors; Jesus's royal entrance into Jerusalem; and the events at the cross that are infused with tension between Jesus, the Jewish leaders and the representatives of the Roman Empire.

The concept of the kingdom that forms the core message of Christ preaching, especially in the parables, is probably the most pervasive symbol-political concept in the Gospels. The term kingdom (*βασιλεια*) depicts in the original Greek the fact and act of God's reign rather than a geographical area. It is a dynamic term depicting the liberating power of God's reign breaking through in the world. The kingdom points to the person of Christ in whom the new aeon enters the world. He breaks the power of Satan, servitude to the Law and the violence of worldly rulers. The kingdom that Christ establishes is both a present and future, immanent and transcendental, internal and external reality. Though the kingdom of God enters the world in Christ and is in the words of Welker a "perpetual emergent power" through the work of the Spirit, the New Testament canon em-

---

110 Ibid., 102.
111 Ibid.
112 Ibid., 108.
113 Cf. Theißen, Gerd, "Jesus und die symbolpolitischen Konflikten seiner Zeit. Sozialgeschichtliche Aspekte der Jesusforschung," *EvTh* 57/4 (1997), 378–400.

phasizes that God's kingdom does not replace or obliterate worldly kingdoms.[114] However, it does relativize worldly power and it eventually relates all exercise of power to the judging reign of God.[115]

There are strong counter-imperial impulses in the writings of Paul. Paul states quite emphatically that even though the new aeon has yet to be fully established, its presence can already be experienced.[116] For Paul, Christ's reign radiates into worldly realms of power and can therefore not be dismissed as a purely spiritual reality without any significance for public realms.[117] Hence, in his letter to the Romans, Paul challenges the newly converted Gentile Christians to denounce the worship of Roman gods, which is nothing other than submitting their bodies to sin; and to rather enter into the worship of Jesus, who was raised from the dead.[118] In a world where Caesar was proclaimed as Savior and Messiah, Paul announces Jesus as the Savior and Lord; the one in whom the whole of humanity finds its appointed destiny and in whom God's justice is revealed.[119] Yet, Paul was also cautious not to allow eschatology to suspend the structure of social and political relationships. He therefore exhorts the Christians of Rome in Romans 13:1–7 to honor the state, though he qualifies this exhortation by stating that the state is a servant of God who will be accountable to God. According to Paul, Christians may not engage in anarchy because anarchy would subvert the order that God has created. To God alone belongs the right to remove the rulers of this world.

Augustine followed the Pauline line of thought. He distinguished between two cities, namely the city of God and the city of the world. These two cities live in a dialectical tension. The church is an eschatological community that is an exile in the city of the world. Though it is in the world, it is not of the world. While surrounded by the disbelief of the world, the church has the calling to stay true to its distinctive identity until the consummation. The city of the world is essentially a pagan world within which the saved live. The government of the city of the world is concerned with maintaining order and curbing the disorder that sin brings. This being the case, Christians have the duty to obey worldly governments. Augustine, hence, opposed any form of violent insurrection against the state.

114 Cf. Matthew 22:21, Romans 13:1, Titus 3:1. Cf. Welker *God the Revealed*, 228.
115 Cf. Romans 13:3, Colossians 1:16.
116 Cf. 2Corinthians 5:17, 1Corinthians 10:11.
117 Cf. Colossians 1:16.
118 Cf. Romans 1:18–32.
119 Cf. Wright, Nicholas Thomas, "Paul's Gospel and the Roman Empire," in: Richard A. Horsley (ed.), *Paul and Politics*, Harrisburg, Pennsylvania: Trinity Press, 2000, 168.

Eusebius of Caesarea was the first theologian who propagated the idea of a Christian empire. This notion entailed that the state is regarded as the guardian of the church as institution, while the Christian faith is established as the official religion of the state. After the fall of Rome and the collapse of the Western Empire, Eusebius's imperial theology lost traction, yet eleventh-century reformers would again revive the notion of imperial Christian reign.[120] During the medieval and early modern period, state and church were closely affiliated. Emerging rulers of the new European nations effected mass conversions, while the papacy exerted considerable coercive power over the continent.[121]

Bonaventure and Thomas Aquinas were in the thirteenth century instrumental to renewed interest in the natural law tradition. They held that God's eternal law is impressed on the human soul. All people are therefore capable of moral discernment and rational reflection. This philosophical premise had important implications for the relation between freedom and authority. The duty of obedience is not primarily grounded in moral precepts founded by positive human law, but in God's natural law that participates in God's eternal law. This suggests that there are limits to obedience and occasions when the subordinate does not need to obey authorities, but has the duty to exercise his own moral judgement and choice in accordance with God's natural law.[122] By subjecting positive human law to natural law, and by locating a sense of the natural law in all human beings, medieval natural law theorists prepared the way for a greater emphasis on individual human choice that would eventually emanate in human rights theories based on natural law premises.

Natural law theory also had a decisive influence on the political thinking of the Reformers. Luther famously developed a two-kingdoms doctrine on the basis of his distinction between the human being's outer and inner person to explicate the relationship between the spiritual freedom and civil authority. According to this doctrine, God instituted two forms of governments, namely the spiritual government of Christ that produces righteous believers who live in obedience to God and the temporal government of the state who restrains sin in the world. The spiritual government relies on the revelation of God's Word, whereas the temporal government is ruled based on reason and the natural law. Whereas the spiritual government can make people free, the temporal government cannot bring freedom. It, after all, exists precisely because people are unfree. The temporal gov-

---

120 Welker, *God the Revealed*, 228.

121 Cf. Freeman, Charles, *A New History of Early Christianity*, Yale: Yale University Press, 2009, 319.

122 Cf. Porter, Jean, "Natural equality: Freedom, Authority and Obedience in Two Medieval Thinkers," *Annual of the Society of Christian Ethics* 21 (2001), 290.

ernment ought not to interfere with the spiritual government because the spiritual government is an expression of the sovereign freedom of Christ, while the obedience of Christians to temporal government is an expression of their inner freedom. Insurrection against temporal governments is unacceptable, because it reflects a mistaken effort to locate freedom in the outer and external conditions of the world.[123] John Calvin's two-kingdoms doctrine displayed similarities with Luther's doctrine, but he made a greater attempt to relate the spiritual and civil realms to each other. Calvin used the analogy of the relation between soul and body to explain his stance. The spiritual kingdom relates to the affairs of the soul and the civil kingdom to external and material affairs (the bodily realm). Different "kings and laws" preside over the two realms and they therefore need to be kept apart.[124] Yet, as the soul and body form one human person, so the spiritual and civil kingdoms are two regiments of the one kingdom of God. As the body provides habitation for the soul and the soul *anima* to the body, the spiritual and civil kingdoms are not 'adverse' to each other, but keep each other in tact without being absorbed into each other. The spiritual kingdom maintains our spiritual lives by preaching the Word, while the civil realm upholds the spiritual realm by preserving order and protecting external worship and sound doctrine.[125]

Reformed Orthodoxy developed in the seventeenth century a covenantal theology that distinguished between two kinds of covenants, namely the covenant between God and people and between the ruler and people. The covenant between ruler and people is analogically aligned to the covenant between God and people and contains a set of mutual obligations. The ruler ought to be a guardian of the freedom of the people according to the ordinance of God and the people ought to obey rulers as representatives of God. This covenantal notion of authority had a profound influence on the later development of social contract theories and constitutionalism in the Western world.

For Bonhoeffer, Christian responsibility entailed that the Christian lives within the bounds of God's commandments, which embrace the whole of life. God's commandments do not limit us, but free us to experience the fullness of life.[126] When worldly exercises of power conflict with God's commandments, a decision

123 Cf. Chester, Stephen, "Who is Freedom For? Martin Luther and Alain Badiou on Paul and Politics," in: Paul Middleton; Angus Paddison/Karen Wenell (eds), *Paul, Grace and Freedom*, London: T & T Clark, 2009, 101–102. Cf. LW 45.91.

124 Calvins, *Institutes* 2.14.1.

125 Ibid., 4.20.1.

126 Cf. Nickson, *Bonhoeffer on Freedom*, 68.

should be made for Christ.[127] Bonhoeffer, therefore, justified resistance against the Nazi regime on the basis that Christ freed believers from their conscience so that they can incur guilt for the sake of others in the same way that Christ incurred guilt for us.[128] Christian freedom entails that the liberated become liberators of the oppressed and those that suffer.

Reinhold Niebuhr's notion of political realism exercised considerable influence in the United States from the 1930s to the 1960s. This approach was strongly informed by the Augustinian understanding of freedom as a choice between greater and lesser being. Realism's understanding of politics recognizes the limits of human judgement and highlights the importance of responsibility. Human nature is limited not only because it is finite and flawed, but also because judgement ultimately belongs to God. Only God can have the final say in history. Human judgements and political arrangements are therefore always preliminary and conditional and can only be exercised within limits and under certain conditions of responsibility.[129] We cannot give ultimate meaning to history, nor can we determine the future, because we are ultimately only human. Niebuhr subsequently posited that the best political systems balance power with "countervailing power."[130] The task of the Christian is to display a critical attitude towards all political systems while upholding a responsible attitude. Such an attitude recognizes on one hand that we can only make preliminary judgements, conversely it affirms that we have a duty to make choices between greater and lesser evils when we find ourselves in ambiguous moral contexts.[131]

4 Main Differences Between Contemporary Catholic, Protestant and Orthodox Approaches to Freedom

The main modern Christian traditions largely agree that we are saved by God's grace alone; that freedom cannot merely be defined as freedom *of*, but that it also has a strong positive dimension in that we are freed *for* service to God

127 Bonhoeffer, *Ethik*, 283.
128 Ibid., 279.
129 Cf. Lovin, Robin W., "Christian Realism for the Twenty-First Century," *Journal of Religious Ethics* 37/4 (2009), 669–682, 669–671.
130 Cf. ibid., 670.
131 Cf. Niebuhr, Reinhold, "Theology and Political Thought in the Western World," *The Ecumenical Review* 9 (1957), 253–262, 253–54.

and humanity; and that the church as body of Christ is a redeemed community who is an agent of God's liberating work in the world. However, there are some divergences when it comes to the respective views on the relation between divine sovereignty and human agency, the church and the liberty of the believer, as well as the relationship between religion and public freedoms.

With regard to the relationship between divine sovereignty and human agency, Roman Catholic theology largely upholds the notion of *analogia entis*, that is, the human being's existence is analogous to God's being. The *imago Dei* is subsequently understood as consisting of an ontological relation between God and human beings. Mainline Protestantism, in contrast, emphasizes the radical difference between God and creature and understands God's involvement in creation in terms of God's revelation that expresses his will. Protestant theologians tend to regard the *imago Dei* as a relational concept that indicates the ability of the human being to respond to God. Eastern Orthodoxy understands the *imago Dei* as consisting in humanity's common transcendence that emanates from God's being and act. The *Ekklesia* participates in divine life and is as such a "sophianic" community.[132]

These different understandings of God's sovereign involvement in creation and the human's relation to God necessarily result in different understandings of the nature of human freedom. In mainline Roman Catholic theology, the human person is seen as a transcendental being characterized by an openness towards God and possessing a freedom to reach out to God in her spiritual movement. Freedom is not simply a quality of action, but a mode of being that allows us to reach out to absolute being and to actualize ourselves.[133] Consequently, Roman Catholic ethics are characterized by a strong teleological orientation. Freedom is not so much a question of self-determination, but rather of attuning yourself to your ultimate end.[134] Mainline Protestantism, in line with its voluntarist understanding of God's involvement in creation and relational understanding of the *imago Dei*, tends to entertain a relational understanding of freedom. Freedom does not reside, as is the case with the Roman Catholic *analogia entis* doctrine, in human capacity or potentiality; but in a relation enabled by God's grace. Freedom is a divine gift communicated to us through Christ, while the human person is an intentional agent that can respond in gratitude to God's grace. Eastern Orthodoxy, for its part, resists legalistic and external notions of freedom and morality. Freedom is not about self-realization or the exer-

---

132 Williams, Rowan S., "Eastern Orthodox Theology," in: David Ford (ed.), *The Modern Theologians. An Introduction to Christian Theology since 1918*, Malden: Blackwell, ^{3}2005, 574.
133 Cf. ibid., 21–22.
134 Cf. Burrel, David, *Faith and Freedom. An Interfaith Perspective*, Oxford: Blackwell, 2004, 187.

cise of human autonomy, but entails that humans participate in divine life and respond to God's gifts through acts of repentance and self-limitation.

A second difference concerns the relation between church authority and human freedom. The Roman Catholic tradition understands the pope to be Christ's representative on earth and therefore as possessing the authority to develop Christian teachings *ex cathedra* and to impose constraints on Roman Catholic preaching. Subsequently, the Roman Catholic tradition aligns the authority of Scripture closely with tradition and tends to entertain a hierarchical understanding of church government. Eastern Orthodoxy holds that the church is a non-legalistic "organically evolving community" that ought to draw all of humanity into a Christian community.[135] Whereas, the church structure in Roman Catholicism is centralized and hierarchical in nature, the Orthodox tradition, at least in theory, entertains a decentralized notion of church governance.[136] Mainline Protestantism largely stresses the sole authority of Scripture and subordinates tradition to Scripture. This results in a greater emphasis on the individual liberty of the believer. Luther emphasized the believers' freedom from the law, Calvin the freedom of the Christian conscience, and Liberal Protestantism the autonomy of the individual and his freedom to choose.

Lastly, Roman Catholicism, Eastern Orthodoxy and Protestantism diverge on the relation between religion and public freedoms. Whereas both Roman Catholicism and Eastern Orthodoxy traditionally viewed religion and the common good of society as inseparably intertwined, and understood Christianity as a publicly confessed way of life, the Reformers developed the two-kingdom doctrine that sought to distinguish between religion and politics. Following Luther and Calvin, seventeenth century Protestants in the Dutch Republic and the United States developed the notion of freedom of religion in order to emancipate religious institutions from political institutions. This, inevitably, and perhaps unintendedly, contributed to the modern distinction between private and public spheres life, as well as the privatization of religion.

5 Christian Concepts of Freedom in Relation to Judaism and Islam

The Western notion of toleration has had the unintended consequence of creating parallel societies in which communities tolerate each other, but live isolated

135 Williams, "Eastern Orthodox Theology," 574.
136 Cf. Pollis, "Eastern Orthodoxy and Human Rights," 351.

from one other. As can be seen in the rise of radical Islam, this has had a destructive effect on social cohesion because second and third generation migrant communities do not integrate sufficiently with their adopted societies. This leads to feelings of alienation, loss of identity and resentment. Toleration is indeed a very thin moral concept and seems inadequate to address the realities of globalization. As a consequence, we might need to find 'thicker' mediatory notions that can bridge the divide between religions and communities with different value systems. This identification of 'thicker' mediatory notions requires a mutual exchange that unlocks the civilizing potentialities of religions without assimilating the various religions into one grand narrative.

The divergences between Christian, Judaist and Islamic soteriologies are considerable and do not display an underlying unity. For example, Christian understandings of the Trinity and groundings of human salvation in the life, death and resurrection of Christ are not reconcilable with Jewish and Islamic God-concepts or soteriologies. We will therefore do well to heed the following warning of McGrath:

> Respect for the integrity of the world's religions demands that the distinctive shape of a religion's understanding of salvation including its basis, its mode of conveyance and appropriation, and its inherent nature must be respected.... It is essential to respect and honor differences here, and resist the ever-present temptation to force them all into the same mold.[137]

The discussion that follows identifies some features of the Christian understanding of freedom that overlap with Islamic and Jewish concepts of freedom. These overlapping notions might encourage interreligious dialogue and assist us in developing 'thicker mediatory notions' that empower us to bridge the divide between religious societies.

First, Christianity shares with Judaism and Islam the notion that God is the Creator of all things, that he created all things *ex nihilo* and that he is sovereign, holy and transcendent. All three religions maintain that there is a radical difference between God's essence and creation, though this difference does not mean remoteness. The Hebrew Scriptures, Christian canon and the Qur'an affirm that God created by speaking the creative word. Creation originated through the free creative acts of an intentional Agent who himself is not dependent upon creation. This common understanding of divine freedom is important for articulating human freedom. David Burrel[138] identifies two implications of this stance for the

137 McGrath, *Christian Theology*, 327.
138 Burrel, *Faith and Freedom*, 153.

freedom of the creature. Since the Creator is an intentional agent, he is open to a personal relationship with created beings. Moreover, since the Intentional Agent is the source of the existence and well-being of created persons, he is owed obedience and gratitude.

The precise relation between divine sovereignty and human freedom is an issue with which all three monotheistic religions grapple and therefore ought to serve as an important impulse for interfaith discussions. The three religions agree that divine sovereignty does not compromise human freedom, yet they all struggle with the question on how the relationship between God's sovereignty and human freedom can be formulated in intelligible terms.

Secondly, all three monotheistic religions uphold the 'oneness of humanity' and the innate capacity of human beings to distinguish between right and wrong. This common theological precis is important for discussions on human freedom, because it upholds the sacredness of the human person, the essential equality of all people and the ability of the human to respond to God. Some might argue that the Islamic and Jewish traditions emphasize obedience to God's law to a much greater extent than Christianity. However, Christian doctrines on salvation by grace and justification by faith should not be misunderstood as circumventing the importance of human obedience to God's law, nor as legitimizing permissive behavior. The difference between Christianity and the other two religions does not lie in the question of whether the human person ought to obey God, but rather in Christianity's grounding of obedience in a gratitude for God's gifts in Christ that emanates in a life of conformity to God's law.

Thirdly, while the respective religions are essentially religions of Scripture, various traditions within Christianity and Judaism recognize the existence of a natural law, discernible by all human beings, while the Islamic faith recognizes the notion of *fiṭra*. Sachedina[139] defines *fiṭra* as follows:

> The sense of unity in human beings in spite of their different cultural, ethnic and religious identities represents one of the most important principles of Islam. This unity is based upon the concept of *fitra* (noble nature) with which God has endowed every human being. The notion of *fitra* has important epistemological implications that concern the nature of human beings. *Fitra* represents the primordial nature of human beings that allows them to develop ethical and spiritual knowledge. Muslim theologians have defined *fitra* as an innate natural disposition and as properties that are endowed by God to all human beings at the moments of their birth ... the notion of *fitra* implies the existence of an universal human nature that is shared by all human beings and from which they can derive their human rights.

139 Sachedina, Abdulaziz "Continuing the Conversation About Comparative Ethics," *Journal of Religious Ethics* 43/3 (2015), 552.

The notions of natural law and *fiṭra* share the assumption that moral law is universal and that humanity not only shares a common descent, but also possesses an equal dignity. This common assumption might enable the three religions to develop shared moral concepts of political and social freedoms that can be employed in increasing plural and multi-faith societies.

Fourthly, the three monotheistic religions are salvific religions that confess belief in a God who redeems. A central and recurring theme in the Hebrew Scriptures is the description of God as the Redeemer who liberated Israel from the slavery of Israel.[140] He is the God who protects and liberates the oppressed, weak and marginalized.[141] Messianism within Judaism contains a strong redemptive-eschatological element in that it awaits the coming of a Messiah that will reconcile God with his people and bring salvation to Israel and mankind. The Christian canon depicts Christ as the Messiah promised by the Old Testament prophets. He is the true fulfilment of Jewish expectations, the Son of David, the Anointed of God, the Lord and Savior who was incarnated to re-establish God's reign on earth and to liberate humanity from the bondage of sin.[142] Islam depicts Allah as a merciful God who awards repentance and obedience with eternal blessings.[143] Faith and good works are seen as closely linked. As noted earlier, the three religions diverge considerably as far as their soteriologies are concerned, but they do share a common understanding of God as Liberator and human beings as in need of salvation.

Fifthly, all three religions relate freedom closely to justice and mercy. Since they recognize that every human being carries the imprint of God's image, they correlate vertical obligations to God with horizontal obligations to human beings.[144] Freedom is seen as closely tied to a life of justice in obedience to God that is manifested in serving the well-being of others, specifically the poor and weak. This shared understanding of the relation between freedom, justice and mercy has had a profound influence on the development of welfare systems in various countries and serves as an important catalyst for the future development of shared perspectives on socio-economic rights.

Lastly, when it comes to the relation between church and state, Judaism and Christianity share overlapping perspectives, while Islam mainly diverges. Modern

---

140 Deuteronomy 5:6.

141 Deuteronomy 24:17–22.

142 John 1:29; Matthew 1:1–3; Mark 1:2.

143 Qur'ān 33:43.

144 Cf. Hollenbach, David, "Comparative Ethics, Islam and Human Rights. Internal Pluralism and the Possible Development of Tradition," *Journal of Religious Ethics* 38/3 (2010), 580–587, 582.

Christianity and Judaism generally support the separation between religion and state and emphasize the importance of freedom of religion and freedom of conscience, whereas Islamic traditions are more inclined to uphold theocratic ideals that conflate religion and politics. As Abdulaziz Sachedina[145] rightly points out, these different approaches are, among others, due to the different social contexts within which these religions developed. Islam developed within tribal communities and sought specifically in the seventh century ways to establish political societies that would transcend kinship, whereas Christianity originated within a well-organized empire where the political conditions demanded the recognition of the legitimacy of secular authority. The New Testament, accordingly, exhibits impulses that support a separation between state and religion. Judaism, in a similar vein, developed within diasporic contexts where believers were always a minority. The different contexts resulted in Judaism and Christianity being more inclined to acknowledge the validity of the secular domain and to embrace the principles of liberal democracy and western human rights discourse, whereas Muslim scholars are less inclined to embrace the notion of secular public domains. This does not mean that Islam unequivocally rejects the notion of human rights. Various Muslim scholars are currently attempting to develop an Islamic approach to human rights that recognizes the universality of certain human rights norms, while also addressing the specific needs of Islamic societies. Interfaith dialogue on human rights is probably one of the most promising areas for developing 'thicker' mediatory understandings of human freedom.

6 The Current Use and Impact of the Concept of Freedom within Christianity

The Catholic, Protestant and Eastern Orthodox traditions in Christianity are by no means homogeneous in nature. We, in fact, find various schools of thought within these mainline traditions that employ a wide variety of hermeneutical, philosophical and theological methods to address their contexts and specific burning issues. The most important contemporary developments in Christianity have been the rise of liberation theologies, Pentecostalism and postmodern theology. Each of these theological traditions has had some effect with regard to the Christian understanding of freedom.

145 Sachedina, "Continuing the Conversation About Comparative Ethics," 543–556.

6.1 Liberation Theology

From the 1960's Christianity has seen the growth of liberation theologies that were shaped in the struggle against colonialism, repression, racism and gender discrimination. At the core of these theologies lies a search for social justice and freedom. Theologies such as feminism, eco-feminism, political liberation theology and black theology argue that the biblical traditions have carried forward androcentric, misogynist, patriarchal and hierarchical patterns of thought that have subsequently been uncritically appropriated by Christian traditions.

Feminist theology challenges the patriarchal modes of thought that underlie much of Christianity's theological formulations. Traditional theology, for instance, largely used male pronouns to describe God; medieval and early modern theologians generally accepted that males reflect God's image to a larger degree than females; and the maleness of Christ has often been understood within traditional theology as constitutive of his identity, thus strengthening the notion that femaleness amounts to be less than an ideal human being.

Eco-feminism is a recent development in theology that ascribes the ecological disaster facing the world to the hierarchical thought patterns of male-dominated societies. It argues that patriarchal lines of thought have to be replaced by anthropocene values, that is, values that recognize that reality does not consist of hierarchical patterns of relationship, but that every creature possesses a dignity and value of its own within the wider scheme of things.

Political liberation theology originated in the 1960's and 70's in Latin America in response to the repressive regimes of the region. They specifically focus on the structural effects of sin and the social and political dimensions of salvation. In identifying structural sins, liberation theology utilizes Marxism as a tool of social analysis. Liberation theology employs theological narratives in Scripture, such as the exodus motive in the Pentateuch to develop God-concepts that emphasize God's option for the poor, weak and vulnerable. Since God is on the side of the poor, all theology should begin with a perspective from below, that is, a stance from the side of the sufferings of the weak. The focus of liberation theologies is praxis rather than intellectual reflection, since it attempts to transform societies through action rather than providing religious explanations of reality.

Black theology came to prominence in the United States in 1960's and 70's from where it spread to countries such as South Africa and Zimbabwe. The aim of black theology is to emancipate black people from racist oppression by upholding black dignity amidst white racism. Black experience serves as the central resource for black theology, while blackness serves as an idiom for being oppressed. Jesus is depicted as the black Messiah, that is, as the Savior of the oppressed.

The abovementioned liberation theologies have made a major contribution to the development of a Christian ethos of freedom. They shifted the focus from doctrine to praxis and from reflection to action; and they identified and criticized the patriarchal and hierarchical modes of thought that underlie much of traditional Christianity. In doing so, they brought attention to the plight of the poor and weak in Latin America, the United States and Africa, as well as to environmental degradation. The most outstanding feature of contextual liberation theologies is the wide array of attempts made to develop contextualized Christologies that are deemed as useful for political and social engagement. Though liberation theologies have made an important contribution to theological discourse on freedom, Michael Welker rightly warns that the functionalization of Jesus Christ for political and moral goals can easily lead to new kinds of distortions and ideologies.[146]

6.2 Pentecostalism

The growth of Pentecostal movements during the twentieth century is probably the most significant modern development within Christianity. According to Anderson,[147] Pentecostalism refers to a wide variety of movements that share the common feature of emphasizing the gifts of the Spirit. It includes Pentecostal denominations, charismatic movements within Catholic and Protestant churches and independent 'neo-charismatic' churches. Pentecostal movements tend to attach importance to signs, wonders and miracle healings. They are generally suspicious of academic and dogmatic theology and rather emphasize the experiential and personal aspects of faith. Emphasis is placed on the uniqueness of redemption in Christ; the authority of Scripture; the need for personal conversion; the 'baptism of the Holy Spirit' and the urgency of mission. Pentecostal services are usually spontaneous in nature, with members not only participating in, but also contributing to worship rituals.

The Pentecostal movement influenced the Christian understanding of freedom in various ways. First, it is a movement that originated within the lower classes of American society and has subsequently proven itself as able to provide a sense of belonging to the marginalized in society. The rapid growth of Pentecostalism within the impoverished areas of Sub-Sahara Africa bears testimony

146 Cf. Welker, *God the Revealed*, 37.
147 Anderson, Allan, "Pentecostalism, The Enlightenment and Christian Mission in Europe," *International Review of Mission* 95 (2006), 276.

to this. Secondly, Pentecostalism relates salvation to the direct and immediate presence of the Spirit in the life of the believer. The Spirit is bestowed by Christ on every believer without preconditions, and God is seen as present in every area of life, ready to liberate the faithful from the afflictions that they experience. God's direct presence in the lives of the faithful breaks down all dualistic distinctions between the arcane and mundane, as well as the hierarchical distinctions between clergy and laity. Because the supernatural is directly involved in the natural and directly present in the lives of the believers, the Christian community is viewed as essentially free and equal in dignity. Thirdly, Pentecostalism relates human freedom closely to a sense of communal belonging. Amidst the individualism of secular culture, Pentecostalism nurtures the importance of the church as a therapeutic community where people can experience love and healing.[148]

6.3 Postmodern Theology

Postmodernism emphasizes the situatedness of all human thinking and the relativity of linguistic discourse. As a result, postmodern thinkers resist the Enlightenment ideal of creating totalizing metanarratives and challenge the search for universally fixed and absolute truths. Postmodernists consciously embrace diversity, pluralism, particularity and relativity and actively attempt to deconstruct all systematic metanarratives that are perceived as driven by authoritarian agendas to exercise power. Postmodern theology, in a similar vein, is characterized by a search for the recovery of neglected forms of religious discourse such as the prophetical and mystical, as well as a deep concern for those repressed by totalizing systems.[149]

During the last decade, postmodern theologians have been driving a post-humanist agenda that attempts to develop a concept of freedom that takes seriously the ecological embeddedness of humanity. Post-humanist theologians reject modernism's separation of the object and subject in favor of a concept of agential realism that takes seriously the interaction of reality. We only become ethical agents through meeting others and interacting in, with and through our surroundings.[150] Protesting against individualist understandings of freedom, this approach emphasizes the need for a positive understanding of freedom as

---

148 Cf. Anderson, "Pentecostalism, Enlightenment and Mission," 281.

149 Vanhoozer, Kevin H., "Theology and the Condition of Postmodernity," in: Kevin Vanhoozer (ed.), *The Cambridge Companion to Postmodern Theology*, Cambridge: Cambridge University Press, 2003, 19.

150 Rowe, "Freedom is not Free?," 66–67.

an existence with and for others, including non-human entities.[151] The human being exists on the same continuum as animals and is therefore embedded in creaturely reality.

7 Practical Application and Future Relevance of the Christian Concept of Freedom

Judeo-Christian concepts of freedom played a significant role in the development of the economic and welfare structures of especially Western societies, the codification of legal systems such as the Roman-Dutch legal code, the enrichment of human rights discourses and the establishment of political democracy. The tendency to assign the origins of human rights discourse and democracy exclusively to Enlightenment rationalism amounts to a gross simplification of Western intellectual history. Max Stackhouse rightly states:

> Intellectual honesty demands recognition of the fact that what passes as "secular", "Western" principles of basic human rights developed nowhere else but out of key strands of the biblically rooted religions.[152]

Concepts such as rights, the sacral dignity of the human person, freedom and fraternity were established terms in the Christian tradition long before enlightenment philosophers such as John Locke and Immanuel Kant entered the scene. However, the Enlightenment couched the rights language found within the Judeo-Christian tradition into a coherent, universal, humanist and non-religious moral and political discourse. Braulik[153] rightly points out that the Enlightenment humanists were forced to do so because the "Christian" societies of the time were profoundly unchristian. John Locke and his followers knew about "rights" from their Christian upbringing and background, but they had to find a universal philosophical premise in order to oppose the sectarian and oppressive Christian societies of the time. The notion of the autonomous individual who possesses inherent rights was well suited for this purpose. Christianity therefore served as both a resource for human rights discourse and democratic

151 Ibid., 62.

152 Stackhouse, Max, "Why Human Rights Need God: A Christian Perspective," in: Elizabeth M. Bucar/Barbra Barnett (eds), *Does Human Rights need God*, 25–41, Grand Rapids: Eerdmans, 2005, 33.

153 Braulik, "Deuteronomy and Human Rights," 226.

theory, and an adversary against which the human rights discourse and democratic political theory of the times were directed.

Whereas Christianity played an ambiguous and often conflicting role in the early development of human rights discourse, various Christian traditions have made valiant attempts in the post-World War II era to give practical application to their theologically rooted concept of freedoms. Different traditions have drafted human rights declarations, anchoring human rights language in ultimate reality and promoting the common dignity of humankind. The various Christian declarations on human rights and the many Christian human rights organizations that arose are clear testimonies to this. Important Christian human rights declarations and studies that appeared after World War II were Pope John XXIII's Encyclical *Pacem in Terris* (1963), the *Standing Conference of Canonical Orthodox Bishops* statement in support of the *Universal Declaration of Human Rights* (1978), the comprehensive 1977 study on human rights by the *Lutheran World Federation* entitled *Theologische Perspektiven der Menschenrechte*, the 1976 document of the *World Alliance of Reformed Churches* entitled *The Theological Basis of Human Rights* and the *Reformed Ecumenical Synod's* comprehensive study that appeared in 1983 (*Testimony on Human Rights*).

The question that modern Christians face is: Do religious concepts of freedom really matter in practice? Do Christian concepts of freedom carry any potential for the future? Influential secular thinkers such as Richard Rorty,[154] Richard Dawkins,[155] Slavoj Žižek,[156] Alain Badiou[157] and others, do not necessarily deny the rootedness of both Eastern and Western civilizations in religious thought, but they argue that modern societies do not need God concepts to flourish. They insist that metaphysical and theological notions of reality are rationally obsolete and scientifically outdated and have become increasingly implausible to the modern mind.

The confines of this chapter do not allow us to entertain the question in depth or to provide an extensive critique on secular thought. My simple response is that the human person, human societies and the human realm cannot flourish or function properly without the concept of a transcendent God that reigns over material reality. Though the existence of God can neither be proved nor dis-

154 Cf. Rorty, Richard, "Human Rights, Rationality and Sentimentality," in: Stephen Shute/ Susan Hurley (eds), *On Human Rights*, 111–134, New York: Basic Books, 1993, 126.

155 Dawkins, Richard, *The Selfish Gene*, Oxford: Oxford University Press, 2005.

156 Žižek, Slavoj, *The Fragile Absolute, Or, Why is the Christian Legacy Worth Fighting For?*, London: Verso, 2000, 1–2.

157 Badiou, Alain, *Saint Paul and the Foundation of Universalism*, Stanford: Stanford University Press, 2003.

proved in an empirical natural scientific sense, it is quite telling that philosophies, worldviews and political theories that dispense with the concept of God are prone to sliding into nihilism and materialism.

The value of Christian concepts of freedom, in my view, lies in them correlating the *I*, *We*, *It* and *They* to a *Thou* who gives cohesion and direction to these relationships. Whenever the *Thou* is discarded, the relational framework in which human life is embedded seems to become distorted and a materialist struggle for resources appears to ensue. In recent years, Christian thinkers such as John Milbank have argued extensively that secular notions of reality cannot be sustained, because of their tendency to degenerate into nihilism.[158]

In various modernist and postmodernist secular narratives, the *I* has become the ultimate norm for human existence. The classic liberal tradition uses the notion of human autonomy to protect the political vulnerable spheres of human life such as physical integrity, the freedom to choose and the right to own property against external power abuse. Yet, absolute applications of the principle of human autonomy and freedom, as found in neo-liberal economic theory, have emanated in the development of extreme forms of individualism, hedonism, license and permissiveness in various societies. The deformation and erosion of social institutions fundamental to the social fabric of society and the rise of excessive individualism is a concerning sociological phenomenon in especially Western cultures. The abovementioned extremes are the result of a concept of freedom that was dislodged from the *Thou* and grounded in human nature itself, which is its own norm. However, when the *I* is seen as the ultimate norm, the *we*, *they* and *it* can only function as peripheral and often unimportant actors in my life whom I only recognize when they serve my own interests. A further result of the secular culture's rejection of the concept of God has been that the notion of guilt has been replaced by intuitions of shame. I am ashamed because I have been caught out acting immorally, but I do not experience a sense of guilt towards a transcendent *Thou* who demands obedience to his law and searches the depths of my heart. This shame rather than guilt culture has had a profound effect on the moral fabric of some communities and exhibits itself especially in the problem of corruption that is so endemic to many societies. Modern secular culture's utilitarian and expressivist notions of freedom have, indeed, cultivated extreme forms of individualism that threaten to deform and destabilize social institutions and societal spheres. To protect social cohesion, better-nuanced and integrated concepts of freedom are needed that can relate various social spheres to one other without absorbing them into one another.

---

158 Cf. Milbank, *Theology and Social Theory.*

Social systems that make the *We* the ultimate norm tend to descend into collectivism, communalism and tribalism. The *We* is often defined over and against the *They* who represents the other, the enemy or the opposite to the ideal represented by the *We*. In Communist and Marxist narratives capitalists and religion were identified as the archenemies, in Nazism the Jews, in Apartheid ideology the 'black danger' and in African nationalist ideologies the 'colonialists' or 'white monopoly capital.' The *We* ideologies are no less materialistic than their individualist and anthropocentric *I* counterpart. In fact, the superiority of the in-group is often grounded in material reality itself: unique bodily characteristics, technological sophistication or a superior language. Consistent with its materialist presuppositions, the *We* as ultimate norm needs to secure its future against the invasive forces of the *They* by ensuring political dominance, curtailing freedom of expression, acquiring the land needed for survival, expanding weapon arsenals, protecting the integrity of the in-group's culture or ideology, destroying or subjecting so-called "subversive powers" and even engaging in ethnic cleansing or genocide. The danger inherent to *We* ideologies is not only the superiority complex that guides it, but its tendency to utilize all available tools of power to control and survive in an adversarial world where *they* threaten *me* and *us*.

The disastrous potential of materialist-oriented ideologies is becoming increasingly clear in the ecological disaster that humanity faces. When the *I* or *We* are seen as the ultimate norm, the *It* is bound to suffer. The *It*, after all, cannot speak, demand respect or challenge human power. Environmental degradation is a direct result of the instrumentalist rationality that the Enlightenment introduced. No longer was nature seen as a theater of God's works, but as an instrument to be shaped by rational acting agents for the sake of progress and self-advancement. This instrumentalist rationality combined with the nihilist human quest for the control of natural resources has been a major cause of overdevelopment, pollution and natural exploitation.

When it comes to the sins of past and present generations with regard to freedom, the Christian tradition is by no means exempt from blame. Various Christian churches, traditions and groups have abused the Christian message for violent purposes, oppression and exploitation. We only need to refer to the European religious wars, Christian justifications of slavery and gender inequality, Christian defenses of Nazism and Apartheid, the disastrous effects of prosperity theology on poor African communities and the violence preached by some political liberation theologians. Eschatological Christian notions of this earth as penultimate and passing in nature; and dualist Christian-Aristotelian anthropologies that devalued the material realm certainly contributed to environmental degradation.

However, I would argue that these distortions do not only misrepresent the Christian faith, but stand in fundamental opposition to the authentic message of the Gospel accepted by the vast majority of Christian traditions. The Christian faith should be judged by its message, not the actions of individuals or groups who hijacked the Christian faith for malicious purposes to justify acts of hatred and abuse.

In my view, contemporary culture can learn much from Christian concepts of freedom. Over and against the individualist and anthropocentric *I culture*, Christianity proclaims that human nature is neither autonomous nor ultimate in nature, but is created to glorify God and serve fellow human beings by loving them as we love ourselves. True human existence is a decentered existence for others, not free from others; it is an existence that recognizes the *Thou*, *They* and *It* as constitutive parts of our own reality. Authentic faith requires self-limitation, altruism and a sober non-materialistic lifestyle that returns God's gifts by living a life of gratitude. Repentance and sanctification through self-correction are proclaimed as essential parts of the Christian life and demands that the selfish desires of the *I* be constantly subjected to the will of God and the interests of others.

In contrast to the *We culture*, Christianity proclaims that all human beings, also non-Christians, are created in the image of God and ought to be respected as such. Every human being possesses inviolable and innate individual rights, such as a right to life that emanates from his or her God-given status as image of God. The *I* is important and should out of respect for the Creator not be violated in the name of altruism or group interests. The *We* is also important because God created human as social beings. However, the *We* is reprimanded in Biblical literature to respect the *They*. Loving the enemy, protecting the weak, doing good to all people and refraining from violence are core messages of the Christian faith and serve as a means to counter distorted and self-inflated *in-group* ideologies that proclaim violence.

In opposition to the instrumentalist rationality of modernism, the Christian faith recognizes the significance of the *It*. In Pauline literature, for instance, creation is depicted as fundamentally part of God's restorative grace and the consummation of all things. Creation is the arena of God's works, it signifies his majesty and should be respected as such. Humans acts as stewards, not owners, and they have no right to abuse or exploit nature. Human beings are themselves creatures, and are embedded in nature.

Lastly, in response to the emptiness and nothingness of nihilist and materialist doctrines, Christianity proclaims redemption, forgiveness of sins, reconciliation with God and our participation in the death and resurrection of Jesus Christ. Most Christians acknowledge that their faith rests on a transcendental outlook on life rooted in the witness of Scripture and their experience of God's presence in their life; not verifiable, empirical facts. However, they argue that knowledge is not exclusively attained from 'hard science,' but that spiritual intuition and rational philosophical reflection also serve as sources of knowledge. From an intuitive, spiritual and rational point of view, I am convinced that concepts of freedom cannot function properly without recognizing the existence of a transcendent Creator who acts as the norm of all things.

8 Conclusion

As is the case with Islam and Judaism, the Christian concept of freedom has evolved through centuries and has adapted itself to various social contexts and cultures. It has learned to tread the fine line between collectivism and individualism; theory and context; freedom and anarchy; right and duty; difference and relation. If modern culture is to survive the challenges of globalism, xenophobia, hyperpluralism and tribal conflicts, it will have to develop concepts of freedom that can sustain societies. Christian concepts of freedom generally share an integrated understanding of freedom that differentiates between various societal spheres, the individual and community, rights and duties in order to relate them to each other. This approach might prove to be better in sustaining societies than the excesses that utilitarian and expressivist notions of freedom brought us. Further studies on religious notions of freedom and their utility for modern society are consequently urgently required.

Bibliography

Anderson, Allan, "Pentecostalism: The Enlightenment and Christian Mission in Europe," *International Review of Mission* 95 (2006), 276–281.

Arminius, James, "Analysis of the Ninth Chapter of St Paul's Epistle to the Romans," in: *The Works of James Arminius*, vol. 3, trans. William Nichols, Grand Rapids: Baker Book House, 1986.

Badiou, Alain, *Saint Paul and the Foundation of Universalism*, Stanford: Stanford University Press, 2003.

Barth, Karl, *The Epistle to the Romans*, trans. E. Hoskyns, London: Oxford, 1968.

Barth, Karl, *The Humanity of God*, trans. Thomas Wieser, Louisville: Westminster John Knox Press, 1960.

Blochner, Henri, "Biblical Metaphors and the Doctrine of Atonement," *Journal of the Evangelical Theological Society* 47/4 (2004), 629–645.

Bonhoeffer, Dietrich, *Sanctorum Communio*, vol. 1, *Dietrich Bonhoeffer Werke (DBW)*, Joachim von Soosten (ed.), München: Chr. Kaiser Verlag, 1986.

Bonhoeffer, Dietrich, *Ethik*, vol. 6, *Dietrich Bonhoeffer Werke (DBW)*, Ilse Tödt et al. (eds), München: Chr. Kaiser Verlag, 1992.
Bonhoeffer, Dietrich, *Creation and Fall. A Theological Exposition of Genesis 1–3*, vol. 3, *Dietrich Bonhoeffer Works*, John De Gruchy (ed.), trans. Douglas Steven Bax, Minneapolis: Fortress, 2000.
Bonhoeffer, Dietrich, *Letters and Papers from Prison*, vol. 8, *Dietrich Bonhoeffer Works*, John De Gruchy (ed.), Minneapolis: Fortress Press, 2010.
Braulik, Georg, "Deuteronomy and Human Rights," *Skrif en Kerk* 19/2 (1998), 207–229.
Burrel, David, *Faith and Freedom. An Interfaith Perspective*, Oxford: Blackwell, 2004.
Calvin, John, *Institutes of the Christian Religion*, trans. Henry Beveridge, Peabody: Hendrickson, 2008.
Chester, Stephen, "Who is Freedom For? Martin Luther and Alain Badiou on Paul and Politics," in: Paul Middleton/Angus Paddison/Karen Wenell (eds), *Paul, Grace and Freedom*, London: T & T Clark, 2009, 98–118.
Dawkins, Richard, *The Selfish Gene*, Oxford: Oxford University Press, 2005.
Duff, Nancy J., "'Stages on the Road to Freedom': A Brief Introduction to Dietrich Bonhoeffer," *Theology Today* 71/1 (2014), 7–11.
Dunn, James, *Christology in the Making. A New Testament Inquiry into the Origins of the Doctrine of the Incarnation*, London: SCM Press, 1992.
Ferguson, Everett, *Backgrounds of Early Christianity*, Grand Rapids: Eerdmans, 2003.
Freeman, Charles, *A New History of Early Christianity*, Yale: Yale University Press, 2009.
Groppe, Elizabeth, "Creation ex Nihilo and Ex Amore: Ontological freedom in the Theologies of John Zizioulas and Catherine Mowry Lacugna," *Modern Theology* 21/3 (2005), 463–495.
Guroian, Vigen, "Human Rights and Modern Western Faith. An Orthodox Christian Assessment," in: Elizabeth M. Bucar/Barbra Barnett (eds), *Does Human Rights need God*, Grand Rapids: Eerdmans, 2005, 41–48.
Harris, R. Laird/Archer L. Gleason/Waltke, Bruce K. (eds), *Theological Wordbook of the Old Testament*, Chicago: Moody Press, 1980.
Hengel, Martin, *The Son of God: The Origin of Christology and the History of Jewish Hellenistic Religion*, trans. John Bowden, Philadelphia: Fortress Press, 1976.
Hesselink, John, "John Calvin on the Law and Christian Freedom," *Ex Auditu* 11 (1995), 77–89.
Hick, John, *Evil and the God of Love*, London: MacMillan Press, 1977.
Hollenbach, David, "Comparative Ethics, Islam and Human Rights. Internal Pluralism and the Possible Development of Tradition," *Journal of Religious Ethics* 38/3 (2010), 580–587.
Hunsinger, George, "A Tale of Two Simultaneities. Justification and Sanctification in Calvin and Barth," in: John C. McDowell/Mike Higton, *Conversing with Barth*, Hampshire: Ashgate, 2004, 68–90.
Hurtado, Larry W., *Lord Jesus Christ. Devotion to Jesus in Earliest Christianity*, Grand Rapids: Eerdmans, 2003.
Iwand, Hans Joachim, "The Freedom of the Christian and the Bondage of the Human Will," trans. Jacob Corzine, *Logia* XVII/2 (2008), 7–15.
Jones, F. Stanley, "Freedom," in: David Noel Freedman (ed.), *The Anchor Bible Dictionary*, vol. 2, New York: Doubleday, 1992.

Largen, Kristin, "Freedom From and Freedom For. Luther's Concept of Freedom for the Twenty-First Century," *Dialog: A Journal of Theology* 52/3 (2013), 232–243.

Louw, Johannes/Nida, Eugene A., *Greek-English Lexicon of the New Testament Based On Semantic Domains*, vol. 1, Cape Town: Bible Society of South Africa, 1989.

Lovin, Robin W., "Christian Realism for the Twenty-First Century," *Journal of Religious Ethics* 37/4 (2009), 669–682.

Luther, Martin, *Luthers Werke*, Arnold E. Berger (ed.), Leipzig: Bibliographisches Institut, 1917.

Marko, Jonathan S., "'Free Choice' in Calvin's Concepts of Regeneration and Moral Agency. How Free Are We?," *Ashland Theological Journal* 42 (2010), 41–60.

McGrath, Alister E., *Christian Theology. An Introduction*, Oxford: Wiley-Blackwell, 2011.

Milbank, John, *Theology and Social Theory. Beyond Secular Reason*, Oxford: Blackwell, 2006.

Milbank, John, "Participated Transcendence Reconceived," *Stanton Lecture* 5 (2011), 1–32, http://theologyphilosophycentre.co.uk/2011/03/12/john-milbanks-stanton-lectures-2011/comment-page-1/ (Accessed Nov 2, 2011).

Moltmann, Jürgen, "Sun of Righteousness Arise! The Freedom of a Christian – then and now – for the Victims and Perpetrators of Sin," *Theology Today* 69/1 (2012), 7–17.

Nickson, Ann L., *Bonhoeffer on Freedom. Courageously Grasping Reality*, Oxford: Ashgate, 2002.

Niebuhr, Reinhold, "Theology and Political Thought in the Western World," *The Ecumenical Review* 9 (1957), 253–262.

Prodromou, Elizabeth H., "Orthodox Christian Contributions to Freedom. Historical Foundations, Contemporary Problematics," in: Timothy Samuel Shah/Allan D. Hertzke (eds), *Christianity and Freedom. Volume 1: Historical Perspectives*, Cambridge: Cambridge University Press, 2016, 301–332.

Pelagius, *Pelagius's Commentary on St Paul's Epistle to the Romans*, trans. Theodore De Bruyn, Oxford Early Christian Studies, Oxford: Oxford University Press, 1993.

Pollis, Adamantia, "Eastern Orthodoxy and Human Rights," *Human Rights Quarterly* 15 (1993), 339–356.

Porter, Jean, "Natural equality: Freedom, Authority and Obedience in Two Medieval Thinkers," *Annual of the Society of Christian Ethics* 21 (2001), 275–299.

Quash, Ben, "Exile, Freedom and Thanksgiving. Barth and Hans Urs van Balthasar," in: John C. McDowell/Mike Higton (eds), *Conversing with Barth*, Hampshire: Ashgate, 2004, 90–120.

Rahner, Karl, *Foundations of Christian Faith. An Introduction to the Idea of Christianity*, trans. W.V. Dych, New York: Seabury, 1978.

Rorty, Richard, "Human Rights, Rationality and Sentimentality," in: Stephen Shute/Susan Hurley (eds), *On Human Rights*, New York: Basic Books, 1993, 111–134.

Rowe, Terra S., "Freedom Is Not Free? Posthumanist, Ecological Reflections on Christian Freedom and Responsibility," *Dialog: A Journal of Theology* 54/1 (2015), 61–71.

Sachedina, Abdulaziz "Continuing the Conversation About Comparative Ethics," *Journal of Religious Ethics* 43/3 (2015), 543–556.

Slater, Jennifer, "Freedom: The Liberative Value and Ethical Credential for Christian Living in South Africa," *Journal of Theology for Southern Africa* 148 (2014), 48–64.

Stackhouse, Max, "Why Human Rights Need God: A Christian Perspective," in: Elizabeth M. Bucar/Barbra Barnett (eds), *Does Human Rights need God*, Grand Rapids: Eerdmans, 2005, 25–41.

Theißen, Gerd, "Jesus und die symbolpolitischen Konflikten seiner Zeit. Sozialgeschichtliche Aspekte der Jesusforschung", *EvTh* 57/4 (1997), 378–400.

Thomas Aquinas, *Disputed Questions on the Virtues*, E.M. Atkins/Thomas Williams (eds), trans. E.M Atkins, Cambridge: Cambridge University Press, 2005.

Uertz, Rudolf/Schmidt, Lars Peter Schmidt (eds), *Die Grundlagen der Lehre der Russischen Orthodoxen Kirche über die Würde, die Freiheit und die Menschenrechte*, Moscow: Auslandsbüro der Konrad-Adenauer-Stiftung, 2008.

Van de Beek, Abraham, *Een Lichtkring Om Het Kruis. Scheppingsleer in Christologisch Perspectief*, Zoetermeer Boekenzentrum: Meinema, 2014.

Vanhoozer, Kevin H., "Theology and the Condition of Postmodernity," in: Kevin Vanhoozer (ed.), *The Cambridge Companion to Postmodern Theology*, Cambridge: Cambridge University Press, 2003, 3–26.

Vorster, Nico, "The Nature of Christ's Atonement," in: Eddy van der Borght/Paul van Geest (eds), *Strangers and Pilgrims on Earth. Essays in Honour of Abraham van de Beek*, Brill: Leiden, 2013, 129–147.

Welker, Michael, *God the Revealed. Christology*, Grand Rapids, Eerdmans 2013.

Williams, Rowan S., "Eastern Orthodox Theology," in: David Ford (ed.), *The Modern Theologians. An Introduction to Christian Theology since 1918*, Malden: Blackwell, 32005, 572–588.

Wright, Nicholas Thomas, "Paul's Gospel and the Roman Empire," in: Richard A. Horsley (ed.), *Paul and Politics*, Harrisburg, Pennsylvania: Trinity Press, 2000, 60–184.

Žižek, Slavoj, *The Fragile Absolute, Or, Why is the Christian Legacy Worth Fighting For?*, London: Verso, 2000.

Suggestions for Further Reading

Aulén, Gustav, *Christus Victor. An Historical Study of the Three Main Types of the Idea of Atonement*, trans. Hebert A.G, London: SPCK, 2010 [1931].

Brinkman, Martien E., *The Tragedy of Human Freedom. The Failure and Promise of the Christian Concept of Freedom in Western Culture*, trans. Harry Flecken and Henry Jansen, Amsterdam: Rodopi, 2003.

Hollenbach, David, *The Global Face of Public Faith. Politics, Human Rights and Christian Ethics*, Washington, DC: Georgetown University, 2003.

Küng, Hans, *Christianity and The World Religions. Paths of Dialogue with Islam, Hinduism and Buddhism*, trans. Peter Heinegg, New York: Doubleday, 1986.

Moltmann, Jürgen, *The Crucified God. The Cross of Christ as Foundation and Criticism of Christian Theology*, trans. R.A. Wilson and John Bowden, London: SCM Press, 1974.

Ochs, Peter, "Judaism and Christian Theology," in: David Ford (ed.), *The Modern Theologians. An Introduction to Christian Theology since 1918*, Malden: Blackwell, 32005.

Siddiqui, Ataullah, "Islam and Christian Theology," in: David Ford (ed.), *The Modern Theologians. An Introduction to Christian Theology since 1918*, Malden: Blackwell, 32005.

Maha El Kaisy-Friemuth

The Concept of Freedom in Islam

The issue of human freedom in Islam has become highly polarizing. Can it be said that Islam prevents or limits the freedom of individual Muslims? Can Muslims choose their own beliefs? Can Muslims use critical methods to address religious issues? Does freedom lead to immorality and does Islam limit the freedom of Muslim women?

Investigating these question starts with first defining this term in the Qu'rān. However, the Qu'rān, in general, is mainly concerned about the community of believers and their collective understanding of religion. It answers different theological questions such as the nature of resurrection, the nature of God and the importance of prophecy. On the social level, the Qu'rān provides answers to all questions concerning punishments pursuant to particular crimes as well as family problems. It also grants the believer a right to armed self-defense. However, it hardly deals with the individual's problems and rights. Its aim is to protect the community of believers and deepen their belief in God and the afterlife. Thus, the term freedom is not mentioned in the Qu'rān, as its primary concern was rather with slavery and its abolishment. Establishing the rights and duties of the individual was the concern of Islamic law, *fiqh*. Through establishing the authority of the Hadith, the early Muslim jurists could construct a Divine Law under the concept of *sharīʿa*. The *sharīʿa*, on the one hand, secured and canonized the rights of individuals, while on the other hand, it ensconced these rights with the standards of the second Islamic century culture.

In order to examine the development of the concept of Freedom in Islam, we need to survey its origins in the Qu'rān, its integration into the study of *kalām* (Islamic theology), and its conceptual explication in Islamic Philosophy, while tracing its importance into the modern period, especially in securing the right of choosing an own belief.

Thus, in this chapter, I will examine the following issues:

1) the understanding of the concept of freedom in pre-Islamic Arabia and its foreshadowing in the Qu'rān.
2) its development in the Islamic theology, or *kalām*
3) its conceptualization amongst the Muslim philosophers
4) the Sufi concept of freedom
5) the rise of the concept of freedom amongst modern thinkers
6) the freedom of women in Islam
7) the problem of apostasy as eliminating free choice
8) critical free thinking versus *taqlīd*

https://doi.org/10.1515/9783110561678-004

9) freedom in the Shīʿite thougth
10) freedom, ethics and its limitation: "commanding right" (*al-amr bi-l-maʿrūf*)

1 The Perception of Freedom in Pre-Islamic Arabic Culture and in the Qur'ān.

The term of freedom as we understand it today in Arabic *ḥurrīya* is not to be found in Qu'rān or in Islamic theology, *kalām*. However, a variation of it is depicted in the two pair terms *the free and the slave* (*al-ḥurr wa-l-ʿabd)* on the one hand and *predestination and free will (al-jabr wa-l-ikhtiyār)*, on the other hand. The pair *al-ḥurr wa-l-ʿabd*, are derived from the pre-Islamic context of slavery. The tribal system of the Arabs of Hijāz is best described in the 10 volumes work of Jawād ʿAlī *al-Mufaṣṣal fī tārīkh al-ʿarab qabl al-Islām, The Detailed History of the Arabs before Islam.*[1]

Jawād ʿAlī informs us that the Arabs largely considered themselves as the slaves of the gods. They must obey and please them in order to obtain a good, wealthy, and healthy life. Being a slave for someone who is great, powerful and just was not a shameful position. The individual in Hijāz could only be seen as a part of the clan living under the tribal laws, *ʿurf.* Although Mecca and Medina, at the rise of Islam, were considered towns, tribal customs governed the daily life. According to Jawād ʿAlī, Mecca was a trading town while Medina flourished with agriculture land. A large Jewish community was living in Medina and had influenced the customs and laws of the Medinan tribes.[2] Mecca and Medina were idolatrous communities, which worshipped many different gods. Tribes considered the gods as owning the whole of the land with its animals and human inhabitants. The names of ʿAbd al-Lāt, ʿAbd Manāf or ʿAbd Shams were known as names of individuals as well as names of tribes. These theophoric names denote the position of humanity as slaves of the gods *al-Lāt, Manāf* or *Shams.* Priests were considered the servants of the gods and those who protect their rights. Thus, all offerings of thanks should be presented at the temples.[3]

The relationship between the members of the clan and of the tribes was tied to certain laws and customs known as *ʿurf.* The authority within the tribes lied manly in the hands of male members, though there are some hints that matrilin-

---

1 ʿAlī, Jawād, *Al-Mufaṣṣal fī tarīkh al-ʿarab qabl al-Islām*, 10 vols, Baghdad: Baghdad University Press, 1993.

2 ʿAlī, *al-Mufaṣṣal*, vol. 4, 343–50.

3 ʿAlī, *al-Mufaṣṣal*, vol. 6, 17–19.

eal customs were older and still valid in some Bedouin clans. However, with the emergence of Islam, the patrilineal tendency prevailed.[4] Thus, the ranking was established in the following fashion: the gods existed at the top of the scale owning both animals and humans. The priests came in second as the servants of the gods. The tribal chiefs protected the rights of their tribes and served as fathers that cared and owned their children. At the bottom of the scale, they situated the slaves who hardly owned any rights. Children and most women held similar positions in which the father could sell them as slaves if he was in severe financial troubles. They could also kill their children as offerings for the gods.[5] We know from Ibn Isḥāq that the grandfather of prophet Muhammad, ʿAbd al-Muṭṭalib vowed to offer one of his sons to the god *Hubal.* Upon conferring with the gods, he chose his youngest son ʿAbd Allāh, the father of the prophet. Yet he and his relatives deployed a ruse whereby they payed a ransom instead of offering ʿAbd Allāh.[6] This story demonstrates the value of the individual in tribal life. Though a person can be a free man/women, they are owned by their families and possess no individual freedom.

These tribal laws were quite strict concerning the ransom of a noble free man. If the killer himself is a noble man, the family of the one killed has the right to kill a noble man from the clan of the killer. The Qurʾānic saying "a free man by a free man and slave by slave"[7] is a tribal costum which demonstrates that the revenge must be equal. This means that a person could be killed for an act that he or she did not commit. In this community the individual can only be counted as a part of the tribe. The welfare of the tribe/clan/family comes first.[8]

In these tribal communities the noble men and women consisted of those who do not earn their nobility through handwork. In Mecca noblemen were traders who owned caravans and had the opportunity to become chiefs of the tribe. Killing them through a slave or a poor man would have to be conducted by means of ransom via the owner of the slave or the nobles of the poor man's tribe. Thus, even the freedom of revenge was carefully customized.[9]

Furthermore, any free man could be enslaved through captivity. Even noble man/women could end up in slavery. However, the position of slave is not always one of complete supplicant that would imagine today. Due to the fact that every

---

4 ʿAlī, *al-Mufaṣṣal,* vol. 4, 550–60.
5 Ibid., 541–50.
6 ʿAlī, *al-Mufaṣṣal,* vol. 6, 192–3.
7 Qurʾān, 2:178.
8 ʿAlī, *al-Mufaṣṣal,* vol. 5, 482–85.
9 ʿAlī, *al-Mufaṣṣal,* vol. 4, 563.

member of the tribe could potentially be held captive, no one could completely rely on his or her own freedom. The threat of slavery was always one to be taken seriously.

If a person became embroiled in a conflict within the tribe and could not find someone to defend him, he could be expelled from the tribe. In this case he would have no worth as regarding to ransom money and anyone could kill him without punishment. No one could survive outside the tribe.[10]

Conflicts between clans or tribes are usually solved through arbitrators. These wise men or women were known as judges and were able to solve conflicts. This kind of justice, which was only possible in these communities, could guarantee some kind of freedom. Freedom was also bound to responsibility. Free men and women are responsible for their family's children and slaves.[11] The concept of vicegerent in the Qu'rān is also known in tribal costumes. Priests, whether they be male or female, were the ones who represented the gods and protected their rights and interests. Tribal chiefs and noble men, *al-ashrāf*, came in second. Justice in this case referred to the collective welfare of the tribe; all other forms of freedom were sacrificed for its sake.

It is in this context that the Qu'rānic concept of freedom should be evaluated. The Qu'rān is in dialogue with these communities and is attempting to mirror their known and accepted values. Therefore, the term *ḥurrīya* is not found in the Qu'rān. On the contrary, the Qu'ān confirms the pre-Islamic notion of freedom and speaks of men as *al-ḥurr wa-l-ʿabd*, the free and the slave "O ye who believe! The law of equality is prescribed to you in cases of murder: the free for the free, the slave for the slave, the woman for the woman. But if any remission is made by the brother of the slain, then grant any reasonable demand, and compensate him with handsome gratitude." (2:178)[12]

However, the Qu'rān attempts to improve this situation by introducing the concept of the *taḥrīr raqaba*, ransoming or liberating slaves as a bonus through which believers can earn high rewards and compensate for their sins. Yet in the case of killing a believer by mistake the murderer must free a slave: "Never should a believer kill a believer; but (If it so happens) by mistake, (Compensation is due): If one (so) kills a believer it is ordained that he should free a believing slave, and pay compensation to the deceased's family, unless they remit it freely." (4:92)

---

10 Ibid., 564–65.

11 Ibid., 565–66.

12 English translations from the Qur'ān according to the translation of Abdullah Yusuf Ali (modified).

The act of liberating slaves was therefore the first serious step towards abolishing slavery. Every rich believer is called to buy slaves and subsequently liberate them.

Although the Qu'rān recognizes the concept of freedom versus slavery, as discussed above, it also presents another conceptual interpretation of freedom. Starting with the story of creation, God declares the human being as vicegerent and above all other creatures, "Behold, thy Lord said to the angels: 'I will create a vicegerent on earth.'" (2:30) God taught Adam all "names," which means that He provided him with divine knowledge, as it is said "And He taught Adam the names of all things" (2:31). The concept of vicegerent here expresses freedom in connection with responsibility, which is established through knowledge. In this way God provides the guarantee that human beings will represent Him and will not destroy the earth as the angels expressed in 2:30. However, when Adam and Eve disobeyed God and ate from the forbidden tree, they were not alienated from God's mercy. Verses 2:36–9 demonstrate this dramatic event: "We said: 'Get ye down, all (ye people), with enmity between yourselves. On earth will be your dwelling-place and your means of livelihood – for a time.' Then learnt Adam from the Lord words of inspiration, and his Lord Turned toward him; for He is Oft-Returning, Most Merciful. We said: 'Get ye down all from here; and if, as is sure, there comes to you Guidance from me, whosoever follows My guidance, on them shall be no fear, nor shall they grieve. 'But those who reject Faith and belie Our Signs, they shall be companions of the Fire; they shall abide therein.'"

Az-Zamakhsharī asks in his commentary on these verses whether Adam's sin here is a major or a minor sin. Since Adam is a prophet, as it is believed among the commentators, his sin cannot be a major one. Yet, if it were a minor sin, God would not have expelled him and his wife from paradise. The solution for him is that Adam did not commit a major sin, but that the sin here is considered as major in order to emphasize its nature and its consequences. Thus, some of the traditional commentators highlight the position of Adam here as a prophet who still possess dignity and the freedom of choice since God at the end of these verses declares that "whosoever follows My guidance, on them shall be no fear, nor shall they grieve. But those who reject Faith and belie Our Signs, they shall be companions of the Fire; they shall abide therein." (2:38–39)

The Qu'rān also deviates from Pre-Islamic customs and presents new values. The free man or woman is the one who acts righteously and worships God truly: "O mankind! We created you from a single (pair) of a male and a female, and made you into nations and tribes, that ye may know each other (not that ye may despise (each other). Verily the most honoured of you in the sight of God is (he who is) the most righteous of you." (49:13)

This is indeed a revolutionary concept for pre-Islamic customs of ranking and inequality. The shift between the duality of free men and slaves to the equality of believers in righteousness demonstrates the nature of the challenge that the Qu'rān is setting here: only those who reach righteousness experience equality.

Freedom and equality are two heavily related concepts: a person is free only when he or she is equal to other free persons. Muḥammad Shaḥrūr in his book *al-Kitāb wa-l- Qu'rān* reflects on the two concepts *īmān – islam* and *Muslim – believer.* He shows that the Qu'rān intends the term Islam to mean the worshipping of the one God and therefore a person is a Muslim even if he or she is also a Christian or Jew or from another religion. Thus when the Qu'rān mentions that Moses and Jesus and other prophets were Muslims it means that they all believed in the one God. However, Shaḥrūr here mainly emphasizes the equality which the Qu'rān bestows on every believer whether they be a prophet or merely a believer.[13] This is the explanation of the verse 2:62 "Those who believe, and those who follow the Jewish (scriptures), and the Christians and the Sabians,– any who believe in God and the Last Day, and work righteousness, shall have their reward with their Lord; on them shall be no fear, nor shall they grieve."

Indeed this verse implies a high quality of freedom and equality. Instead of the pre-Islamic concept of *al-ḥurr wa-l-ʿabd* here the Qu'rān declares that all who believe in God will be equally liberated from all burdens in the afterlife. Furthermore, verse 3:64 is clearly an invitation for dialogue and the recognition of equality: "Say: 'O People of the Book! come to common terms as between us and you: That we worship none but God; that we associate no partners with him; that we erect not, from among ourselves, Lords and patrons other than God.'" It seems here that the Qu'rān is emphasizing the importance of maintaining a sense of equality with those members of different religions when all recognize the omnipotence of God. The aforementioned verse, however, ends by allowing freedom of choice "If then they turn back, say ye: 'Bear witness that we (at least) are Muslims (bowing to God's Will)." (3:64)

13 Shaḥrūr, Muḥammad, *Al-Kitāb wa-l-Qur'ān*, Damascus: Al-Alī li-n-nashr wa-ṭ-ṭibāʿa wa-t-tawzīʿ, 1990, 716–17.

2 The Concept of Freedom in Islamic Theology (*ʿilm al-kalām*)

Another form of freedom is highlighted in the Quʾrān through the concept of rational reflection. Humans should perceive the Divine present within the created world and appreciate its beauty, "Do they see nothing in the government of the heavens and the earth and all that God hath created?" (7:185) and also "Then let man look at his food, (and how We provide it): For that We pour forth water in abundance, And We split the earth in fragments, And produce therein corn, And Grapes and nutritious Plants, And Olives and Dates, And enclosed Gardens, dense with lofty trees, And fruits and fodder, – For use and convenience to you and your cattle." (80:24–32)

These verses call for reflection on God's creation and the process of development. The power of thinking, which was indeed the starting point of Islamic theology *kalām*, is also mentioned in Quʾrān as a power which God created in humans in order to recognize creation as the product of Divine design and therefore submit not to other gods: "So set thou thy face steadily and truly to the Faith: (establish) God's handiwork according to the pattern on which He has made mankind: no change (let there be) in the work (wrought) by God" (30:30).

Consequently, *ʿilm al-kalām*, and especially the Muʿtazilite theologians, studied the power of choice which all humans equally possess. They called this ability *istiṭāʿa*, which all humans possess for acting or refraining according to own choice. The terms *jabr wa-ikhtiyār*, predestination and free will, are another pair of dual terms which are relevant for the concept of freedom in Islam. The Quʾrān adopts both tendencies and lays the roots for the *kalām* discussion of this issue. There are several verses which affirm predestination, and they are as follows:

> To Him belongs the dominion of the heavens and the earth: It is He Who gives Life and Death; and He has Power over all things. He is the First and the Last, the Evident and the Immanent: and He has full knowledge of all things. He it is Who created the heavens and the earth in Six Days, and is moreover firmly established on the Throne (of Authority). He knows what enters within the earth and what comes forth out of it, what comes down from heaven and what mounts up to it. And He is with you wheresoever ye may be. And God sees well all that ye do. (57:2–4)

> No soul can believe, except by the will of God, and He will place doubt (or obscurity) on those who will not understand. (10:100)

> Some He hath guided: Others have (by their choice) deserved the loss of their way; [...]. (7:30)

> God hath set a seal on their hearts and on their hearing, and on their eyes is a veil; [...]. (2:7)

M. Watt considers the predestinational tendency in the Qu'rān to reflect the pre-Islamic notion of natural decree, which is expressed in the concept of *ad-dahr*, the time endless.[14] In contrast, Wolfson suggests in his great work *The Philosophy of Kalām* that the Qu'rānic decree pictures the mightiness and the omnipotence of God against the idols of the unbelievers.[15] In this way, Wolfson argues that this kind of Qu'rānic predestination is a literary image intended to express the majesty of the Divine rather than limiting human freedom of choice.

This can be also observed in the verses which demonstrate humans' free choice: "Say, 'The truth is from your Lord': Let him who will believe, and let him who will, reject (it) [...]." (18:29) "But there is no blame on you if ye make a mistake therein: (what counts is) the intention of your hearts [...]." (33:5) "Those who believe not in the Signs of God,– God will not guide them [...]". (16:104)

Wolfson considers that verses which denote liberty were first studied when polemical debates between Muslim and Christians started to take place at the end of the Umayyad period. He argues that it was John of Damascus (d. 750 CE), who in his work *Disputatio Saraceni et Christiani,* staged a debate between a Muslim and a Christian, who shed light on the importance of free choice. In this debate, the Muslim asks the Christian whether he believes in free will. The Christian answers that God has formed him with free will and that this free will enables him to choose between good and evil.[16]

It is also probably true that the issue of causality and secondary causes was studied under the influence of Christian theologians. While the Qu'rān emphasizes the connection of God with every natural event, John of Damascus, in his aforementioned book, argues that God created the world (including the creation of the human) in six days through intermediate causes. This connection between causality and the problem of the free will reflects God's delegation of power to natural law, which allows the humans to act through their own power.[17]

This theory of causality which the church fathers adopted from Greek philosophy influenced the Baghdadi Mu'tazilites theological school with its two important masters Abū Ishāq Ibrāhīm b. Saiyār an-Naẓẓām and Mua'mmar b. 'Abbād.

14 Watt, W. Montgomery, *Free Will and predestination in Early Islam*, London: Luzac and Company Press, 1948.

15 Wolfson, Harry Austryn, *The Philosophy of Kalām*, Cambridge et al.: Harvard University Press, 1976, 602–4.

16 Ibid, 607.

17 Ibid, 617–623.

An-Naẓẓām, although he admits that human sustenance (*rizq)* and deadly termination (*ajal*) are both predetermined, argues that the human soul has power and knowledge per se generated by its own self, thereby rendering all human acts the products of their own creation. However, this total independence from divine determination was debated among the Muʿtazilites.[18]

Baṣrian Muʿtazila, for example, connected free will with responsibility and called the human "*mukallaf*", i.g. responsible person. They studied this issue under the rubric of understanding the nature of human acts (*al-afʿāl*). Freedom of action can only be understood when analyzing the process of how humans act. The famous theologian ʿAbd al-Jabbār defines the act as: "what comes into existence from someone who has been capable of it"[19]. This means that an act is completely related to the one who performed it, *taʿalluq al-fiʿl bi-l-fāʿil*. He also considers it impossible that one (and the same) act can be produced by two actors. Therefore, human actions cannot be attributed to God.[20]

Further, we must ask here whether humans possess the capacity to produce an act according to their own wishes. Here ʿAbd al-Jabbār differentiates between three levels in performing an act: the intention of the act, the power to act and the act itself. The intention of the act denotes the idea present in the mind before its existence. This level belongs directly to the person and only he or she can preconceive of the act. On the second level the person needs a certain power which can enable them to perform the desired act termed *istiṭāʿa*. If these two parts of the acts exist, then the act will happen in the way the person intended it to.[21]

Baṣrian Muʿtazilis differ from the Baghdadis as to whether the person internally possesses freedom or acquires it from an external source. They all agreed that *istiṭāʿa*, the power to act, is given by God. Yet in contrast to the Ashʿarī traditionalists, they considered this power to be given to humans a considerable amount of time prior to the act. The Ashʿarites believed that this power is substantiated concomitantly with the human act. The difference here is that the Muʿtazilite is assured that he or she will perform the act as intended, while the Ashʿarites believed that each action is either blessed or condemned by God.[22]

However, Baṣrian Muʿtazilites connected human freedom with responsibility. The guarantee that God delivers the power to act a considerable amount of time prior to such an act taking place (it probably was inscribed at birth) implies that

18 Ibid.
19 ʿAbd al-Jabbār, *Sharḥ al-uṣul al-khamsa*, Cairo: Maktabat Wahba, 1996, 324.
20 Cf. El Kaisy-Friemuth, Maha, *God and Humans in Islamic Thought*, London: Routledge 2011.
21 Cf. El Kaisy-Friemuth, Maha, "The Free Thinkers of Islam. The Muʿtazila," *Common Ground Journal* 12, no. 2 (2015), 38–40.
22 Ibid.

this power should or even must be used in order to fulfill one's religious obligations.

Alternatively, the Ash'arite school developed a theory termed *kasb*. This theory is indeed quite obscure. God provides human beings with the power to act at the time and place of an individual action, and humans acquire the capacity to act when he or she receive this power. Thus, the human is free to think but is not free to act.[23]

To conclude, there are three main positions concerning freedom in Islamic theology:

- Humans are fully free and independent from divine influence because they possess their own power and knowledge to act freely. This the opinion of Baghdadi Mu'tazilites.
- The second position is that humans are free agents as long as God provides them with this freedom in order to perform their *taklīf* (religious responsibility). This is the position of the Baṣrian Mu'tazilites.
- The third position is the position of the Ash'arites who considered human beings to be free to think but not free to act. They are therefore fully dependent on the power which God provides at the time of the action.[24]

2.1 Freedom and Responsibility

Although the Mu'tazilites became famous for their concept of free will, they consider this freedom to be bound with the obligations of *taklīf*. These obligations are two-sided. On the one hand, humans are guided to a righteous life, while on the other hand the conditions for reward and punishment are set. The Mu'tazilites contended that humans are created in order to receive different benefits, the highest of which being the deserved ones. For God to bestow this kind of benefit, he must grant humans the divine law, thereby revealing the importance of reward and punishment. This law is communicated through rational and revealed knowledge such that all humans can be guided to know God and thus avoid performing those actions which entail punishment. Thus, human beings for the Mu'tazilites have the attribute of being responsible *mukallaf* who are created with certain qualities that enable them to fulfil the divine law.[25]

23 Ibid.

24 Cf. El Kaisy-Friemuth, *God and Humans*, 47–51.

25 'Abd al-Jabbār, *Al-Mughnī fī abwāb at-tawḥīd wa-l-'adl*, vol. XI, Cairo: Wizārat ath-thaqāfa wa-l-irshād al-qawmī, al-idāra al-'āmma li-th-thaqāfa, 1965, 387–390.

Thus, although the Muʿtazilites are famous for their concept of free will claiming that God cannot and will not compel them to do what they do not themselves approve of, they consider the human as obliged to know God through his *taklīf.* Otherwise he or she will face punishment. This punishment ensues because human beings have neglected to reflect on the wisdom of life and the reasons for their own creation. The appreciation of this kind of thinking is what they call *rational taklīf,* which means that humans are rationally able to reflect and discover God and the wisdom of His creation. This capacity is known among Muʿtazilites as *tamkīn* (enabling-capability). They analyze the human act in order to demonstrate that God has given the humans all the powers they need for leading an intellectual life which enables them to recognize the existence of God and his divine law. *Tamkīn* ensues in the following fashion:

1. The first quality, which all humans possess, is the desire to act. This is the first attribute created in the body that motivates humans to act and recognize the importance of obtaining benefits. If the purpose of *taklīf*, obligatory duties, is to reward humans and to warn them against doing evil, they must first be motivated to act. This motivation, Muʿtazilites claim, is created in them.

2. The second quality is the power of choice which provides the ability to commit an act along with its very opposite. This ability allows the person either to perform an act or refrain from it. Such an ability is created in the person long before the act in order to enable him or her to choose between different possibilities of action. They believe that humans can only be judged based on the acts which they freely chose; constrained acts cannot receive praise or blame. Thus, free will and the ability to perform a certain act and its opposite are the preconditions for human beings to be rationally responsible for achieving *taklīf.*

3. Humans must also be provided with certain intuitions that offer them the possibility for developing ideas. The humans must possess basic ideas about the world, ideas which give them a clue as to where to start. All cultures and ideas begin through an intuition that is given.[26] God for the Muʿtazilites is the source of all reliable intuitions. The first intuition is that the world was created for a certain purpose. It is possible that the human starts from this basic premise and reflects further on the different consequences ensuing from it. The second intuition is that this power, which we would call God, must be good and desire to benefit his creatures. Indeed, that is the reason why he created them. So the gift of receiving intuition is a quality possessed by humans which supports their capacity for free will. They are not given the free will without any guidance. Rather, God gives them hints as to where to go. This intuition, which is also called *ʿaql* or *nec-*

26 ʿAbd al-Jabbār, *Al-Mughnī*, XI, 387–90.

essary knowledge, consists of the certain basic and immediate knowledge considered as the basis on which rational knowledge is built. This basic knowledge comes from God and identifies the person as rationally mature and qualified to act rationally. The term connoting rational responsibility is *kāmil al-ʿaql*, and it is reached by the age of 14/15 years. Achieving it means that the person now is mature and capable of judgement. This state of maturity implies freedom in their eyes because from now on a person is responsible for their deeds.[27]

The Muʿtaziles demonstrate here that humans are created with certain qualities that indicate a higher purpose behind their own creation, that is, they have the quality of being responsible *mukallafūn* and commanded to fulfil certain duties.[28] Thus, the Muʿtazilites consider human beings to be free rational creatures responsible, in the sense of being *khalīfa,* vicegerents for the spread of goodness and the prevention of evil on earth.

2.2 The Freedom of God in Islamic Theology

In this context the Muʿtazilites also asked whether God is totally free or bound to certain duties. The Baghdadi Muʿtazilites developed the theory of "*al-aṣlaḥ*", which means the choice of the best option. They argued that God works always for the best in the world and therefore He provides the best possible option for his creations. However, according to this theory, God then possess certain duties that he must fulfil. In order to produce "the best," God must provide certain elements such as: a) human beings with all the tools necessary in order to be able to think and perform according their own individual will. b) God must also provide the guidance for those who are not able to use their ability of thinking properly and thus remain dependent on clear divine guidance. God provides this through the deployment of prophets and holy texts. c) God also must compensate those who suffer through the defect of bodily abilities: those who are born with a handicap or are injured in natural disasters.[29]

Thus, for the Muʿtazilites there is no freedom without responsibility, meaning that freedom is bound to some coerced acts and that freedom is only given in order to spread a greater good in the world. Freedom to spread evil does not constitute freedom for them because evil doers disturb God's plan for his creatures.

27 Ibid., 371–387.

28 Hourani, George F., *Islamic Rationalism. The Ethics of ʿAbd al-Jabbār,* Oxford: Oxford University Press, 1971, 17. Cf. also, *Al-Mughnī* XII, 13, 25.

29 Cf. El Kaisy-Friemuth, *God and Humans*, 50–52.

Muslim theologians in general considered religion as necessarily leading to the increase of goodness and decrease of evil. The Muʿtazilites insisted quite vehemently on an ultimate result of goodness. God not only acts for "good result," but he is in and of himself pure goodness. Therefore, freedom mainly leads to goodness, whereas committing evil for the sake of evil implies subservience to ignorance which prevents the person from acting righteously. Freedom is thus the discovery of the power of goodness, which is indeed the power of God. Goodness is the aim of *taklīf.* Hence, ethical behavior lies is the perception and performance of goodness. This is the highest form of freedom for the Muʿtazilites.

3 Freedom and Individuality among the Muslim Philosophers

In harmony with the Muʿtazilites, the Muslim philosophers considered God to be pure goodness, *al-khayr al-maḥḍ*. However, they move here from the study of the freedom of human action to a search for the inner freedom of a person. This inner freedom connotes a mental grasping goodness, whether in action or in the world. Their aim is not the fulfilment of the divine law but rather joining the "Upper World" and experiencing perfect happiness. The human, however, is hindered through his bodily desires from grasping this goodness. Thus, the human rational faculty is the only part of the human being capable of perceiving this goodness, therefore leading him or her to happiness. In order to reach this rational faculty, Ibn Sīnā (d. 1037/428) studied the nature of the human soul.[30]

The soul for him constitutes an expression of all human activities. It has different faculties, each of which has a specific role to fulfil. This conception of the soul is very much influenced by the Aristotelian tradition. It recognizes the importance of the soul as the power which moves the body and initiates its activity. The Aristotelian tradition considered the body, as matter, to be able neither to think nor to act, thus it is always passive. In contrast, the soul is the power which enables the body to act. Human and animal souls are considered to have "higher" qualities which initiate activities according to the will.[31]

Ibn Sīnā, following Aristotle, considers that the soul as a power in the body functions through three main faculties: the vegetable soul, which governs the growth and nourishing the body; the animal soul, which governs the sensory, imaginative and estimating faculties; and finally the rational soul, which leads

30 Cf. El Kaisy-Friemuth, *God and Humans*, 94–5.
31 Goodman, Lenn E., *Avicenna*, New York/London: Routledge, 1992, 153.

the other two souls and forms human knowledge.[32] Ibn Sīnā, however, differs from the Aristotelian tradition in his conception of the independence of the soul from the body, a facture which grants it eternal life. Therefore, the soul is the power which initiates thinking and reflection.

In his two works *an-Najāt*[33] and *ash-Shifā'*[34], Ibn Sīnā commences upon a long discussion on the manner in which the human being gains knowledge through the rational soul. The human intellect perceives knowledge of the world through the senses and the power of material imagination. The intellect receives this imaginative knowledge and abstracts a higher form of knowledge from it. The intellect, however, can reach this abstract knowledge only when it is free from the desires of the body.[35] Thus, freedom on this plane implies freedom from bodily disturbance. The desires of the body enslave the human and turn him or her away from wisdom.

However, the human, in Ibn Sīnā's eyes, is not able to reach all favorable results through the power of the rational soul alone. He or she does need outside assistance. This assistance is constituted necessarily through a connection to a higher active intellect, providing the human being with intuition and inspiration. In any case, Ibn Sīnā considers that the relationship with the active intellect is dynamic because ideas come in successive fashion, one form after another, and each intelligible gives way to the next. In contrast to the Mu'tazilites, Ibn Sīnā considers that humans are not able to reach all knowledge through their own mature rational faculties, but rather they need divine assistance from the divine world.

Most philosophers adopted the dual theory of body and soul. The soul is the main power that differentiates the individual, and for this reason they also call it *al-anā*, the "I". This power of the soul is known to the individual even when all of his or her senses are cut off. To illustrate this fact, Ibn Sīnā tells the tale of a floating man who recognizes himself and his individuality even when all his of bodily senses have been cut off. Consequently, freedom for most philosophers constitutes the liberation of the soul from bodily desires and disturbances. This liberation, however, only happens when the rational soul is in full control of the

32 Ibid., 62–3.

33 Ibn Sīnā, Abū 'Alī al-Ḥusain ibn Abd Allāh, *An-Najāt fī-l-ḥikma al-manṭiqīya wa-ṭ-ṭabī'īya wa-l-ilāhīya,* Cairo: n.p. 1938.

34 Ibn Sīnā, Abū 'Alī al-Ḥusain ibn Abd Allāh, *Ash-Shifā', al-Ilāhīyāt,* 2 vols, ed. G. C. Anawati et al., Cairo: Al-Hai'a al-'āmma li-shu'ūn al-maṭābi' al-amīrīya, 1960.

35 Nāder, Alber Naṣrī, *An-Nafs-al-basharīyah 'ind Ibn Sīnā,* Beirut: Dār al-mashriq, 1986, 54–6 (collection of some texts on the human soul from *Najāt* and *Shifā'*).

body. Thus, the rational soul is the key conduit for freedom, as the human is only free when he or she thinks rationally, while ignorance only leads to enslavement.

4 The Sufis and the Concept of Freedom

The Sufi concept of freedom lies at the crux of their belief system. Sufis generally acknowledge the dual concepts of freedom versus captivity or slavery. As observed above, slavery for the pre-Islamic Arabs indicated a status and a rank, whereas for the theologian it was facilitated through a blind following of the religious leaders *fuqahā*ʾ. For the Muslim philosophers, freedom constituted the ability to prevent bodily desires from disturbing rational capacity. Sufis, in a manner similar to the philosophers, recognize slavery as the satisfaction of bodily desires. They also adopted the duality of the soul and body, thereby denouncing the power of the body. Their starting point is similar to the Christian belief that they consider the human being is corrupted and needs salvation. Though they do not believe in an original sin, they consider humans to be immersed in the desires of the material world. In order to understand their concept of freedom, I will present here al-Ghazālī's (1058 – 1111/450 – 505) concept of the human soul, its capture and liberation.

Most Sufi writings show a great interest in grasping the role of the human soul in the mystical approach of knowing God. Al-Ghazālī demonstrates in *Mīzān al-ʿamal* that while the soul dominates the body with its intellectual faculty and directs it to act in accordance with the religious laws, it also searches for the higher world of the *malakūt*.[36] The soul therefore is the key subject for understanding al-Ghazālī's search for the knowledge of God.[37]

Although the human soul exists in the material world, it does have another origin. Al-Ghazālī demonstrates in *The Alchemy of Happiness* that the human soul was created before the body in eternity and it was sent to earth in order to gain knowledge and experience. He based his idea on the Quʾrānic verse: "When thy Lord drew forth from the Children of Adam – from their loins – their descendants, and made them testify concerning themselves, (saying): 'Am I not your Lord (who cherishes and sustains you)?'- They said: 'Yea! We do testify!' (This), lest ye should say on the Day of Judgment: 'Of this we were never mindful'" (7:172).

---

36 Al-Ghazālī, Abū Ḥāmid, *Mīzān al-ʿamal*, edited by S. Dunyā, Cairo: Dār al-māʿārif, 1965, 199 – 200.
37 Ibid., 207 – 9.

The idea of the higher origin of the soul in relation to this Qu'rānic verse is used among many Sufis such as al-Junayd (d. 980/298), al-Ḥallāj (d. 922/309) and al-Bisṭāmī. On the other hand al-Ghazālī uses this verse here in order to disclose the relationship between the soul and the divine world with the soul's natural yearning to return to its origin.[38] In the meantime he refers here to the origin of *fiṭra*, interior knowledge, which discloses that human nature in its purest form knows God.

The human soul, however, becomes estranged within the body from this knowledge and therefore it needs purification in order to recall its origin. This is a central idea in al-Ghazālī's mysticism. The human, as is observed above, is created in a free and pure form. God testified and presented himself to all human souls before their emergence into their respective bodies. The souls testified and admitted to their knowledge of God. In this case al-Ghazālī declares that humans are born free from evil. When, however, they are connected to their material bodies, this knowledge becomes veiled from their original *fiṭra*. The freedom which was hereby given to them and which enabled them to recognize the truth is now captive in the material body, thus preventing the perception of the soul. Al-Ghazālī, however, declares in *The Alchemy of Happiness* that the purpose of creating the human soul in this material world is to enable it to receive knowledge and experience.[39] At the same time, he admits that the ability to obtain true knowledge is granted only to some mystics and a few scholars.

Al-Ghazālī attributes different qualities to the human soul; all are very close to the qualities which he attributes to God. The following passage shows these similarities:

No one can understand a king but a king; therefore God has made each of us a king in miniature, so to speak, over a kingdom which is an infinitely reduced copy of His own. In the kingdom of man God's 'throne' is represented by the soul; the Archangel by the heart, 'the chair' by the brain, the 'tablet' by the treasure chamber of thought. The soul, itself unlocated and indivisible, governs the body as God governs the universe. In short each of us is entrusted with a little kingdom, and charged not to be careless in the administration of it.[40]

---

38 Al-Ghazālī, *Iḥyā' 'ulūm ad-dīn*, Cairo: Al-Mujallad al-'Arabī, 1998, vol. I, 116–7. (*Kitāb al-'ilm*). Cf. also Al-Ghazālī, *Mīzān al-'amal*, 335 and *The Alchemy of Happiness*, tr. by Claud Field, rev. and annotated by Elton L. Daniel, London: Octagon Press (for the Sufi Trust) 1980, 35. Cf. also El Kaisy-Friemuth, *God and Humans*, 129–137.

39 Al-Ghazālī, *The Alchemy*, 35.

40 Ibid., 19.

In this beautiful passage al-Ghazālī says that the role which the soul plays in the body is analogous to the role which God plays in the world. Its nature is also invisible, indivisible and not to be located in any one place, similar to the nature of the essence of God. While this soul is created by God, it does not emanate from him. In *Mishkāt al-anwār* he explains that this nature is also the nature of the angels and that they are the closest creatures to God.[41] The main difference between the angels and the human soul is that the angels are constrained to obey God and the human soul is free but captured by the bodily desires.[42] This freedom, however, prevents the human from concentrating on his or her inner voice.

These similarities between God, the angels and the human soul are expressed by the repeated Hadith: "he who knows himself knows God"[43] or the Hadith "God created Adam in His likeness".[44]

Another quality of the soul is mentioned by al-Ghazālī in the treaty *On the Meaning of the Intimate Knowledge of God.* He emphasizes here the individuality of each human soul. He explains that it is not possible for any two persons to become identical even if they reach the same level of knowledge and mystical experience.[45] Each human soul, he believes, is an individual entity which can never be identical to any other entity.

On the whole, Sufism is the journey of liberating the soul from its captivity in the body. Following this journey al-Ghazālī studies the several faculties of the soul in order to identify avenues for its liberation. The human soul consists of different powers, some of which govern the body while others lead the soul to fulfil its purpose of achieving liberation from bodily desires.[46]

The rational acquisition of divine knowledge, however, is not available to everybody; there are only few scholars within whom this knowledge is deeply rooted. The achievement of such a level of knowledge, according to al-Ghazālī, lies in liberating the soul from five different types of veils which separate us from the truth. First of all, it depends on the level of our intelligence and maturity, as hu-

---

41 Al-Ghazālī, Abū Ḥāmid, *The Niche of Lights*, trans. David Buchman, Provo Utah: Brigham Young University Press, 1998, 13–14; Al-Ghazālī, Abū Ḥāmid, *Mishkāt al-anwār*, in: *Majmūʿat rasāʾil al-Imām al-Ghazālī*, Beirut: Dār al-mashriq, 1986.

42 Al-Ghazālī, *Iḥyāʾ*, vol. III, (*kitāb ʿAjāʾib al-qalb*), 8.

43 This hadith is found in as-Suyūṭī, Jalāl ad-Dīn, *Al-Ḥāwī li-l-fatāwī*, 2:412, Beirut: Dār al-kutub al-ʿilmīya, 1982.

44 Cf. al-Bukhārī, Muḥammad, *Ṣaḥīḥ al-Bukhārī*, *Bāb al-istiʾdhān* and Muslim, *Ṣaḥīḥ Muslim*, *Bāb al-birr wa-ṣ-ṣila.*

45 Al-Ghazālī, Abū Ḥāmid, "On the Meaning of the Intimate Knowledge of God," in: John Renard (ed.), *Window on the House of Islam. Muslim ibn al-Ḥajjāj, Sources on Spirituality and Religious Life*, London, 1998, 355–8.

46 Al-Ghazālī, *Mīzān*, 201–3.

mans are endowed with different degrees of intelligence. The second difficulty lies in the fact that human beings are immersed in worldly desires. The third is the lack of interest in contemplating questions related to the nature of God and his relationship to the world. The fourth veil consists of those previous beliefs and convictions inherited from parents or teachers. This obstacle prevents us from directing our efforts fully towards the search for God's truth and the divine world. Finally, it is also a problem for many seekers to ascertain in what direction the truth should be explored. In other words, they are ignorant of the kinds of sciences and methods which lead to the knowledge of God.[47]

5 Modern Thinkers and the Concept of Freedom

In our modern times, several Muslim thinkers have demonstrated great interest in studying and defining the nature of the human being. In the colonial period, many Muslim thinkers enjoyed access to Western culture and thought. However, it was quite disappointing to acknowledge that the human being in this culture does not exist anymore as a relative of God but rather simply a relative of the apes as conceived by a secularistic Darwinism. Our origin was not in the heavens but in the deepest earthily forests, our manner of memory is not derived from a knowledgeable God but rather our animalistic origins. The first Muslim thinker who, while accepting the scientific proofs of the theory of evolution, but rejecting its psychological meaning was Jamāl ad-Dīn al-Afghānī (1838-9 – 1897/1254 – 1314). He reasoned that our intelligence originates in God through His inbreathing of the human soul into the human body. In this way, al-Afghānī attempted to save the dignity of the humans through relating their souls and intellects to the cognizance of divine origins, while acknowledging the evolution of the material bodies.[48]

Remarkable here, however, is the view of Sir Muḥammad Iqbāl (1877 – 1938), the Indian philosopher and poet. Iqbāl believed that the inner human being, for which he uses the Persian *khudī*, is that which characterizes the distinctiveness of each individual. In *Asrār-i hhudī*, the *Secrete of the Self*, he explains that the human ego also passes through evolution: egos move from primitive stages

47 Al-Ghazālī, *Iḥyā'*, vol. I, (*al-'Ilm*), 18 – 19.
48 Rūsān, Ẓāhid, *Manhaj al-Afghānī al-ʿaqlī fī difāʿih ʿan al-Islām*, Majallat jāmiʿat Dimashq, vol. 24 (2008), 14 – 16.

where they do not realize their individuality to the highest stages when they experience their uniqueness of being an individual and a person.[49]

Iqbāl used here the Persian word *khudī* instead of the Qu'rānic terms *nafs* or *rūḥ* because of its etymological origin which denotes not the self but that which gives the self its distinctive personality. In other words, Iqbāl uses the term *khudī* to express the Western concept of individuality or the ego.[50]

The ego for Iqbāl consists of several opposing powers which keep it in a state of tension. This tension is not destructive but is necessary for its development. The ego here has the task of composing a symphony out of these tensions. In this schematic, each instrument plays a different melody but together they produce the most beautiful music. In Iqbāl's philosophy, the highest form of ego is the one which is deeply aware of itself. Thus, the most perfect ego is the ego of God – God is indeed is the most unique individual.[51]

The most advanced human is the one who has deep awareness of his or her individuality which can be reached through understanding the individuality of God. At this stage, Iqbāl argues, the human will understands the beauty of submitting itself to God, which is the meaning of the word *Islam*. This form of submission means enslaving yourself to God. It is a full understanding of who God is and a full understanding of one's own individuality and existing as a God-like human. Indeed, only in this form of captivity can the human acknowledge his or her true freedom. Freedom here means knowing yourself, knowing God and acknowledging your own true position towards God.[52]

5.1 Maḥmūd Muḥammad Ṭāha (1909–1985)

Ṭāha is considered one of the most consequential modern Arabic thinkers. He was born in Sudan in 1909 and was ultimately executed under an-Numeirī regime in 1985. He faced the accusation of apostasy several times, but with Ṭāha's opposition to the September law of 1985 declaring Islamic *sharī'a* as the official law of Sudan, this charge of apostasy became very serious. Ṭāha was a reformist who understood that Islam reliant on the status quo cannot contribute towards the development of modern thought and is of no help to the in-

---

49 Iqbal, Muḥammad, *The Secrets of the Self (Asrār-i khūdī). A Philosophical Poem*, trans. with introduction and notes by Reynold A. Nicholson, London: Macmillan and co. Limited, 1920.
50 Ibid., 16–18.
51 Ibid., 18–23.
52 Iqbal, *Secrets*, 43–48.

novative Muslim thinker.[53] Therefore, he called urgently for increasing our efforts towards reform. He developed an interesting hermeneutical theory in which he divided the Qu'rān into two moments of revelation. The first moment is illustrated in the "Medinan" chapters and is deeply ensconced in the structures governing the Arab society of the seventh century. These chapters contributed heavily towards the construction of an Islamic nation and provided a majestic structure. The second moment of revelation occurs in the subsequent Meccan chapters. These chapters are of a more universal nature and depict the true Islam. These preach tolerance, wisdom and equality between men and women. He explains that these selections were neglected and not utilized by the *fuqahā'* in their structuring of the *sharīʿa* law. The Meccan chapters constitute, in his opinion, an effective hermeneutical blueprint for the future of Islam. He was of the opinion that it was now time to focus on their potential, a position which would thereby abrogate the Medinan ones.[54]

It is in the context of this very important project that Ṭaha put forth his opinion on the nature of freedom in Islam. He differentiated between two kinds of freedom: limited and absolute. Limited freedom is the freedom of the individual as regards to his or her connection with the broader society. Freedom must emphasize responsibility and respect for the freedom of other individuals. This kind of freedom is controlled by state law and aims at ensuring justice.[55]

The second kind of freedom is of a more universal and absolute nature. It does not distinguish between people or religions. Its criterion of truth consists of the belief in God and the recognition of one's own position in the universe as God's creature. Ṭāha is of the opinion that God has created human beings in order to acknowledge and receive this absolute freedom, a fact which ultimately liberates him or her from all kinds of material subjugation. This kind of freedom requires a basic form of relationship with God which ensures divine forgiveness. This divine forgiveness will assist human beings with the imperative to forgive to their neighbors. Thus in this form of freedom the human being will realize that a relationship to his or her fellow man is fundamentally characterized by forgiveness. This absolute freedom is felt in and characterized by good deeds. Therefore, Ṭāha emphasizes that absolute freedom in this regard is essentially defined by God's plan for human beings, a plan which moves from the limited freedom controlled by law and *sharīʿa* to the unlimited absolute freedom which can be reached in a mature state characterized by the acknowledgement

53 Ṭāha, Maḥmūd Muḥammad, *ar-Risālah ath-thāni min al-Islām*, Sudan: n. p., 1971, 8–10.
54 Ṭāha, *ar-Risālah*, 130–139.
55 Ibid., 39–42.

of one's own responsibility to forgive. Indeed, the maturity of the believer is stressed in Ṭaha's concept of rituals. He believes that rituals, like prayer, are prescribed in a traditional fashion to the people until they become true believers. At such a level, the believer should possess a direct and more personal form of prayer directed toward God, thereby making an alternate form of prayer imperative. Thus, maturity in belief leads to freedom of thought and action. Now the human being recognizes his or her actual relationship to God and feels confident in his or her behavior towards himself and others.[56] It is deeply sad that such maturity of belief had been characterized as a form of apostasy!

5.2 Ṭāha ʿAbd ar-Raḥmān (b. 1944)

In contrast, the Muslim thinker Ṭāha ʿAbd ar-Raḥmān (b. 1944) from Morocco explains that freedom in reality does not exist since the human being is always constrained by different forms of slavery. Human beings, in reality, do not enjoy freedom because they belong to their creator.[57] Since creation must possess a purpose, all humans are bound by a certain responsibility in fulfilling this purpose. In order to enjoy freedom humans must recognize three rules:

1) The rule of remembrance: To a large degree, humans consider themselves as the most noble of creatures with nothing existing above themselves. Consequently, they seek their utmost freedom without harming other people. ʿAbd ar-Raḥmān insists, however, on humans ignore the existence of the divine world *al-ghaybīyāt*, and do not recognize a higher authority. This fact is mentioned in the Quʾrān when it relays that God has established a covenant with all humans before the emergence of their existence on earth rooted in their belief in him, as it is mentioned above in verse 7:172.

Thus, the imperative of remembrance is essential for the enjoyment of one's own freedom due to the fact that one needs to recognize his or her own origin. This reality determines the status of human beings and therefore the possibility of their freedom.

2) The second rule is the law of the human nature (*qānūn at-taʿnīs*). In light of the first rule, humans are indeed created with certain qualities, one of which is the natural ethics, *al-akhlāq al-fiṭrīya*. Each human is born with a sense of recognition of good and evil, thereby providing the capacity for judgment.

56 Ṭāhā, *ar-Risālah*, 41–53.

57 ʿAbd ar-Raḥmān, Ṭāhā, *Suʾāl fī l-ʿamal*, Beirut: Al-Markaz ath-thaqāfī l-ʿarabī, 2012, 150–191.

Thus freedom must follow this instinct, and every human being should evaluate one's freedom in this light. This intuitive sense of ethics delineates the limits of freedom and presents a wider picture of freedom that includes both the welfare of the society as well as the welfare of an immediate other.

3) The third and last rule relates to slavery. This rule reveals the truest sense of freedom. ʿAbd ar-Raḥmān considers human beings to be born with an inclination towards slavery. Human beings are slaves to their own desires, slaves to others, and slaves to their love of power. In fact one moves from one form of slavery to another, thereby precluding any true sense of freedom. The only path towards the enjoyment of freedom consists in the worship of God as a higher form of slavery. In this form of worship, human beings will recognize their own reality and free themselves from being slaves to other humans. Closeness to God opens the eyes to the fact that God created the human being as a free person, thereby engendering the freedom of choice. This freedom of choice can only be recognized through a form of worship rooted in the will which removes the veil of darkness and promotes the recognition of true freedom.[58]

This concept of willed worship put forth by Ṭāha ʿAbd ar-Raḥmān is reminiscent of the concept of veils in al-Ghazālī's *Mishkāt al-anwār.* Al-Ghazālī asserts at the beginning of chapter three in *Mishkāt* that God in himself is always manifest to all beings, yet humans veil themselves through darkness, light mixed with darkness or a veil of light. Lifting up these three kinds of veils in order to see God is achieved via the ascent from the sensory world to the divine world of light.[59] Only at this level can the human recognize absolute freedom.

5.3 Freedom and Liberation

In the search for delineating a concept of freedom in Islam, one must examine the terms *ḥarrara* and *taḥrīr*, both defined as "liberation." As explained above, the liberation of a slave is essential for understanding freedom in the Qu'rān. However, the concept of liberation is also connected with most prophets in the Qu'rānic narration. The liberation of people from evil authority figures is especially emphasized in the stories of Moses and Noah. Exodus is a powerful form of liberation in which God provides "way out" of an evil situation. More-

58 ʿAbd ar-Raḥmān, *Su'āl*, 150–59.

59 Cf. El Kaisy-Friemuth, *God and Humans*, 130.

over, the Qu'rān also mentions liberation in the sense of raising up the marginalized and the weak to a newly found powerful status. This search for a liberation theology in Islam is the concern of the South African Muslim theologian Farid Esack (b. 1959). He considers liberation theology as the vehicle with which he can interpret the relevance of the Qu'rān in the South African context. Esack hears the voice of God as a liberating power in which, he declares his indignation towards oppression and exploitation. He contextually conceives the core message of Islam as one that liberates the true believers, namely the poor slaves and the weak merchants in the seventh century suffering on account of both their Meccan oppressors and the exploitative aristocratic Qurayshian.[60] In order to address this oppressed community, God revealed his message to Muhammad and commanded him to fight against the oppressors and establish justice. With this new reading of the Qu'rān, Esack interprets the plight of South African Muslims in the apartheid period.[61]

A revealed text is not written in vacuum, Esack insists, but it addresses certain people in light of relevant historical events and problems, thereby gaining salience with the addressed community. The text achieves a certain dynamism through its interaction with the lives of the believers and the change it can produce. Hermeneutic methodology here, explains Esack, should bridge this gap between the past and present. It should seek to engender a text that addresses both a certain historical period that nonetheless remains imminently relevant to our situation today. In this fashion, Esack implements a hermeneutic of historical reception which differentiates between two levels. The first level consists of understanding a certain text within its original historical context, while the second relates the text to a particular historical and communal situation, thereby creating an imminent moment of revelatory event. In this sense, our understanding of God's intention relevant to our own situation becomes a part of the text itself.[62]

The hermeneutic of liberation is defined through the selection of six hermeneutical keys, each of which provides and broadens a concept of liberation. These are: *taqwā* (awareness of God's presence), *tawḥīd* (belief in the unity of God) *an-nās* (the masses), *al-mustaḍʿafuna fi l-arḍ* (the oppressed), *ʿadl* (justice) and *jihād* (struggle and praxis). Most of those notions are deeply embedded within Christian liberation theology, namely the masses, the oppressed, justice and praxis. These key concepts in Christian liberation theology attempt to change

60 Tatari, Muna, *Gott und Mensch im Spannungsverhältnis von Gerechtigkeit und Barmherzigkeit. Versuch einer islamisch begründeten Positionsbestimmung*, Münster: Waxmann Press, 2016, 198–200.
61 Tatari, *Gott und Mensch*, 203–5.
62 Ibid.

the Christian message from one of salvation to one of liberation. In Christian liberation theology, God does not remain anymore at the center of events, but it is rather the masses and the oppressed that constitute the narrative fulcrum. This new reading of the gospels emphasizes God as existing in solidarity with the poor and oppressed. God calls upon them to be activists in the struggle against oppression and exploitation. Only through this struggle can they be saved, not merely in theory but also in praxis. Without a doubt, these elements of Christian liberation theology impressed Esack and assured the unity of God's message with an aim of social harmony.[63]

Turning to examine Esack's hermeneutical keys, *taqwā*, the first key, is used in many passages in the Qu'rān such "O mankind! reverence your (*etteqū/ taqwā)* Guardian-Lord, who created you from a single person" (Q. 4:1). Esack interprets *taqwā* as an awareness of the presence of God rather than a fear of him. This is a form of liberation which warns the oppressors and assures the believers that they possess a certain strength from having God on their side. *Tawḥīd*, in this hermeneutical method, has a broader meaning than the unity of God. It points here to the unity of human beings as the creatures of God, emphasizing an absolute equality. This is ensured through the next key, *an-nās*, or the masses. The Qu'rān emphasizes the role of God as being the God of the masses without any differentiation between human beings.[64] From *an-nās* the Qu'rān places the weak and the marginalized that need the strength of God in a distinguished position. This hermeneutical key is mentioned in many verses such as: "Say: I seek refuge with the Lord and Cherisher of Mankind, The King (or Ruler) of Mankind, The God (or judge) of Mankind, – From the mischief of the Whisperer (of Evil), who withdraws (after his whisper), – (The same) who whispers into the hearts of Mankind, – Among Jinns and among men." (sura 114). Further, the important hermeneutical key of justice emphasizes the aim and the content of the divine massage. Justice and liberation must come paired together. People experience liberation and freedom solely within a just community. Justice is a vital element in ensuring freedom. Finally, *jihād* in this context places emphasis on the believer as an activist who practices his or her beliefs. All these six keys point towards the importance of liberation in the Qu'rānic massage and present a new understanding of Islam's definition of freedom.[65]

---

63 Tatari, *Gott und Mensch*, 206–7.
64 Ibid, 207–11.
65 Ibid., 211–15.

6 Freedom and the Rights of Women in Islam

The question of how Islam treats women came to the fore when secular education was introduced in the 19th century, thereby replacing the religious education which was provided in small group settings within village and city mosques. In Egypt, Muḥammad ʿAli (1769–1849), an Albanian ruler under the Ottomans, started to engender a modern form of education by opening different forms of schools such as military academies, medical and engineering schools, and language-learning institutes. Subsequently, he opened a school that taught the art of a midwife in order to train female gynecologists. No preparatory or secondary schools, however, were opened for their elementary education. Early-childhood education was conducted at home. Indeed, only very few upper-class women could join the school for midwives, and even then they were shuttled by the government into arranged marriages with male doctors. The couples received housing in various towns and villages across Egypt. Public education for women began in 1870, but girls were nevertheless required to remain fully covered with the *niqāb*. Women until 1870 were mostly secluded and could only go out in the company of their male guardians.

When seeking to understand the rights of women as dictated by Islam, we must start in the seventh century and examine the status of women before and after Islam.

The first question that faces a researcher in examining the position of women before Islam regards the sources we currently have available from this period. Leila Ahmed is one of the earliest Muslim feminist theologians who has worked in this field. The main difficulty facing her while engaging the available sources regarding the pre-Islamic period was that all these texts were written by Muslim males.[66]

The most important and earliest source regarding these matters is the biography of Muhammad written by Ibn Ishāq (d. 767/150) who died about 135 years following the passing of Muhammad. Additional texts include the Hadith works of al-Bukhārī (810–870/194–256), Muslim b. al-Ḥajjāj (d. 875/202) and the *Kitāb al-Aghānī* by Abū l-Faraj al-Iṣfahānī (897–967/284–356). Of course we also have the Qu'rān itself.[67]

There is no doubt that Arabia before Islam consisted of Bedouins and settled tribes. Ibn Isḥāq tells us that Muhammad was sent to a Bedouin tribe for some years as an infant and a young boy in order to experience Bedouin life. This in-

66 Ahmed, Leila, *Women and Gender in Islam*, New Haven/London: Yale University Press, 1992.
67 Ibid.

dicates that around the time of Muhammad's birth, Bedouin customs were dying out and being replaced by the settled culture of large tribes.[68] In examining marriage customs reported by Ibn Isḥāq, we realize that women had great freedom in choosing their husbands and divorcing them. Indeed the woman largely remained in her tribe when she married someone outside of the tribe. She received both a dowry and marriage gifts. Al-Iṣfahānī informs us that when women wanted to leave their husbands, they turned their tent upside down such that the door would be facing the other side of the tent. When the husbands saw this, they realized that they had been divorced, thereby rendering their continued stay within those tribe impossible.[69]

Noble women also had the custom of asking males for their hand in marriage. Ibn Ishāq reports of many circumstances in which women had asked the prophet to marry them. In nearly all marriages entered into by the prophet, his wives were the initiator of the marriage.[70] In many cases women had also enumerated several conditions within the marriage contract and it was not uncommon that they married several times even after becoming widowers.[71] Many such marriage contracts initiated by women took place after the rise of Islam. Um Salama, a wealthy widow, had initiated a marriage contract with the young man Abū l-ʿAbbās as-Saffāḥ, who proceeded to follow it. In her marriage contract, she stipulated that he refrains from taking a second wife or seeking out a concubine. Al-ʿAbbās accepted her condition and was faithful to her even when he in 749 became the first caliph and the founder of the Abbasid dynasty. That means that marriage initiated and conditioned by women carried on for at least the first 100 year after the rise of Islam.[72]

On the other hand, other sources show that in more established towns like Mecca and Ta'if, where trade flourished, a patriarchal culture dominated. The son, who was considered a valuable investment, belonged to the tribe of the father. Thus the value of women depreciated. It was also assumed that the instances of infanticide proved that the birth of girls was a source of shame within a patriarchal system. However, it seems that the impetus for infanticide was connected to economics more than anything else. Poor nomadic tribes at the mercy

68 Ibn Isḥāq, Muḥammad, *Sīrat Ibn Isḥāq*, Fez: Maʿhad ad-dirāsāt wa-l-abḥāth li-t-taʿrīb, 1976, 31–35.

69 Ahmed, *Women*, 41–64.

70 Ibn Isḥāq, *Sīrat*, 359–400.

71 Ibid.

72 Ahmed, *Women*, 41–64.

of persistent hanger during the year used to kill some of their infants in order to prevent them from suffering.[73]

Thus we face here a pre-Islamic Arabian community possessing matriarchal as well as patriarchal cultural traits. The emergence of the Quʾrān from this particular culture has had clear consequences. It must, namely, address both aspects of culture. Linguistically, it addressed women in their gendered form when referring to believers.

According to Naṣr Ḥāmid Abū Zaid (1943–2010), one of the most prominent modern scholars of the Quʾrān, the Quʾrān consists of a dialogue between the addresser and the addressee. Therefore, women were clearly addressed in a gendered fashion.[74] One example can be found in the following verse:

> For Muslim men and women,– for believing men and women, for devout men and women, for true men and women, for men and women who are patient and constant, for men and women who humble themselves, for men and women who give in Charity, for men and women who fast (and deny themselves), for men and women who guard their chastity, and for men and women who engage much in God's praise,– for them has God prepared forgiveness and great reward. (33:35)

However, as I demonstrated above, the period in which the Quʾrān witnessed a transition from a matrilineal to patrilineal culture. The Quʾrān was therefore obliged to take into account these new cultural conditions facing its believers. Its treatment of this problem is quite praiseworthy and was fully accepted by both kinds of believers. In fact, in order to appreciate the position of the Quʾrān towards women, one should be very much aware of the pre-Islamic culture conditions. On the whole, the Quʾrān neither improved nor damaged the position of women, but simply mirrored it. Thus, the Muslim judges who formed the Islamic *sharīʿa* in the first three hundred years of Islam had the choice of determining the direction of this new body of law. The following Quʾrānic passage, for example, simply sought to depict the current situation in Medina. Instead, it was used to create a precedent for the encouragement of polygamy, a rule that contradicted its original intention Quʾrān 4:3: "If ye fear that ye shall not be able to deal justly with the orphans, Marry women of your choice, Two or three or four; but if ye fear that ye shall not be able to deal justly (with them), then only one, or (a captive) that your right hands possess, that will be more suitable, to prevent

73 Ibid.

74 Abū Zaid, Naṣr Ḥāmid, *Dawāʾir al-khawf: qirāʾah fī khiṭāb al-marʾah,* Beirut: Al-Markaz ath-thaqāfī l-ʿarabī, 2008.

you from doing injustice." Further Qu'rān 4:129: "Ye are never able to be fair and just as between women, even if it is your ardent desire".

By insisting on the preservation of justice, the Qu'rān is attempting here to establish a form of monogamy that was probably not desired in this period. The decision to favor monogamy over polygamy was left to the discretion of the community. This shows that the Qu'rān does not lay legal conditions, but instead sets the main ethical and moral guideposts. The main goal of the passage was to emphasize justice and to warn against the misuse of an orphan's wealth by the guardians to whom this money is entrusted. Leila Ahmed informs us that this rule was not followed in early Islam and men from patriarchal tribes married more than four women.[75]

Many traditions also mention the position of 'Umar ibn al-Khaṭṭāb towards women. 'Umar was a very important member of the early Muslim community and became the second. He came from one of the most influential and nobel patriarchal tribes of Mecca. Although he was known as a wise and just caliph, his position towards women was quite fanatical. Many commentators reported that the famous verses concerning the veiling of the wives of the prophet and the believers reflect the position taken by 'Umar and other early patriarchal believers requesting the prophet to demand modesty of Muslim women. This is reflected in Qu'rān 33:35 and 33:54. During 'Umar's rule following the death of the prophet from 634–644, he placed strong restrictions on the wives of the prophet. He also did not allow women to attend mosque services. Although 'Ā'isha and Umm Salama, two of the prophet's wives, were well known as imams, he did not allow them to teach men. All these rules were abrogated during the reign of the third caliph 'Uthmān b. 'Affān. In summary, this discussion demonstrates the struggle between patriarchal and matriarchal components within early Islam. Patriarchal notions finally prevailed when Islam was transported into the Persian and Christian cultural milieus north of Arabia.[76]

6.1 The Commentators and Their Culture

Islam spread from its cultural setting in Arabia to the Persian and Mediterranean cultural contexts in the span of a mere decade following the death of the prophet. Leila Ahmed, depicts the situation of women within Persian culture in the following fashion:

75 Ahmed, *Women*, 41–50.
76 Ibid.

Although women, to some extent, enjoyed a degree of respect in ancient Persian culture, the dominance of Zoroastrianism in the Sassanid Empire reduced their status severely. Women and slaves in Zoroastrianism were considered as property and not persons. Women were totally subjugated to their fathers and husbands. They needed to obey their husbands fully, required to declare "I will never cease all my life to obey my husband". Women were obliged to extend their arms in greeting their husbands just as performed by in their worship of Ohrmazd. A husband could obtain a "certificate of disobedience" from the court if his wife disobeyed him.[77]

Although monogamy was widespread among the masses in the Sassanid period, polygamy and concubines were common amongst the royal families. Thus, Arab caliphs developed their harem mainly when they ruled from Baghdad in Iraq.

From Syria to Egypt, Greek-Christian culture was prevalent. Greek culture in the Middle East was of a patriarchal nature and women had very little to say. They were mainly secluded in the home and considered biologically inferior to men. This was influenced by Aristotle's view of women in Book 10 of his Metaphysics. For him, a man's nature is the most well-rounded and complete. He compared the relationship between men and women to the relationship between the soul and the body. Just as the soul has full control over the material body, so should men have complete control over women.[78]

Thus, in the north of Arabia, the patriarchal position prevailed and was highly influential in the articulation of the new religion. The transition between patriarchal and matriarchal norms in Islamic society after the death of the prophet was finally executed when Islam became the dominant religion in the Middle East and moved its center of authority permanently to Damascus and Baghdad. Commentators such as aṭ-Ṭabarī (839–923/224-5–310), considered amongst Muslims as a preeminent source of Qu'rānic knowledge, used a great deal of Judeo-Christian material known as the Israeliyyat in the interpretation of many of parts of the Qu'rān. The story of creation, for example, is interpreted fully in light of its equivalent in the Genesis book of the Old Testament. According to aṭ-Ṭabarī, Eve is created from Adam's ribs, although the Qu'rān clearly offers the enjoinder to "reverence your Guardian-Lord, who created you from a single person, created, of like nature, His mate, and from them twain scattered (like seeds) countless men and women" (4:1). Nowhere in the Qu'rān can one derive

77 Ibid., *Women*, 11–25.
78 Ibid., 25–39.

an understanding of Eve's creation as emerging from a part of Adam's body, an important fact which has several implications.

Aṭ-Ṭabarī also considers women to be responsible for the original sin by virtue of eating from the Tree of Knowledge. Yet the Qu'rān clearly says "Then began Satan to whisper suggestions to them, bringing openly before *their* minds all their shame that was hidden from them (before) ... So by deceit he brought about *their* fall" (7:20, 22, emphasis by the author). Although it is clear both here and in other passages that Adam and Eve together were responsible for the original sin, aṭ-Ṭabarī invoked a tradition from Wahb ibn Munabbih (a Jewish convert, 654-55 – 728/34 – 109) testifying that it was the women who ate first from the tree and thereby convinced Adam to do the same. Although aṭ-Ṭabarī mentions this story only in the interpretation of one passage (2:36) amongst the different passages reciting the story, this particular interpretation prevailed.[79] Most Muslim men and women solely recall the story of Wahb until today.

Thus by virtue of its entrance into Persian and Mediterranean culture, the Qu'rān suffered from a severe patriarchal form of interpretation which produced negative gendered images of women.

6.2 Liberating the Qu'rān

The Qu'rān, with its dated Arabic diction and style, is difficult for Muslims today to understand. Therefore, they have become fully dependent on the help of the commentators. Translators of the Qu'rān are also fully dependent on traditional interpretations in their understanding of the old Arabic of Mecca. In fact many translations are fully dependent on traditions of interpretation rather than the original language of the Qu'rān itself.

The earliest modern commentator who challenged the authority of the traditional exegetes was Muḥammad 'Abduh (1849 – 1905). He insisted that the Qu'rān must be read as a unified message in a modern context. Its main message concerns the welfare of society dependent on historical context. This should be taken into consideration when reading any part of the Qu'rān. For example, in his interpretation of sura 4:3 on polygamy, 'Abduh considers the condition of justice to be the most important element in building a felicitous society. Therefore,

79 Ibid., 64 – 79.

the notion of marriage inherently and implicitly forbids marrying more than one wife.[80]

Fazlur Rahman, a Pakistani theologian who died 1988, proposed that the Quʾrān must be interpreted on two levels: 1. parts which declare eternal principles and 2. others which describe contingent situations.[81] In this way it is possible to accept parts of the Quʾrān which are connected to the seventh century but examine their working for the changed situation of today, while other parts of the Quʾrān are suitable for every time and context.

6.3 Liberating Women

Let us now move to the interpretations of modern Muslim feminists who struggle to present a novel and female-friendly understanding of Islam. We can divide these modern Muslim writing on gender issues into two groups:

1) Those who are trying to interpret the patriarchal parts of the Quʾrān in order to produce a more moderate position.
2) Those who are of the opinion that today's Muslims need to recognize the culture of the Quʾrānic context and to concentrate on the overall moral intention of the Quʾrān as a guideline for behavior.

Amina Wadud (b. 1952) is an excellent example of the second group. Her book *Women and the Quʾrān* has made a great impact on this field and many of her concepts are considered as sources for a feminist reading of the text.

The Qu'rān for Wadud is both a document and guiding scripture. It facilitates a dialogue with us as well as with its original 7th century audience. It consists of a universal as well as particular discourse. The universal ethos offers the main guidelines which speak to every culture and in every language, while the particular ethos is concerned with 7th century situation in which the text is revealed. Women's attire at that time and their social behavior are not of great relevance to our situation today. To limit the text to a certain period and culture is, in effect, a reductionist position.[82]

While the Quʾrānic text consists of the revealed ideas of God, it must always find ways to speak to the people today in their myriad situations. In her study,

80 Ahmed, *Women*, 127–145.

81 Rahman, *Fazlur, Revival and Reform in Islam. A Study of Islamic Fundamentalism*, Oxford: One World Press, 1999.

82 Wadud, Amina, *Qur'an and Woman. Rereading the Sacred Texts from a Woman's Perspective*, New York: Oxford University Press, 1999, 1–15.

she discovered that there are differences between what the Qu'rān says and what various commentators across the ages have interpreted the Qu'rān to be saying. In the second situation, the Qu'rān is manipulated in order to express what it does not mean to express.

Wadud proposes a hermeneutical method which concentrates on three aspects of the text: 1. The context in which the text was revealed in order to understand which was its first audience and to grasp why the text is saying what is saying. The mode of historical inquiry here does aim to limit the Qu'rān to past traditions, but rather its goal is to reach an understanding of what the text is really saying 2. The grammatical composition of the text in order to be sure that the text is actually saying what might only ostensibly be articulated 3. The comprehensive worldview of the text which strives to unify the text regarding its overall message, thereby guaranteeing potential access its modern readers.[83]

Wadud's hermeneutical approach found wide-ranging acceptance among many Muslim thinkers who have devoted much effort in exploring and articulating the position of women in within Islam such as Asma Barlas, Kasia Ali, Fatima Mernissy and other.

7 Freedom of Belief and Apostasy

Parallel to the rationalistic discussion regarding the freedom of choice in the *kalām* tradition, Muslim jurists involved in the articulation of Islamic law have discussed the concepts of *ḥudūd*, the divinely prescribed punishments, as well as the concept of *at-ta'zīr*, laws which are subject to the judge's opinion. One of these laws concerns the punishment for apostasy.

The freedom of choosing one's own religion or withdrawing from all religious belief is a fundamental right of each human being. Islam faced apostate movements at a very early stage in its history, and the Qu'rān depicted this problem in approximately 200 verses such as:

> They swear by God that they said nothing (evil), but indeed they uttered blasphemy, and they did it after accepting Islam [...]. (9:74)

> Only those are Believers who have believed in God and His Apostle, and have never since doubted [...] (49:15)

83 Ibid.

> A section of the People of the Book say: 'Believe in the morning what is revealed to the believers, but reject it at the end of the day; perchance they may (themselves) Turn back; [...]. (3:72)

Apostasy is not only an Islamic phenomenon, but also appears in the Old Testament in chapter 13 of Deuteronomy, which mention false prophets. The punishment of those who follows false prophets is the death penalty. This is addressed in Deuteronomy 13:6–11,

> If your very own brother, or your son or daughter, or the wife you love, or your closest friend secretly entices you, saying, 'Let us go and worship other gods' do not yield to him or listen to him. Show him no pity. Do not spare him or shield him. You must certainly put him to death. Your hand must be the first in putting him to death, and then the hands of all the people. Stone him to death.

Thus, administrating punishment of apostasy was already practiced among the Jews of Medina. Therefore, when the prophet Muhammad was confronted with this problem, a mode of punishment was already available to him. Therefore the Qu'rān sought to declare another position:

> Let there be no compulsion in religion: Truth stands out clear from Error: whoever rejects evil and believes in God hath grasped the most trustworthy hand- hold [...]. (2:256)
>
> Say, 'The truth is from your Lord': Let him who will believe, and let him who will, reject (it) [...]. (18:29)

Punishment of apostasy in Qu'rān, however, consists of hell when facing the Day of Judgement. Yet, there is hardly any Qu'rānic text prescribing a temporal punishment for apostasy. Muhammad in his life did render a judgement with a sentence of death in two cases, but then recanted this verdict likely due to such Qu'rānic emphasis on punishment occurring the hereafter.

Ṭāha Jābir al-ʿAlwānī (1935–2016) in his book *Let there be no Compulsion in Religion*, explains that the death penalty of apostasy was established in Islamic law in a later period when Muslim jurists were faced with the danger of internal or external foreign influences threatening the authority of Islam as the official religion of lands where Christianity was practiced by the majority of the population.[84]

The jurists found two Hadiths which give them the authority to retain the Jewish sentence of death for apostasy.

84 Al-ʿAlwānī, Ṭāha Jābir, *Let there be no Compulsion in Religion. A Historical Analysis*, IIIT Books in Brief Series, 2012, 3–6.

The Hadiths:

> If any one changes his religion put him or her to death.[85]

Al-ʿAlwānī here argues that this Hadith is a Hadith aḥād, meaning that it does not fulfil the criterion of the mutwāter, which means the chain of the transmitters is known to us.

> Allah's Apostle said, 'The blood of a Muslim cannot be shed except in three cases: In *Qaṣaṣ* for murder, a married person who commits illegal sexual intercourse and the one who reverts from Islam (apostate) and leaves the Muslim group.[86]

Nearly all four Sunni schools of law, alongside a slightly different Shīʿa approach, accepted these two hadiths in favor of the death penalty. Although about 200 verses in Quʾrān discuss this problem and clearly express that those who have abandoned Islam and intended to spread doubt about the truthfulness of Islam will be punished in the afterlife, Muslim jurists insisted on a worldly punishment.[87] This insistence of such harsh punishment was intended to stop anyone from undermining the authoritative nature of Islam in the new Islamic empire. ʿAlwānī tells us that such a form of defence aimed at establishing Islam as the official religion within this period should not be undermined. That is to say that the jurists came to this position pursuant to concern for the welfare of the Islamic nation, *maṣlaḥa,* rather than establishing an eternal form of judgement.[88]

He also indicates that all four schools dealt with this subject not under the rubric of divine punishments, *ḥudūd,* but also under the judge's possibility to render judgement according to his own opinion, *taʿzīr,* or in the interest of the welfare of the *umma.* There is no consensus, however, as to what exactly should be deemed apostasy. Some jurists define apostasy only in terms of causing distress and aiming to spread anxiety amongst Muslims. In this case, such individuals should be put to death because of this particular effect, and not because of apostasy in and of itself. In contrast, others consider anyone who criticizes Islam or attempts to omit any doctrines concerning belief accepted through communal juristic consensus to be an apostate. This opinion of the latter jurists have been cited in recent cases against Muslim writers who have studied Islam critically in

85 Al-Bukhārī, *Ṣaḥīḥ al-Bukhārī,* 4:52:260.

86 Al-Bukhārī, *Ṣaḥīḥ al-Bukhārī,* 9:83:17, cf. also Muslim, *Ṣaḥīḥ Muslim,* 16:4152.

87 Al-ʿAlwānī, *No Compulsion,* 14–16.

88 Ibid., 14–16.

order to apply scientific methods of research such as Naṣr Hāmid Abū Zaid or Farag Foda or Maḥmūd Muḥammad Ṭāha.[89]

Al-ʿAlwānī's main criticism here concerns the following point: how can we accept hadiths which clearly contradict the Quʾrān. Hadith, in his opinion, maintains the function of either interpreting the Quʾrān or to adding to cases which are not dealt with in the Quʾrān. Thus, the two hadiths cited used here do not fulfil this criterion and are harnessed to establish an independent judgement standing in contradiction to the Quʾrān. Therefore, Muslim jurists must consider them to be weak hadiths and cease to cite them as the basis for the death penalty. We should accept the treatment of the *fuqahā*ʾ as historical exceptional judgements. This is exactly what Shaikh al-Azhar Aḥmad aṭ-Ṭayab expressed in a TV interview in which he said: I do not believe in the death penalty for apostasy, as Muslims are free to change their religion in light of the freedom was given to them by the Quʾrān.

8 Critical Free Thinking versus Taqlīd

The problem of critical thinking as the basis for freedom was already established in early theological discussions. The main argument in this case was that every Muslim should understand and examine his or her own beliefs. Simply following others or the elders was deemed as practicing *taqlīd*, which means blindly following without independently perceiving. The discussion around *taqlīd* layed the ground for establishing a system of scientific knowledge capable of defining what knowledge is and how to achieve it. Muʿtazilites and Ashʿarites both encouraged the theologians to develop their own opinions and not to blindly follow their masters. However, Muʿtazilites believed in what they called *taklīf ʿaqlī*, which means that every human is called upon to seek out the true understanding of God and His connection to the world through their rational capacity. This capacity is a divine grace which enables every mature person to find certainty, *al-yaqīn*, in religious and scientific maters. This rational capacity is summed up in the following fashion: intuition which each person receives directly from God such as the capacity to distinguish between good and evil independently without the need of further guidance. The holy text can, in the main, explicate details on the basis of what we already know. God also provides necessary knowledge which establishes the groundwork for our research.[90] Further, humans receive

89 Ibid., 13–14.
90 Cf. El Kaisy-Friemuth, "Free Thinkers of Islam," 37, 40.

the tranquility of the soul, *sukūn an-nafs*, as a sign pointing to correct knowledge and belief. On the basis of such divine gifts, the human being is able to construct his or her own understanding of the world and its creator. Thus, human beings can only develop knowledge through divine grace and their own efforts, as both elements are important for establishing and undergirding opinion and critical thinking. Critical thinking, in the opinion of these early theologians indicated the capacity to ask all kinds of questions and the knowledge required to provide different sets of possibilities as answers. This was and is the basis for freedom, which, in this case, demands that humans not be obliged to follow others, but are rather able to develop their own opinions and make independent decisions. This freedom, however, also constitutes a form of responsibility as it must necessarily lead to goodness and felicity. The role of religion is to provide confirmation of our own knowledge, thereby making it easier for those who find it difficult to embark on the path of rational knowledge. It aims to elucidate in detailed form that which we already know in a universal form, *ʿalā al-mujmal*, and to provide legal judgements.[91]

However, al-Ghazālī did indeed defend *taqlīd* as a possibility for those who are not able or willing to develop their own opinions. Frank, in his article "Ghazālī on Taqlīd", explores al-Ghazālī's position towards the acquisition of true knowledge.[92] He explains that attaining knowledge, for al-Ghazālī, is achieved via three main methods: through the knowledge of others; through demonstrative proofs which are produced by original thinking; or through direct inspiration. Original thinkers, however, are very few and far between; most people follow others and are therefore *muqallidūn*.[93] *Taqlīd*,[94] for al-Ghazālī, constitutes

91 Ibid., 40–42.

92 Frank, Richard M., "Al-Ghazālī on Taqlīd. Scholars, Theologians, and Philosophers," *Zeitschrift für Geschichte der Arabische-Islamischen Wissenschaft* 7 (1991/1992), 209, 215. Frank refers here to the work of Farīd Jabre, *La Notion de Certitude chez Ghazālī dans ses origines psychologiques et historiques*, Paris: Vrin, 1958.

93 Frank, "Taqlīd," 207–8.

94 *Taqlīd*, in al-Ghazālī's opinion, is related to the faculty of *wahm*, or estimation. This faculty is the highest of the practical intellect and although it abstracts images and transfers them to ideas, these ideas are very much related to sensible experience. It presents ideas which are dependent on empirical experience as true rational concepts. They are easy to accept because of their natural appeal to the human mind. This faculty, therefore, is quite deceptive because it makes people believe that their reflections are purely rational, whereas in reality they are fully dependent upon empirical experience. Frank explains that al-Ghazālī's demonstrates in *Munqidh* that even the philosophers are misled by this faculty in their metaphysical principles when they depend on concepts which the mind can accept merely because they are familiar ones. Cf. Frank, "Taqlīd", 248.

a legitimate way of knowing, thereby contradicting the position of the Ash'arite School, which required an individual's rational conviction.[95] Al-Ghazālī's retort to the Ash'arite claim is simply to reference the first Bedouin believers whose assent to the prophet's authority did not depend upon rational demonstration but rather upon a simple acceptance of what the prophet proclaimed. The recognition of the power of this simple assent probably, as Frank points out, lay in al-Ghazālī's belief of the natural knowledge of God present in each soul through the *fiṭra.*[96] However, this theory of *taqlīd* seems to be influenced by Ibn Sīnā's logical theory of *taṣawwur* and *taṣdīq.* At the beginning of the *Najāt* Ibn Sīnā explains that *taṣawwur* requires the independent formation of concepts, whereas *taṣdīq* implies the granting of assent.[97]

Taqlīd, however, comprises many levels according to al-Ghazālī, the lowest of which involves the simple assent of the believer to the prophet and the first caliphs, *as-salaf.* Theologians and philosophers are also considered as *muqallidūn*, explains Frank. For al-Ghazālī, there are very few theologians possessing original proofs, methods and demonstrations supporting their knowledge. Most of the theologians are excellent followers of their teachers and the respective lines of their schools without fully apprehending counter-positions, and examining the principles of their own school.[98]

The issue of critical thinking and its connection to freedom is crucial to the attempts of modern Muslim thinkers to reform Islam. Muḥammad 'Abduh criticized and rejected polygamy. In his estimation, the notion of justice conditional to polygamy in sura 4:3 "If ye fear that ye shall not be able to deal justly with the orphans, Marry women of your choice, Two or three or four; but if ye fear that ye shall not be able to deal justly (with them), then only one, or (a captive) that your right hands possess, that will be more suitable, to prevent you from doing injustice" is interpreted in verse 4:129 "Ye are never able to be fair and just as between women, even if it is your ardent desire", using precisely that initial verse as impossible to achieve. Therefore one is advised to be satisfied with having only one wife.

Critical thinking, however, has been connected in modern times with apostasy. Modern thinkers who have examined religious ideas and beliefs established by earlier theologians are accused by religious and political authorities with the inclination towards apostasy. The two cases are important to examine in this regard are the cases of Muḥammad Khalafallah and Naṣr Ḥamid Abū Zaid.

95 Ibid, 219.
96 Ibid, 213.
97 Ibn Sīnā, *An-Najāt*, 3–4.
98 Frank, "Taqlīd," 241–49.

Muḥammad Khalafallah (1916 – 1991) questioned the historicity of the Qu'rānic stories in his book *al-Fann al-qaṣaṣī fī l-Qu'rān*. He was aiming at presenting a novel reading which would enable these stories to demonstrate wisdom and their applied relevance to modern exigencies.[99]

Naṣr Ḥāmid Abū Zaid (1943 – 2010), in his criticism of ash-Shāf'ī in his book *al-Imām ash-Shāfi'ī* was convinced that the basis upon which ash-Shāf'ī established his jurisprudence contains many difficulties and thus must be re-read critically. The first difficulty lies in the equivalence he established between the Hadith and the Qu'rān, both of which were to be used as the main source of law. In Abū Zaid's opinion, this would mean that the Hadith undermines the authority of the Qu'rān and must then be considered as an expansion of revelation. He also demonstrates that the concept of consensus is not sufficiently elucidated and needs further research. Ash-Shāfi'ī was chiefly interested in expanding the eternal Texts such that they could be used in an expansive range of legal cases.[100]

In addition to the two above cases, in which both authors were accused of Apostasy, Muḥammad Sa'īd Ramaḍān al-Buṭī, the Syrian theologian d. 2013, supported Abū Zaid in differentiating between *aḥkām at-tablīgh* and *aḥkām al-imāma*. The first consist of judgements drawn directly from the Qu'rān, while the second are the judgements left for the Judge and the Umma to render valid in the final sense. Thus he was able to distinguish the eternal from the contingent, thereby rendering the second form of judgement adaptable according to the welfare of a particular society.

The aforementioned examples highlighting the freedom to engage critical thinking among Muslim thinkers in the modern and contemporary periods demonstrate the importance of practicing this kind of freedom.[101] Many of these thinkers were accused of apostasy and al-Buṭī, in particular, was killed during his public lecture in 2013.

---

99 Khalafallah, Muḥammad, *Al-Fann al-qaṣaṣī fī l-Qur'ān al-karīm*, Beirut: Sīnā' li-n-nashr: 1999.

100 Abū Zaid, Naṣr Ḥāmid, *Al-Imām ash-shāfi'ī wa-ta'sīs al-aydiyūlūjīya al-wasiṭīya*, Beirut: Sīnā li-n-nashr, 1992.

101 Al-Būṭī, Muḥammad Sa'īd Ramaḍān, *Ḥurrīyat al-insān fī ẓill 'ubūdīyatihi li-llāh*, Beirut: Dār al-fikr al-mu'āṣir, 1992.

9 Freedom in the Shīʿa Thought

Nearly all Shīʿa sects have followed Muʿtazilite theology and have adopted their notion of the free will. Freedom of will in the classical period valued the important of the human in understanding and interpreting the religion. This ability was and is attributed not only to the Shīʿi imams but also all Shīʿi *mujatahidūn*. In the following passages, I will give two examples of understanding freedom among modern Shīʿi thinkers.

Muḥammad al-Bāqir, a modern Iraqi Shīʿi theologian also known as al-Ḥakīm (1939–2003), laid the basis for a rich concept of freedom in his works: *Falsafatunā*, our Philosophy; and his book *Iqtiṣāḍunā, our Economy,* along with several other short works such as *al-Khiṭāb al-ʿlmānī*, the *Modern Secular discourse*. Al-Bāqir divides freedom into two typologies: the natural freedom bestowed by natural law on all living beings. The second kind of freedom is specifically given to human beings in order to offer them the freedom of choice in a wider and deeper sense than that bestowed upon other beings by natural law.[102]

The freedom which offered to human beings is of a dual nature, namely an inner and outer freedom. The inner freedom consists of the freedom of choice. Since humans have the capacity to act, they possess a free will which allows them to act or not to act. This capacity is offered to the human being in order to allow him or her to choose the good and refrain from practicing the evil which is confirmed in the concept of *al-amr bi-l-maʿrūf wa-n-nahī ʿan al-munkar,* commanding the right and forbidding the wrong. The outer form of freedom constitutes the freedom influenced by external social and political elements. These have positive and negative influences on human freedom.

Freedom to oppose Islamic doctrines is also allowed in al-Bāqir's philosophy. Although he insist that Islam is a truthful religion, he underscores the Quʾrānic notion that there "there is no compulsion in religion".[103] He hereby highlights several Quʾrānic verses, which allow oppositional opinions under the condition that the discussion be qualified by scientific proofs, conducted in a peaceful manner such as "As for those who divide their religion and break up into sects, thou hast no part in them in the least: their affair is with God: He will in the end tell them the truth of all that they did." (6:159)

Al-Bāqir claims that freedom of thought is a basic element in Shīʿi belief. The concept of *ijtihād* is very important in Shīʿi thinking and ensures the possibility

---

102 Ḥamza, Ḥāmid, *Dirāsāt fi l-ḥurīya wa-l-dimuqrāṭīya*, Wāsiṭ: Dār allaṭīf li-l-ṭibāʿa wa-n-nashr, 2006, 5.

103 Ibid., 15–17.

for the imam and his follower to interpret and re-read the holy texts. Al-Bāqir considers this freedom as essential for the Shīʿa because religion must cope with a changing culture. Therefore a group of *mujatahidūn*, reformers, must exist in every historical period. Otherwise a split will emerge between religion and its contextual reality.[104]

Furthermore, social freedom is based on the concept of the welfare of the society, *al-maṣlaḥa*. Following the Muʿtazilites, freedom for al-Bāqir is not separable from responsibility. The freedom of Muslims must be limited to their responsibility for the freedom of others and the welfare of society. Moreover, truthfulness and justice should constitute the groundwork for personal and social freedom. All forms of freedom which lead to *mafsada,* that which is evil, socially discriminatory or exploitive, are not permitted in Shīʿa Islam.[105]

Political freedom is also essential for him. Al-Bāqir considers God's call for the human being to constitute his *khalīfa* or a representative on Earth, as quite crucial. Since the Shīʿa community currently exists without the infallible Imam, his representatives should accordingly take charge. The conditionality of this freedom is ensured by the existence of a democratic system which allows for those representative to come forward and take charge. This could only happen through a form of political freedom which ensures truthfulness and justice.[106]

Finally in *Iqtiṣāḍuna*, *our Economy*, al-Bāqir insists on the personal economical freedom which does not result from exploitation. In contrast to the socialist communist system, economic freedom constitutes an expression of love for one's self which he considers to consist of an instinctive behavior. Humans naturally want to earn and reach a level of luxurious living. While this instinct cannot be eliminated, all forms of exploitation should nevertheless be forbidden.[107] Moreover, Islam did limit these economic desires through prescribing *zakāt*, the compulsory charity system. All believers must pay 2.5% of their wealth to the poor while ensuring the welfare of their parents and relatives.

Further, the philosopher and theologian Mujtathid Shabastari (b. 1936) considers that faith is based on freedom. Since God spoke to humans and established a discourse with them, He declared them to have the ability and freedom to follow and understand His discourse. The religious discourse is building a relationship between God and humans from a person (God) to a person (the human).

104 Al-Ḥakīm, Muḥammad Bāqir, *Dawr ahl al-bayt fī bināʾ al-jamāʿa aṣ-ṣāliḥa*, vol. 1, Iraq: Dār ahl al-bayt, 2003, 120–23.

105 Ibid.

106 Ḥamza, *Dirāsāt fī l-ḥurīya*, 5–18

107 Aṣ-Ṣadr, Muhammad Bāqir, *Iqtiṣādunā*, Iraq: Markaz al-abḥāth wa-d-dirāsāt at-takhaṣuṣīa, 2004, 306–9.

God is an absolute and abstract person while the human is a limited and defined one. This kind of relationship for Shabastari is an emphasis on the importance of the personal freedom. In his article "the Religious Experience",[108] he analyzes freedom to be "freedom from", "freedom in" and "freedom towards". In examining "freedom from", he argues that the outer context is compelling us to follow the traditions, the religious commands and prohibitions and the social pressures, which limit our freedom of actions. Further, the inner pressures of personal desires of the ego prevent us to think and act freely.

Shabastari considers freedom to be the only path to establishing a relationship with God. The capturing of freedom through the outer and inner pressures prevent the person from enjoying and understanding the real freedom which he/she could experience in encountering God. Real freedom is the freedom of God, which is free from all kinds of limitations this kind of freedom is possibly to taste through a person to person relationship with God. He explains that humans communicate with two parties: with things and persons. Relating to things is only one sided since things cannot establish a dialogue or communications with us. Our freedom can only be practiced with persons who we encounter in a dialogue and discourse. Our relationship with God should be of the second kind.[109]

Religious authorities usually present God to us as a thing and not a person. His commands and prohibitions are eternal and not disputable. This picture religion as a judgements court institution with no discourse. Thus, Shabastari calls for renewing the religious discourse which should declare the freedom of thought and act which enable the establishing of a relationship with God. This is the highest form and aim of freedom.

Both al-Hakim and Shabastari emphasize the human freedom of will and action as the ground for reform and new interpretation of Islam. This attitude is very connected to the Shīʿi understanding of revelation and inspiration. Both are revealing to the human the reality about God and about themselves. The Qurʾān as the revealed word of God can only reach the human when it is understood in the human context and culture. Thus the Shīʿa realized the importance of the Imam and the Aytollah in the dynamic interpretation of Islam which is perceived in the specific time and context. Thus, freedom here plays an important role in the Shīʿi reform and *ijtihād*. As a result, the Shīʿi concept of freedom is very much connected to their concept of *imamāt*.

---

108 Shabastari, Mujtahid Muḥammad, *Al-Imān wa-l-ḥurrīya ad-dīnīya*, in: Journal of Qaḍāyā Islamīya Muʿāṣira, no. 51–52 (2012), 132–160.
109 Ibid.

10 Freedom and Its Limitation: *al-amr bi-l-maʿrūf*

The concept of freedom has often been connected in Islamic milieu with immorality. This accusation began in early Islamic period but it also finds its supporters today. The earliest groups who presented this accusation were the Khwārij on the political level, and the Hanbaliten on the social level.

The Kharjites limited the freedom of the caliph to decide in a war situation according to his own opinion and considered his decision as disbelief *kufr*. They constituted an early political group who fought against ʿAlī b. Abī Ṭālib, the fourth caliph, and Muʿaway, the governor of Damascus. Both Alī and Muʿawiya b. Abī Sufyān were fighting each other because of their different position on the punishment of the killers of the third caliph ʿUthman b. ʿAffān. When both parties wanted to engage judges as impartial arbiters to solve the problem in peaceful manner, the Khwārij considered this position to stand against God's determination. They formed a theological subgroup, accusing whoever did not follow their principals as unbelievers. This concept of designating others with the moniker of "nonbelievers" *kufr/takfīr*, also found its way onto the social level. Early Hanbalites constituted the first group who presented a discussion of the Qu'rānic concept of *al-amr bi-l-maʿrūf wa-n-nahī ʿan al-munker*, commanding right and forbidding wrong. The work of Michael Cook *Commanding the Right and Forbidding the Wrong*, is a leading book dedicated towards this theme. The concept is mentioned in many passages in the Qu'rān such as sura 3:104: "Let there arise out of you a band of people inviting to all that is good, enjoining what is right, and forbidding what is wrong". This concept was first conceived as a divine command under Ahmad Ibn Ḥanbal, when his followers requested his guidance, *fatwā*, regarding how to deal with neighbors blaring loud music and drinking alcohol. His advice was to first talk to the neighbors and advise them to cease such sinful behavior. If they did not accept this advice, his followers were instructed to break the musical instruments and pour out the wine. Ibn Ḥanbal, however, was reluctant to use his hands or arms in fighting those who engage in such behavior. He considered this to be the task of the official authorities.[110]

The Muʿtazilites adopted this concept in their five theological principals. Although they supported rational approaches, they were of the opinion that rational believers must practice their beliefs and behave accordingly. However, they stipulated that the practice of this principal can only be supervised by a person who is able to differentiate between good and evil in a universal and detailed

---

110 Cook, Michael, *Commanding the Right and Forbidding the Wrong*, Cambridge et al.: Cambridge University Press, 2004, 87–105.

form. He or she must identify the sinful behaviour and assert its evilness. They differed, however, in the methods required to stop such shameful behavior: some Muʿtazilites supported violence while others preferred more peaceful techniques.[111] Many medieval and modern theologians considered this principal to constitute a duty which Muslim should practice in a peaceful form. Contemporary rational thinkers, however, considered the ensuring of social welfare to constitute the task of the official authorities.

Nevertheless moral freedom in Islam is very much connected with Islamic ethics and morality. The Quʾrān and Hadith are the main source of moral principles. The Muʿtazilites, however, adopted the concept of intuited ethics and asserted that the human can derive universally applicable ethical concepts through their own rational power. The holy law, the *sharīʿa*, mainly provides guidance for forms of punishment in cases proven to involve immorality.

Conclusion

There have been several approaches developed in order to conceive freedom in Islam.

Primary, we have clearly established that the word freedom in the way we understand it today is not used in the Qurʾān. Here liberation meant to be a free man or women who are not possessed by others as slaves. Slavery in this time was considered a community class, which does not have the right of taking own decisions. The freedom of thought and actions was developed later under the Muʿtazili school. Their interest was both juridical to establish justice and theological to awaken the importance of the human in taking own decisions and therefore, being responsible. This freedom of human will was very important in the political changes in the early Islamic empire. Through this kind of free will the Muʿtazilis could limit the authority of the caliph and increase the importance of the, theologians (ʿUlamāʾ). Further the Muʿtazili concept of *taʾwīl*, religious interpretation, is based in their theory of free will which declare the human as rational and able to interpret and reinterpret the religion. This is demonstrated in their five principles, which reject blind following.

Thus, the Muʿtazilite concept of free will gives great value to human ability to perceive God's discourse and to adapt it to the time and context.

Further, the Arab philosophers studied the process of thinking and proved that human beings can grasp the world with its creator. For them this ability

111 Ibid., 224–27.

is comparable with divine will and a prove of the emanation theory. Human freedom is a part of divine freedom and can be realized through the study of philosophy.

Moreover, the Sufis also considered the human soul as a part of the divine universal soul. Freedom for them is the realization of reality of the soul and enjoying the divine freedom in the annihilation process.

Some modern Muslim thinkers realized the centrality of the human and his/her importance for understanding and evaluating the modern concept of freedom. Many of them were influenced by the Muʿtazili classical theories of the free will and used their ideas in adapting them to western modern concept freedom.

Thus, the rationalists consider freedom as a gift of God, which allows humans to reflect upon and choose that which is good, while recognizing that which is dishonorable and ignorant. This kind of freedom distinguishes the free human from the slave of *taqlīd*, blindly following others, and self-interest. Therefore, this form of freedom requires personal responsibility in order to achieve its aim. There are many verses in the Qu'rān which support this kind of freedom.

Traditionalists and Orthodox Muslims, on the other hand, believe that Islam is the source of freedom and draw its limits to their own interpretation of the Qu'rān, thereby standing against any form of change, which could result from the practice of a type of freedom which is not rooted in the holy texts.

In contemporary period, Muslims are debating between these two positions and somehow avoiding taking clear stand. The call for human rights among Muslim scholars is increasing; however, great obstacles are placed in their way.

Bibliography

The Classical Period

ʿAbd al-Jabbār, *Al-Mughnī fī abwāb at-tawḥīd wa-l-ʿadl*, Cairo: Wizārat ath-thaqāfa wa-l-irshād al-qawmī, 1960–68.

ʿAbd al-Jabbār, *Sharḥ al-uṣūl al-khamsa*, Cairo: Maktabat wahba, 1996.

Al-Bukhārī, Muḥammad, *Ṣaḥīḥ al-Bukhārī*, Beirut-Damascus: Dār Ibn Kathīr, 2003.

Al-Ghazālī, Abū Ḥāmid, "On the Meaning of the Intimate Knowledge of God," in: John Renard (ed.), *Window on the House of Islam. Muslim Sources on Spirituality and Religious Life*, London, 1998, 355–8.

Al-Ghazālī, Abū Ḥāmid, *Iḥyā' ʿulūm ad-dīn*, Cairo: al-Mujallad al-ʿArabī, 1998.

Al-Ghazālī, Abū Ḥāmid, *The Niche of Lights*, trans. and ed. David Buchman, Provo Utah: Brigham Young University Press, 1998.

Al-Ghazālī, Abū Ḥāmid, *The Alchemy of Happiness*, trans. Claud Field, rev. and annotated Elton L. Daniel, London: Octagon Press (for the Sufi Trust), 1980.
Al-Ghazālī, Abū Ḥāmid, *Mīzān al-ʿamal*, ed. S. Dunyā, Cairo: Dār al-maʿārif, 1965.
Al-Ghazālī, Abū Ḥāmid, *Mishkāt al-anwār*, in: *Majmūʿat rasāʾil al-Imām al-Ghazālī*, Beirut: Dār al-mashriq, 1986.
Ibn Isḥāq, Muḥammad, *Sīrat Ibn Isḥāq*, Fez: Maʿhad ad-dirāsāt wa-l-abḥāth li-t-taʿrīb, 1976.
Ibn Sīnā, Abū ʿAlī al-Ḥusain ibn Abd Allāh, *An-Najāt fī l-ḥikma al-manṭiqīya wa-ṭ-ṭabīʿīya wa-l-ilāhīya*, Cairo: n. p., 1938.
Ibn Sīnā, Abū ʿAlī al-Ḥusain ibn Abd Allāh, *Ash-Shifāʾ, Al-Ilāhīyāt*, 2 vols, ed. G. C. Anawati et al., Cairo: al-Haiʾa al-ʿāmma li-shuʾūn al-maṭābiʿ al-amīrīya, 1960.
Jabre, Farīd, *La Notion de certitude selon Ghazālī dans ses origines psychologiques et historiques*, Paris: Vrin, 1958.
Muslim b. al-Ḥajjāj, *Ṣaḥīḥ Muslim*, Cairo; Dār al-bayān al-ʿarabī, 2006.
As-Suyūṭī, Jalāl ad-Dīn, *Al-Ḥāwī li-l-fatāwī*, Beirut: Dār al-kutub al-ʿilmīya, 1982.

The Modern Period

ʿAbd ar-Raḥmān, Ṭāha, *Suʾāl fī l-ʿamal*, Beirut: Al-Markaz ath-thaqāfī l-ʿarabī, 2012.
ʿAlī, Jawād, *Al-Mufaṣṣal fī tārīkh al-ʿarab qabl al-Islām*, 10 vols, Baghdad: Baghdad University Press, 1993.
Abū Zaid, Naṣr Ḥāmid, *Al-Imām ash-Shāfiʿī wa-taʾsīs al-aydiyūlūjīya al-wasiṭīya*, Beirut: Sīnā li-n-nashr, 1992.
Abū Zaid, Naṣr Ḥāmid, *Dawāʾir al-khawf: qirāʾah fī khiṭāb al-marʾah*, Beirut: Al-Markaz ath-thaqāfī l-ʿarabī, 2008.
Ahmed, Leila, *Women and Gender in Islam. Historical Roots of a Modern Debate*, New Haven/London: Yale University Press, 1992.
Al-ʿAlwānī, Ṭāha Jābir, *Apostasy in Islam. A Historical and Scriptural Analysis*, trans. Nancy Roberts, London/Washington, 2011.
Al-Būṭī, Muḥammad Saʿīd Ramaḍān, *Ḥurrīyat al-insān fī ẓill ʿubūdīyatihi li-llāh*, Beirut: Dār al-fikr al-muʿāṣir, 1992.
Cook, Michael, *Commanding Right and Forbidding Wrong in Islamic Thought*, Cambridge: Cambridge University Press, 2004.
El Kaisy-Friemuth, Maha, "The Free Thinkers of Islam: the Muʿtazila," in: *Common Ground Journal*, vol. 12, no. 2 (2015), 38 – 44.
El Kaisy-Friemuth, Maha, *God and Humans in Islamic Thought*, London: Routledge, 2011.
Frank, Richard M., "Al-Ghazālī on Taqlīd. Scholars, Theologians, and Philosophers," *Zeitschrift für Geschichte der arabisch-islamischen Wissenschaften* 7 (1991), 207 – 52.
Goodman, L. E., *Avicenna*, New York/London: Routledge, 1992.
Al-Ḥakīm, Muḥammad Bāqir, *Dawr ahl al-bayt fī bināʾ al-jamāʿa aṣ-ṣāliḥa*, vol. 1, Iraq: Dār ahl al-bayt, 2003.
Ḥamza, Ḥāmid, *Dirāsāt fī l-ḥurīya wa-l-dimuqrāṭīya*, Wāsiṭ: Dār al-latīf li-ṭ-ṭibāʾa wa-n-nashr, 2006.
Hourani, George F., *Islamic Rationalism. The Ethics of ʿAbd al-Jabbār*, Oxford: Clarendon Press, 1971.

Iqbal, Muḥammad, *The Secrets of the Self (Asrār-i khūdī). A Philosophical Poem*, trans. with introduction and notes Reynold A. Nicholson, London: Macmillan and co. Limited, 1920.
Khalafallah, Muḥammad, *Al-Fann al-qaṣaṣī fī l-Qur'ān al-karīm*, Cairo/Beirut/London: Ibn Sīnā li-n-nashr – al-intishār al-ʿarabī, 1999.
Nāder, Alber Naṣrī, *An-Nafs al-basharīya ʿind Ibn Sīnā*, Beirut: Dār al-mashriq, 1986.
Rahman, Fazlur, *Revival and Reform in Islam. A Study of Islamic Fundamentalism*, London: Oneworld Publications, 1999.
Rūsān, Ẓāhid, *Manhaj al-Afghānī al-ʿaqlī fī difāʿihʿan al-Islām*, Majallat jāmiʿat Dimshq, vol. 24 (2008), 353–93.
Aṣ-Ṣadr, Muḥammad Bāqir, *Iqtiṣādunā*, Iraq: Markaz al-abḥāth wa-d-dirāsāt al-takhaṣuṣīa, 2004.
Shabastari, Mujtahid Muḥammad, Al-Imān wa-l-ḥurrīya ad-dīnīya, in: *Journal of Qaḍāyā Islamīya Mu'āṣira*, no. 51–52 (2012), 132–160.
Shaḥrūr, Muḥammad, *Al-Kitāb wa-l-Qur'ān*, Damascus: Al-ʿAlī li-n-nashr wa-ṭ-ṭibāʿa wa-t-tawzīʿ, 1990.
Ṭāha, Maḥmūd Muḥammad, *Ar-Risālah ath-thāni min al-Islām*, Sudan: n. p., 1971.
Tatari, Muna, *Gott und Mensch im Spannungsverhältnis von Gerechtigkeit und Barmherzigkeit. Versuch einer islamisch begründeten Positionsbestimmung*, Münster: Waxmann, 2016.
Wadud, Amina, *Qur'an and Woman. Rereading the Sacred Text from a Woman's Perspective*, New York: Oxford University Press, 1999.
Watt, W. Montgomery, *Free Will and Predestination in Early Islam*, London: Luzac and Company, 1948.
Wolfson, Harry Austryn, *The Philosophy of the Kalam*, Cambridge/Massachusetts/London: Harvard University Press, 1976.

Suggestions for Further Reading

Arkoun, Muhammad, *Ayna huwa al-fikr al-Islāmī l-muʿāṣir?*, London/Beirut: Dār as-sāqī, 1993.
Ash-Sharfī, Muḥammad, *Al-Islām wa-l-ḥurrīya*, Damascus: Dār batrā wa-rābiṭat al-ʿaqlānīyīn al-ʿarab, 2008.
Al-ʿAlwānī, Ṭāha Jābir, *Apostasy in Islam. A Historical and Scriptural Analysis*, trans. Nancy Roberts, London/Washington 2011.
Ibrāhīm, Zakarīyā, *Mushkilat al-ḥurrīya*, Maktabat miṣr li-ṭabāʿat al-ūfsat, 1971.
Iqbāl, Muḥammad, *Tajdīd al-fikr ad-dīnī fī l-Islām*, Dār al-kitāb al-miṣrī, 2011.
Jad, Yehiya Reda, *Al-Ḥurriya al-fikrīya wa-d-dīnīya*, ad-Dār al-miṣrīya al-lubnānīya, 2013.
Al-Khaṭīb, ʿAdnān, *Ḥuqūq al-insān fī l-Islām*, Dār Ṭalās li-d-dirāsāt wa-t-tarjama wa-n-nashr, 1992.

Georges Tamer and Katja Thörner

Epilogue

Introduction

In many ways, an examination of the concept of freedom in Judaism, Christianity and Islam constitutes a highly interesting and sophisticated endeavor. With their conception of God as Creator and Almighty Ruler of the universe, these religions, basically, leave little room for the freedom and autonomy of the human being in terms of how these two concepts are currently understood in our age. As these religions teach that God made man from earth, i.e. from the lowest of the four natural elements, they place man in a radical relationship of dependence with a Creator whose nature is fundamentally different from that of his creatures and who exists on the other side of an unbridgeable ontological gap. Man exists in an essentially submissive position vis-à-vis God and powerless against His will – an idea implied in the account of creation in Judaism and Christianity and which finds an even more precise expression in the human attitude expressed in the Arabic word *islām*. Accordingly, every human decision contrary to the will of God is perceived in these three religions in terms of transgression and sin. Therefore, man cannot have freedom in the true sense in the face of God. At most, man can temporarily free himself from divine predestination, such as in the story of Jonah. This time-dependent state of freedom, however, ultimately ends via an act of divine intervention. The three religions believe that God's temporal rule penetrates down to the smallest details. The freedom that man can enjoy only emerges from the substrate implanted within him by divine will.

On this shared basis, the three religions have developed diverse ideas about the freedom that God grants to man. The subsequent part of this epilogue will present a concise summary of the three preceding chapters. Thereafter, common features and differences between the Jewish, Christian and Islamic concepts of freedom shall be highlighted. The final part of the epilogue is dedicated to the tension between different religious and secular concepts of freedom.

https://doi.org/10.1515/9783110561678-005

1 The Concept of Freedom from a Jewish Perspective

In Judaism, the liberation of the people of Israel from slavery in Egypt is a formative event which finds expression, among other contexts, in both the first commandment and the central position of the event in the Passover holiday.

Another characteristic feature of Judaism seems, at first sight to be opposed to the concept of freedom, namely the notion that Judaism is a religion of law. An adequate understanding of God's Law in Judaism, however, leads to an understanding of freedom as consent to laws – via an analogous concept of covenant. The covenant serves to structure social and individual life in a beneficial manner, as God does not issue orders and expect obedience, but rather invites human beings to cooperate with him. This is evident in some of the most prominent narratives of the Torah. Even figures famous for their piety like Abraham and Moses protest against God's commandments and thereby demonstrate their independence. From a Jewish perspective, it is not a rhetorical statement that God demands consent; human beings are required to deliberate and follow God's Law with inner assent.

As an example of how Jewish law is connected to the concept of freedom, it is helpful to have a look at the issue of Sabbath observance. In contrast to slaves, free men are not defined by labor and can choose to rest. The hierarchical structures and unquestioned aims of daily life are temporarily suspended. The Sabbath repose offers a glimpse of the Hereafter where human beings are delivered from the burden of daily work. Therefore, Sabbath observance can function as an instrument for the attainment of genuine freedom completely independent of God.

Given that Judaism is a monotheistic religion, God as the Creator possesses the attributes of omnipotence and omniscience that exist in tension with the idea of human freedom of action. In a purely theoretical manner, even great thinkers like Maimonides did not succeed in harmonizing divine foreknowledge and free will. Indeed, it appears to be an irreconcilable task to put stock in both concepts simultaneously without restricting one's allegiances to one part or the other. The idea of repentance, however, comes here into play, thus assuming an important role within Judaism. Human beings may not have an arbitrary and unpredictable will, but they are to impose laws on themselves and feel responsible for their deeds. Moreover, human beings are fallible and able to feel guilty when they transgress self-imposed laws. The act of repentance demonstrates the will to change one's way of life, and this cannot be dictated – even by an almighty God. Forgiveness opens up a future that is relieved from the burden of the past. This idea is also entailed in the concept of messianism, understood as the belief that there is always a better time to come, a notion deeply rooted in Jewish thought in terms of God's promises to Abraham and the People of Israel.

2 The Concept of Freedom from a Christian Perspective

One central dimension of the concept of freedom in Christianity is reflected through the acknowledgement of human liberation from sin via the incarnation, crucifixion and resurrection of Jesus Christ. In this respect, Christianity can be characterized mainly as a salvific religion. From a Christian perspective, human beings – even they are created as free – are caught in the bondage of sin and death and not able to redeem themselves. Given that God desired to deliver humanity from this bondage, he revealed himself in Jesus Christ. The idea of redemption through the suffering and death of Jesus Christ on the cross is both paradoxical and provocative. At the same time, the fact that God does not intervene even if he has to sacrifice his own Son demonstrates an ultimate freedom bestowed onto human beings even in their performance of the worst deeds. To solve the paradox, crucifixion has to be seen in union with Christ's resurrection as the triumph over death and sin as well as a demonstration of his life-affirming power and mercy for humanity. Thus, freedom is considered as a gift of God's mercy, which then demands a response of gratitude.

This entails that, in Christianity, human beings were considered from the very outset of the faith as persons with the capability of free agency and responsibility. Therefore, Christian theologians were required to deal with the question of how to reconcile human free will with God's sovereignty. Quite different concepts have been developed in order to handle this problem, from the idea of double predestination in the Reformed Theology of John Calvin to Process Philosophy, where God is to some extent limited by the decisions of each creature.

The emphasis on the relief and salvation offered by Jesus Christ has often been opposed to the yoke of the (Jewish) Law. The obedience to God's Law has been transformed into the idea of an inner tribunal of conscience. In contemporary times, this idea is rather understood in terms of responsibility and it is still subject to intensive debates concerning to what extent Christians are obligated to intervene in the public and the political sphere. In the 20th century, the political dimensions of the Christian idea of freedom had a great impact on political and social movements in Africa and Latin America in the context of Liberation Theology. Yet whereas the peak of Liberation Theology's influence seems to have been reached, Pentecostal movements focusing on the liberating work of the Holy Spirit are still growing and have been acquiring even more political influence, especially in Latin America and Africa.

3 The Concept of Freedom from an Islamic Perspective

The Arabic term for freedom, *ḥurriyya,* does not occur in the Qu'rān. Instead, there are two affiliated, yet dichotomous terms, which play an important role in the Qu'rān and Islamic theology: the free and the slave. The Qu'rānic notion of freedom mimics the pre-Islamic custom of dividing human beings into the free and the slaves. Yet it also establishes new valuations for organizing this social relationship. The Qu'rānic notion is innovative due to its consideration of the believers as righteous and equal before God regardless of their status as noble men or slaves. God is the omnipotent ruler of both this world and the afterworld, thereby diminishing the social significance of the aforementioned demarcation of status.

The notion of God as an almighty ruler, which is very much emphasized in Islam in contrast to pre-Islamic views, leads to the conflict of predestination and free will (and respectively free choice) that was subsequently debated quite controversially within the different schools of Islamic theology. Whereas the Mu'tazilites, who constituted the dominant stream of theology in the formative period of Islam, highlighted the free will of human beings, the Ash'arite school adhered to the idea that God is the ruler of every single event in the world, thereby rendering free will into an illusory notion.

The emphasis on the freedom and deliberative nature of human action is always connected to the obligation to adhere to God's Law. Given that the Mu'tazilites and the Muslim philosophers conceive of God as pure goodness, the obedience to God's Law has been construed as a path of inner liberation. Particularly in the Sufi tradition, this process was mentioned as a process of liberation from the slavery of bodily desires that disturb the inner freedom of the individual.

These motifs recur in modern debates and were mingled, to a greater or lesser extent, by Muslim thinkers of the colonial and postcolonial period with "Western" concepts of freedom. The emancipatory aspects of the concept of freedom as it was developed over the course of the French Revolution gained influence and lead to an emphasis on the civil rights and liberties of the individual. At the time, the notion of secularism which is – in the Western context – closely connected to the development of individual civil rights and liberties has been recognized as a threat. The controversy over this topic is still going on.

4 Common Features and Differences

The following part will highlight the commonalities and differences between the Jewish, Christian and Islamic concepts of freedom.

In Judaism, the God-given freedom of the Jewish people from slavery is, above all, a collective historical event that is commemorated on every Sabbath. It is this memory that forms a core component of Jewish identity. On the other hand, Christianity places individual freedom from the yoke of sin at the center of the new *conditio humana* made possible through the resurrection of Christ, the Christian Pascha, celebrated every Sunday. Again, Islam differs from the two older religions in that it considers freedom to be more of a social and political issue, which must be granted to certain groups of society due to the fundamental equality of all people as expressed through the concept of *fiṭra*.

According to the three religions, however, man has the freedom to believe or, conversely, to reject faith. From a Christian point of view, belief achieved via freedom exceeds the observance of religious commandments and prohibitions. For the latter constitute external acts that can be practiced without having to stem from faith. On the contrary, the observance of religious laws in Judaism and Islam possesses a higher importance as it is considered a concrete expression of faith with important social consequences that have considerable impact on the religious community as a whole. Yet, in Christianity, the observance of the laws is based on the freedom of the children of God, which is a theological foundation established by the incarnation and salvific acts of Christ, as St Paul emphasized in several of his epistles.[1]

The freedom to believe is considered the highest form of human freedom in all three religions. If you believe, you voluntarily renounce self-centered freedom and submit yourself to God's will. The renunciation of self-centered freedom in the act of faith is, ideally speaking, not based on the interest to derive benefits of any kind from it, but rather on the human love of God, which is represented especially in Christianity as the human response to the divine love preceding it. Islam, for its part, teaches that the renunciation of freedom in devotion to God is a response to his mercy.

1 Cf. for instance Romans 8:21.

In all three religions, freedom is intrinsically connected to rationality. Reason shall lead the human faculty to voluntary actions. Out of the symbiosis of freedom and rationality, responsibility emerges. It lets man voluntarily avoid harmful actions towards him, herself or others. Likewise, from the point of view of the three religions, man is responsible to enjoin the good and avoid evil. Responsibility leads to repentance should such actions have a negative impact. Repentance, conceived via the notion of freedom, is a necessary condition for forgiveness and liberation from guilt, a means of restoring inner peace and functioning relationships between people.

It is also common of the three religions to emphasize the inner freedom of the human being, which is eminently articulated in having distance from worldly things. In Judaism, this includes the Sabbath rest, and for Christians the rest on Sunday, "the day of the Lord". These two perpetuating ritualistic practices differ qualitatively and quantitatively from the dissociation of mystics, Sufis and hermits. Here, inner freedom reaches a climax that allows people to voluntarily renounce worldly life in the longer term and instead seek spiritual goods that allow for the highest bliss, according to the three traditions. They also agree on the view that the renunciation of bodily desires cannot happen without divine assistance. At this point, a specific difference between the three religions, as well as between the different denominations within the one religion, emerges regarding the interpretation of renunciation. Based on a traditional dichotomy of the body and the soul, it is viewed as an agony and chastisement of the body in favor of the soul; or, based on a harmonious perception of body and soul, it is considered in terms of a spiritual elevation of the holistically conceived human being.

Expressed as a form of a religiously pleasing way of life, inner freedom is oriented towards the Hereafter in these three religions. Its fruits go beyond this limited life. The ultimate goal of inner freedom is to seek rewards in the afterlife, which significantly exceed any temporal state in duration and intensity. Therefore, inner freedom can be seen as a bridge between this world and the Hereafter. In Judaism, the appearance of the Messiah is the moment when full freedom is given to man. Only then, people (the Jews) will be reconciled with God and they will receive the salvation longed for. In Christianity, salvation has been granted by Christ whose redeeming deeds have freed man from the yoke of sin and related death. In Islam, the merciful God rewards people for obedience and fear of God.

The three religions consider inner freedom from sin as a central dynamic. Given by God to man, it is essentially linked to the responsibility for contributing to the liberation of others. The believers – Jews, Christians and Muslims – shall derive from their faith the power to act in the world as agents of emancipation in every context necessary. In this sense, the Hebrews were required to "proclaim liberty throughout the land to all its inhabitants" in the year jubilee, thus celebrating their liberation from Egyptian slavery and oppression.[2] Freedom shall be given to others in response to received freedom. Supported by the Holy Spirit, Christians should unfold the spirit of freedom in their environment. In a famous saying attributed to the second rightly-guided caliph Umar, people are born free and no political authority is permitted to restrict their freedom on the condition that they do not commit to anything which would require such a restriction.[3]

The three religions agree that people cannot enjoy freedom if they renounce justice. These religions also teach unanimously that humanity possesses an equal dignity and that moral law is universal. In this sense, freedom consists not only in the self-referential negation of foreign domination, control and limitation, but equally encompasses the extension of freedom to others – even if this attitude, in socio-theological terms, did not lead religious communities in earlier times to a commitment to abolish slavery as a social institution.[4] Judaism, Christianity and Islam, however, are salvific religions which believe that real salvation is eschatological; it is freedom concomitant and coterminous with an eternal God.

The Christian concept of God-given freedom from the normativity of sin is specifically based on a radical contradiction which Judaism and Islam do not share. For the cross, through which the liberation of sin was accomplished, was itself a means of punishment, deprivation of freedom and an instrument of death. Paradoxically, with Jesus' voluntarily accepted crucifixion, the cross became a tool of liberation. The community of the believers in Jesus Christ achieved freedom as a result of a voluntary act of liberation, whose instrument was used to produce the opposite of freedom.

All three religions teach that God created man in an original state of freedom, which means the human ability to choose between obedience and disobedience towards God's first prohibition. As the first human couple disobeyed God, the human ability to make free choices in accordance with God's will became distorted by sin. The negative consequences of the original sin of Adam and Eve for the entirety of humanity are emphasized more strongly in Judaism and Christianity than in Islam. The need of humanity to be repeatedly admonished

---

2 Leviticus 25:10.

3 There are several variants of this saying. Cf. e.g.: ʿAbbās Maḥmūd al-ʿAqqād, *ʿAbqariyyat ʿUmar*, Cairo: Nahḍat Miṣr, [10]2006, 40: "*Bima istaʿbadtum an-nās wa-qad waladathum ummahātuhum aḥrāran?*".

4 As example of this attitude is St Paul's attitude towards Philemon.

by prophets, however, particularly as it is emphasized in the Qur'ān, is part and parcel of the human condition resulting from the first sin.

According to Christian faith, justification is bestowed upon man as a result of the belief in the salvific acts of Christ. Justification is a divine gift that cannot be obtained in result of observing religious laws but has become possible through the voluntary death of Christ and subsequent human faith. The forgiveness which was made possible to man, in this way, may appear from a Jewish point of view as divine appropriation of human autonomy. For in Judaism, the theological assumption prevails that God and man are two free agents facing each other. Nothing can be granted to man; he or she must hope for the justification of their own freedom of agency via fulfillment of religious law. In Islam as well, observance of religious law enables the attainment of salvation. It is the responsibility of man to fulfill God's obligation with a sense of complete responsibility.

While in Christianity the ability of man to differentiate between good and evil is viewed as corrupted by the original sin of Adam and Eve, the Qur'ān considers the major problem of man, in this regard, in terms of forgetting God's commandments and prohibitions. Thus, it is not an intentional act of violating God's will, but the human weakness of forgetfulness which leads man not to freely choose the Good.

In Christianity, man's obedience to God is not a duty required by law, but rather an act of gratitude to God's manifold grace, particularly the grace which was revealed in Christ. In Islam, the observance of religious commandments is a duty, the fulfillment of which is necessary because of an original covenant between God and man.[5] In Judaism, this duty takes wider dimensions, as the commandments, and especially those contained in the Decalogue, were given to the Jews directly by God.

In the Qur'ān, the human ability to reflect on nature constitutes a means of making free decisions. The first decision relates to the belief in God the Creator. On the other hand, the Qur'ān contains verses that indicate a strong preference for divine predestination, a factor which led Islamic theology in many instances to drastically restrict human freedom against divine power. These verses, however, can be understood as sharp rhetorical formulations against the prevailing view in pre-Islamic Arabia of the omnipotence and destructive power of time. The Qur'ān emphasizes God's omnipotence in order to free the pagan Arabs

5 Cf. for instance Q 2:115; 36:60.

from the influence of a notion of "fateful time" (*ad-dahr*).[6] Regarding the views of early Muslim *mutakallimūn* on the topic of human free will, scholars have pointed out a possible influence of Christian theologians, especially John of Damascus, on their contemporaneous Muslim counterparts.[7]

5 The Confrontation with Secular Ideas of Freedom in Modernity

In the age of Enlightenment in Western societies, the concept of freedom has been closely linked to secular ideas such as liberalism, autonomy, independency and emancipation. These concepts are not in and of themselves opposed to religion, but they have been often used as battle cries against the oppressive power of religious authority. In political and ethical theories, the concept of freedom has developed in an increasingly independent fashion from the notion of God and other religious concepts like sin, salvation or divine providence.

Given that change of paradigm, theologians and other religious thinkers have had the option to react in at least two different ways: to dismiss and ignore this development, or to track down common conceptual genealogies while integrating new ideas into their own religious framework. These two ways of handling the emergence of secular concepts of freedom can be found in Christianity given its status as the dominant religion in Western societies in the age of Enlightenment, along with the works of Jewish thinkers like Moses Mendelssohn. These controversies were transferred into the realm of Islamic thought when modern Western ideas of freedom and liberalism became influential in the mid-19th century (at the latest) beginning in Egypt where Muslim thinkers adopted them via reference to related concepts within the Islamic tradition.

---

6 Cf. Q 45:24–26. An extensive Interpretation of this passage can be found in Georges Tamer, *Zeit und Gott. Hellenistische Zeitvorstellungen in der altarabischen Dichtung und im Koran*, Berlin, New York: Walter De Gruyter 2008, 193–197.

7 This question lies beyond the scope of the present context and cannot, therefore, be tackled here. Cf. for instance: Harry Austryn Wolfson, *The Philosophy of Kalam*, Cambridge/London: Harvard University Press, 196, 58–64, 608, 613–614, 617–620, 663; William Montgomery Watt, *Free Will and Predestination in Early Islam*, London: Luzac & Company LTD., 1948, 58, 63, 145.

5.1 Religious Freedom and Political Liberalism

In classical works of political liberalism, the freedom of the individual lies at the heart of the political constitution. For John Stuart Mill, the "only purpose for which power can be rightfully exercised over any member of a civilized community, against his will, is to prevent harm to others. His own good, either physical or moral, is not a sufficient warrant [...] Over himself, over his body and mind, the individual is sovereign."[8] Sovereignty over the own mind implies the rejection of any limitation to free-thinking by doctrines. In conjunction with the principle of equality, political liberalism also implies the rebuttal of one privileged religion in favor of religious tolerance – an idea which was also fostered by the results of the European wars of religion. The claim of separation of church and state in Western European societies – whether in its more hostile or friendly forms[9] – was one fiercely disputed result of this development. Although the distinction between the realm of the spirit and the realm of the world was given conceptual cogence by theologians such as Augustine and Luther, Christian thinkers in liberal democracies have had to redefine the relationship between religion and the public sphere. As Jews have constituted a political minority for a large part of their history, Judaism was never closely connected to political power until the foundation of the state of Israel. Islam, on the contrary, was linked with political power and leadership in its formative period. This does not mean, however, that the differentiation between a worldly sphere and the sphere of God is not within the realm of possibility or reflects a notion completely alien to Islam. The limitation of power and influence, not only in the sense of political power but also in the sense of authority regarding moral behavior and basic beliefs, seems, on the one hand, to threaten the unity and continuation of religious communities in liberal societies. On the other hand, it can be seen as liberation from worldly affairs. Such a temporal freedom allows one to concentrate on the core of monotheistic belief, i.e. the relation between God and human beings. That does not imply a total separation of private belief and public affairs, but rather constitutes, in the ideal case, a balanced reciprocity consisting of adjustment and self-limitation. In fact, there are many tensions between secular ideas of freedom, on one side, and the notions of freedom in Judaism, Christianity and Islam, on the other. Indeed, this is highly evident in the case of women's rights

8 Mill, John Stuart, *On liberty*, New Haven: Yale University Press, 2003, 80–81.

9 Linz, Juan A., "The Religious Use of Politics and/or the Political Use of Religion: Ersatz Ideology Versus Ersatz Religion," in: Hans Maier (ed.), *Totalitarianism and Political Religions. Concepts for the Comparison of Dictatorship*, trans. Jodi Bruhn, London/New York: Routledge, 2004, 109.

or in the case of freedom of conscience. There are, however, also correlations which allow for a sense of mutual reinforcement. The protection of the individual against every form of slavery is a common motif in Judaism, Christianity and Islam and coincides with the roots of political liberalism. Obviously, this can be seen not only in different forms of Liberation Theology, but also in the defense of human dignity and the empowerment of the weakest members of the society.

5.2 Autonomy versus Obedience

Another aspect of freedom that plays an important role in the Enlightenment is the autonomy of the individual. Accordingly, every adult person who is not suffering from debilitating pathologies is able to govern him- or herself and to choose personal ideals that guide his or her actions. The ideal of autonomy also entails the assumption that personally held ideals should be based on free deliberation i.e. independent from any kind of external manipulation. To free oneself from the inner bondages of passion, on the one hand, and from external manipulation on the other, is the ideal of emancipation and individual freedom rooted in human reason. At first glance, this seems fully opposed to the notion of obedience to God and his laws that characterizes to some degree every religion, but in particular characterizes "religions of law" like Judaism and Islam. In Christianity, the strong emphasis on obedience to religious laws was replaced – especially in the Lutheran tradition – by a steadfast faith in Jesus Christ. Therefore, it is not surprising that Christian philosophers of the Enlightenment like Immanuel Kant described "*Jewish faith*, as originally established," as "a collection of merely statutory laws"[10] and denied its very status as "religion." The idea that Jews and even Muslims believe in a God "who demands obedience to such laws solely"[11] is still widely prevalent. This leads to the assumption that these religions are oppressive, depriving their adherents of individual freedom and subsequently inhibiting individual autonomy. In fact, the soteriological aspect of freedom as the result of the salvific suffering and death of Jesus is foreign to Judaism as well as to Islam. From a Jewish and Islamic perspective, the idea that the death of one person redeems the sins of all humanity – or at least of the believers in Jesus Christ – is not infrequently considered as a

---

10 Kant, Immanuel, *Religion within the Boundaries of Mere Reason*, ed. and trans. by Allan W. Wood/Georges di Giovanni, Cambridge: Cambridge University Press, 2012, 154.
11 Linz, *The Religious Use of Politics*, 168.

legitimator of licentious behavior subsequently characterized as non-religious. When we see the obedience to God's Law as well as the redemption in Jesus Christ in a broader context, however, it becomes obvious that there are also commonalities between the concept of freedom in each of these three religions. When we understand obedience as part and parcel of the covenant, it becomes clear that adhering to religious commandments constitutes an act of voluntary inner consent that can be understood as "faith alone". When redemption through Jesus Christ is considered under the rubric of grace, one can understand such a notion of redemption as an acknowledgment of the limitations of the will and as an act of self-submission to God.

The idea of limiting the human will is deeply embedded in the concept of freedom in Judaism, Christianity and Islam, and it may sometimes provide a course correctively to a purely secular concept of freedom. On the other hand, a non-religious person may be more sensitive to tendencies that privatize freedom in the name of religion and to delegate human responsibility to God.

List of Contributors and Editors

Maha El Kaisy-Friemuth, studied Islamic Theology at Birmingham University, Christian Theology at Near East School of Theology (NEST) Beirut and Philosophy at Cairo University. Currently she holds the Chair of Islamic Practical Theology, at the FAU Erlangen-Nuremberg. Her research focuses on Muʿtazilite theology, medieval interreligious dialogue and modern theological discourses. She obtained her PhD from Birmingham University in 2002. Under her publication are *God and Humans in Islamic Thought*, London: Routledge, 2006, together with John Dillon, *The Afterlife of the Platonic Soul in the Monotheistic Religions*, Leiden/Boston: Brill, 2009, and with Mark Beaumont, *Al-Radd al-Jamil: A Fitting Refutation of the Divinity of Jesus from the Evidence of the Gospel*, Leiden: Brill, 2016.

Ursula Männle is Professor for Political Science. Since 2014, she is Chairwoman of the Hanns Seidel Foundation. Prior to this, she was a member of the Federal as well as the Bavarian Parliaments for more than two decades, having also served as State Minister for Federal Affairs. She studied political science, sociology and history at the Universities of Munich and Regensburg and has been author and editor of various publications, with a particular focus on ethical principles and political education. Amongst many other public and social functions, she was for 12 consecutive years elected as Federal Chairwoman of the Catholic Women Alliance of Employed Women and Chairwoman for Europe of the World Union of Catholic Women's Organizations. In 2008, Ursula Männle was appointed as the Honorary Consul of the Kingdom of Morocco.

Kenneth Seeskin is Professor of Philosophy and Philip M. and Ethel Klutznick Professor of Jewish Civilization at Northwestern University. He received his Ph.D in Philosophy from Yale University in 1972 and has been at Northwestern ever since. He specializes in the rationalist tradition in Jewish philosophy with an emphasis on Maimonides. Publications include *Maimonides on the Origin of the World*, Cambridge: Cambridge University Press, 2005, *Jewish Messianic Thoughts in an Age of Despair*, Cambridge: Cambridge University Press, 2012, and *Thinking about the Torah: A Philosopher Reads the Bible*, Philadelphia: The Jewish Publication Society, 2016.

Georges Tamer holds the Chair of Oriental Philology and Islamic Studies and is founding director of the Research Unit "Key Concept in Interreligious Discourses" and speaker of the Centre for Euro-Oriental Studies at the Friedrich-Alexander University of Erlangen-Nuremberg. He received his Ph.D. in Philosophy from the Free University Berlin in 2000 and completed his habilitation in Islamic Studies in Erlangen in 2007. His research focuses on hermeneutics, philosophy in the Islamic world, Arabic literature and interreligious discourses. His Publications include: *Zeit und Gott: Hellenistische Zeitvorstellungen in der altarabischen Dichtung und im Koran*, Berlin: De Gruyter, 2008, and the edited volumes *Islam and Rationality. The Impact of al-Ghazālī*, Leiden: E.J. Brill, 2015, and *Hermeneutical Crossroads: Understanding Scripture in Judaism, Christianity and Islam in the Pre-Modern Orient*, Berlin: De Gruyter, 2017.

Katja Thörner is research assistant in the Research Unit "Key Concept in Interreligious Discourses" at the Friedrich-Alexander University of Erlangen-Nuremberg. She studied Philosophy and German Literature in Trier, Würzburg and Berlin and received her Ph.D. in Philosophy at the Munich School of Philosophy in 2010. She is author of *William James' Konzept eines vernünftigen Glaubens auf der Basis religiöser Erfahrung*, Stuttgart: Kohlhammer, 2011 and published with Martin Turner, *Religion, Konfessionslosigkeit und Atheismus*, Freiburg i.Br. [et al.]: Herder, 2016 and in collaboration with Trutz Rendtorff, *Ernst Troeltsch: Schriften zur Religionswissenschaft und Ethik (1903–1912)*, Berlin/Boston De Gruyter, 2014. Her research focuses on the philosophy of religion, theories of interreligious dialogue and comparative studies of concepts of the Hereafter in Islam and Christianity.

Nico Vorster is Research Professor in Systematic Theology at the North West University's Faculty of Theology (South Africa). He attained his doctorate in 2002 at the Potchefstroom University for Christian Higher Education with a dissertation entitled: *Die kerk en menseregte in Suid-Afrika. Die profetiese roeping van die kerk ten opsigte van die vestiging van'n etos van mensregte in Suid-Afrika.* (The Church and Human Rights in a Constitutional State. The Prophetic Calling of the Church in Establishing an Ethos of Human Rights in South Africa). He served at the NWU as an extraordinary lecturer (2003–2005) and extraordinary associate professor (2005–2011), and was appointed as full professor in 2011. Vorster published two books entitled *Restoring Human Dignity in South Africa*, Potchefstroom: Potchefstroom Theological Publications, 2007, and *Created in the Image of God*, Eugene: Pickwick Publication, 2011. His most recent book is due to appear in 2019: *The Brightest Mirror of God's Works. John Calvin's Theological Anthropology*, Eugene: Pickwick Publications. Vorster's main fields of interest are theological anthropology and public theology. He is specifically interested in the contribution of Christian theology to the interchange between political virtue, moral identity formations and social cohesion in the public sphere.

Index of Persons

Index of Subjects